Roadside History
of Vermont

Peter S. Jennison

Mountain Press Publishing Company
Missoula, Montana

Library of Congress Cataloging-in-Publication Data

Jennison , Peter S.
   The roadside history of Vermont / by Peter S. Jennison
      p.   cm.
   Bibliography: p.
   Includes index.
   1. Vermont—History, Local. 2. Historic sites—Vermont—
Guide-books. 3. Vermont—Description and travel—1981-
—Guide-books. 4. Automobiles—Road guides—Vermont.
I. Title.
F49.J46   1989   89-3434
917.4304 ' 43—dc20   CIP

Mountain Press Publishing Company
P.O. Box 2399
Missoula, MT 59806
(406) 728-1900

In Memory

of

Ralph Nading Hill
(1917 - 1987)

Contents

Introduction

Vermont Won't Come To You

"Vermont is perhaps the only place in America a stranger can feel homesick for— before he has even left it."

—Neil R. Pearce, *The New England States.*

Of all the folkloric jokes about motorists asking directions from stolid old-timers in Vermont ("Does this road go to Greensboro?....Nope; stays right here," et al), the most revealing may be this:

"Does it matter which road I take to Montpelier?" asks the puzzled traveler confronting a choice of routes.

The grizzled codger on the stoop of the general store regards the stranger skeptically. "Not to me it don't."

"The Switzerland of North America," as British historian Lord Bryce called it eighty-five years ago, clings tenaciously to many of the maverick characteristics cultivated during its fourteen years as an independent Republic between 1777 and 1791. Though many of the old-fashioned Norman Rockwell traditions are fading (post-war immigration has nearly homogenized the distinctive nasal twang of the Vermont accent that so amuses Southerners, for instance), the state remains "Contrary Country," to borrow the title of one of Ralph Nading Hill's historical profiles of the state.

Vermonters are as chauvinistic, in their way, as Texans (who also once boasted of their republic): no matter where in the

1

world the sons and daughters of Vermont happen to be living, they regard themselves as Vermonters — not Floridians or Californians. This born-again Vermonter (I returned to my native heath after twenty-five years elsewhere) always used to introduce himself on the lecture circuit as a Vermonter — "like being from Missouri, only more so."

What accounts for this durable mystique? The answer lies in an adhesive compound of geography, original patterns of settlement, an aggressive defense of territorial integrity, vigorous self-government, ingenuity, and a high degree of tolerance for the right of other people to be eccentric or misguided.

Vermont's not just a land of milk, marble, maple syrup and "white gold." Along the highways and byways explored in this book, the mobile or chair-bound traveler can retrace the course of the state's dramatic birth, growth, and achievements, from Revolutionary Bennington to Burlington, the "Queen City", which now resembles a smaller Boston as the state's financial, educational, medical, and communications center. Burlington recently became the state's only 100,000-plus Standard Metropolitan Area.

Here, too, one can meet many of the more colorful and uncommon individuals who influenced the life and times of the state and, indeed, America itself: the Rabelasian free-thinker, Ethan Allen, and his crafty brother, Ira, who led the Green Mountain Boys in guerilla warfare against the Hampshiremen, Yorkers, and "the cruel ministereal tools of George ye Third"; railroad builders like Charles Paine and Frederick Billings; capitalists "Jubilee Jim Fisk," the robber baron who was martyred for love, and Hetty Green, the richest woman in turn-of-the-century America; educators Emma Willard and John Dewey; soldiers and statesmen of the caliber of Admiral George Dewey and Senator George D. Aiken; the protean George Perkins Marsh, ecologist and diplomat; two United States presidents; writers, painters and sculptors of international renown; and inventors like John Deere, maker of the plow that broke the plains. Vermont thus appeals to the tourist who likes to see new places without sacrificing the comforts of home as well as the inquisitive traveler who wants to know what lies behind the brick and frame facades.

After two hundred years of statehood, Vermont is being colonized at a faster pace than all of New England in the 17th century. Still among the smallest in the Union with a population of 550,000 and represented in Congress by a lone Representative, the Green Mountain State is suffering acute growing pains. Many of the most articulate post-World War II refugees from megapolitan centers — unflatteringly called "flatlanders" — are now making common cause with the native "woodchucks" who deplore the invasion of well-heeled condomaniacs and the proliferation of asphalt jungle shopping malls. Even the spiritual descendants of Ethan and Ira Allen, the biggest land speculators of the 1760s, are supporting legislation designed to stem the erosion of the farm land and forests being avidly devoured to satisfy the major ski resorts' insatiable appetite for Lebensraum.

But Vermont lies within two hours' drive of some 35 million people, and if they choose to make the state a playground, there isn't much contemporary Green Mountain Boys can do about it short of adopting a stockade mentality.

Attitudes and political behavior as well as weather are affected by the Green Mountains, born in the mists of the Cambrian age 425 million years ago, and more recently — from one million to 12,000 years — ground down by recurrent glaciers, which reduced Mount Mansfield, the highest peak, from 12,000 feet at birth to 4,393. To Westerners, the Green Mountains are not especially impressive. Some relatives of the author's visiting from Colorado asked where they were. "You've just driven through them," I replied. "Oh. You call those hills mountains?"

Still, they loom large in Vermont history and way of life. As Ethan Allen once said, "The gods of the hills are not the gods of the valleys," a pronouncement more prescient than he knew. One political application was the "mountain rule," which, for nearly 150 years, decreed that the top elective offices should be held alternately by Westerners and Easterners. Residents of the Connecticut River corridor were likely to be more conservative than those of the Lake Champlain valley, and before the proliferation of railroad links in the middle of the nineteenth century, East-West communications were spotty. Stone-strewn hill farms really flourished only during the heyday of pointy-nose sheep raising, as compared to the verdant dairy farms in the broad Champlain basin and along the northern border with Canada.

One of our droll humorists, the late Allen Foley, used to tell this story of the man "from away" watching a farmer at the tedious chore of carting stones from his corn field.

"What are you doing?"

"Pickin' stone."

"Where did all those stones come from?"

"Glacier brought 'em."

"Where did the glacier go?"

"Back for more stone."

The mountains and their "white gold" have sustained Vermont's economy ever since the mid-1930 depression years when Woodstock and Stowe became the ski capitals of the East. And thousands of magnificent public buildings from Washington to Riyadh have been wrested from virtually inexhaustible veins of marble and granite.

Our topography, moreover, has helped "to perpetuate ruralism as the essential social condition," according to Frank Bryan, author of the scholarly *Yankee Politics in Rural Vermont* (1974), and comic *Real Vermonters Don't Milk Goats*. The growth of Vermont was defined by "the homestead and the hamlet." Nearly everywhere a hill lies across the path of togetherness. "For people to live apart from one another among Vermont's never-ending hills is as natural as people living close to one another around New York's harbor, at St.Louis's midwest prairie divide, or on Denver's plateau." The ex-urban gentry who have moved to Vermont in recent years are willing to pay dearly for ruralism because there's so little of it left elsewhere. At the same time, ruralism has honed a "special community ethic...bonds of communal spirit that are very likely matched by few other states."

This bonding is dramatized every March by town meetings, where questions of local self-governance are debated and usually resolved in remarkable displays of civility. Controversial public issues frequently churn to the surface: in 1982, for example, nearly all town meetings in Vermont adopted resolutions supporting a mutual U.S.-U.S.S.R. freeze on the testing, production, and deployment of nuclear weapons.

Public life is, largely, branded by personalism, tolerance, and a sense that the state's social fabric and government are still on a scale small enough to be both workable and humane. Our legislature is the least venal in the nation. In the last

4

twenty years, the century-old Republican political monopoly has been broken by three Democratic governors (Philip Hoff, Thomas Salmon, and Madeleine Kunin), by U.S. Senator Patrick Leahy, and by a current Democratic majority in the legislature — further evidence of independent thinking.

Unlike other northern New England states, Vermont graduated from an agrarian to semi-technological society without being affected by the industrial revolution —from "cow-chips to micro-chips," as U.V.M. professor of Business Administration Ronald Savitt puts it. Although hydro-power is plentiful and once fueled the woolen mills on the Winooski River, the early machine tool factories of Springfield on the Black River, as well as innumerable grist and saw mills along smaller streams (and remains a significant link in today's electrical power grid), Vermont was virtually untouched by the reverberations of industrialism. While dairy farming has declined drastically in the past decade, we remain an essentially agrarian society.

As the market for fluid milk shrank, cheese makers began to prosper, and other Vermont-made comestibles—smoked ham and bacon, preserves, honey-mustards, chocolates and maple sugar products — are being exported to upscale stores in New York and Boston. Ben & Jerry's ice cream, first concocted in a Burlington store-front, has gone national.

Vermont's hospitality, too, has become sophisticated. Luxurious country inns and four-star restaurants can be found in almost every town, many of them staffed by graduates of the New England Culinary Institute in Montpelier.

Education and health care have achieved high standards. Most towns are now willing to fund above-average schools. The University of Vermont is supplemented by a state college system. Private institutions are flourishing: Norwich University has transcended its military academy origins; Middlebury, Bennington, and Marlboro radiate excellence; Goddard College was in the vanguard of free-spirited learning techniques, just as the Putney School has been at the secondary level. Special education for handicapped students has had a high priority; many post-war settlers were attracted by the state's enlightened programs for developmentally disabled children.

The good old country doctor who made house calls in his gig or Model T coupe has disappeared into the vortex of modern medicine, but probably the best medical center north of Boston grows in Burlington; the larger towns have well-equipped hospitals. In Manchester and other resorts, walk-in clinics serve ailing or damaged vacationers; and most communities have fast-squad rescue units as alert and dedicated as their volunteer fire department colleagues.

Natives swear that crossing the border into Vermont induces a subtle change of atmosphere. One's spirits mysteriously rise. Visiting motorists and cyclists begin to notice a vague sense of loss: something is missing. Billboards! Alone among the states, Vermont has banned all off-premise advertising signs, great and small, since 1968—another tangible reminder of the Green Mountain state's contrariness. The once-controversial measure came to symbolize Vermonters' determination to preserve the unadulterated landscape of mountains, lakes, farmland and forests without the distracting intrusion of monstrous ads for personal hygiene, cigarettes, beverages, cars, restaurants and motels.

As a compromise, standardized directional signs for some tourist attractions are posted discreetly along state highways. After twenty years, some inkeepers — and, indeed, a few travelers — grumble, but the great majority of residents and visitors applaud the billboard ban as refreshing to the eye and spirit.

The anti-billboard movement was born in the Thirties. In a 1937 letter to the *Rutland Herald*, Dorothy Thompson, the newspaper correspondent then married to Sinclair Lewis and living in Barnard, wrote: "I noticed this summer, and to my horror and dismay, that the billboard scourge, which has ruined the landscape of half of th United States, is spreading to Vermont. Won't the citizens of Vermont unite to protest?

"If aesthetic considerations do not move us, let us consider the matter from the standpoint of cold cash. Vermont has beauty to sell. Thousands and thousands of tourists come here every summer, for no other reason than that Vermont is lovely. They can see billboards from Connecticut to California. The absence of them is a positive asset."

Vermonters tend to unite with all deliberate speed, but her letter lent impetus to what the Vermont Association for Billboard Restriction was doing at the time. State Representative Horace Brown of Springfield, an artist, fathered legislation requiring the licensing of billboards, restricting their size and specifying the distance they were to be removed from the highway.

Challenges to this law were rejected by the Vermont Supreme Court in 1942. In the 1950s and 60s, Colonel Fairfax Ayers of Shaftsbury and his Vermont Roadside Council lobbied hard for the stronger legislation eventually enacted by a sharply-divided legislature in 1968, for which State Representative Ted Riehle is credited.

Vermont again made environmental news in 1972 by becoming the second state (after Oregon) to ban non-returnable bottles and cans, noticeably reducing roadside litter in annual Green-Up days.

In the post-World War II years, Vermonters continued to boast how they had reaffirmed their independence by rejecting the Green Mountain Parkway, but they could also boast more miles of federal highway per square mile than any other state in the union. In 1953 Governor Emerson pledged his administration to "a policy of matching all available Federal funds" for road construction, which proceeded apace; and in 1956 moved vigorously to take full advantage of the Federally-financed construction of interstate highways I-91 and I-89 as "the very core of Vermont's future development." To secure funding for this expansion, particularly of state highway feeder routes, the state abandoned its "pay as you go" tradition and substituted bond issues.

Vermonters have had to make concessions to the pressures and realities of the late 1980s, some more grudging than others, but the character of the countryside that Bernard DeVoto described as "every American's second home" remains relatively intact, thanks in part to pioneering land-use legislation designed to control growth. As Ralph Nading Hill, the late historian, wrote in *Yankee Kingdom*, our valley towns, "white and serene, seem to have become a universal symbol of nostalgia — of belonging somewhere....The reason is, perhaps, that the people of a rootless age find something admirable about a slice of hillcountry that has resisted being made over into the latest fashionable image."

Finally, as the landscape painter Luigi Lucione remarked, "Vermont is beautiful but not romantic. You have to go to it, it won't come to you."

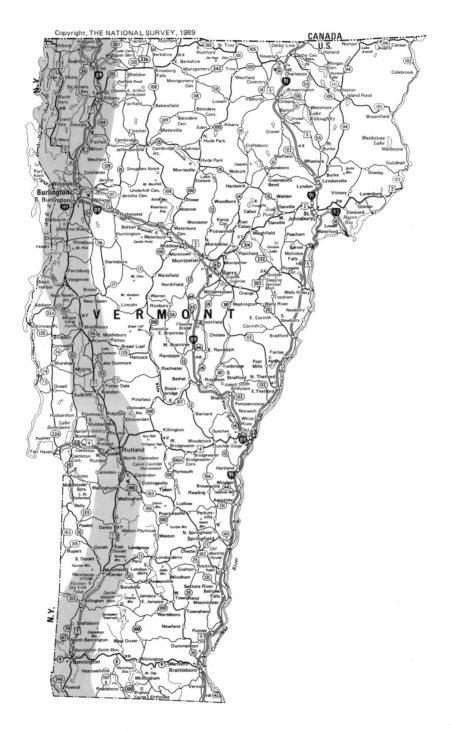

Route 7: From the Catamount Tavern to "Champ"

Chapter One

Route 7 — From The Catamount Tavern to "Champ"

"Vermont has always played far more than her part to which she was by population entitled in the affairs of the country. Vermont has always furnished far more than her proportionate share of leadership because in Vermont you have always kept true to the old American ideals—the ideals of individual initiative, of self help, of rugged independence, of desire to work and willingness, if need, to fight. I feel...that when I come to Vermont I come not to teach but to learn. As a nation we shall succeed very largely in proportion as we show the spirit that this State has ever shown in peace and in war."

> — President Theodore Roosevelt, Burlington, September 1902.

This odyssey through the times and lives of the small state of Vermont, from the harsh wilderness, eighteenth-century settlements, fourteen years as a reluctant republic, statehood, and growth to maturity and national influence, rightfully begins in the southwest corner of the state. Here was the arena where the most dramatic events in the territory's youth were played out — where the protean Allen brothers and their brash young rebels conspired over spirits at the Sign of the Catamount in Bennington, and where the rascally Green Mountain Boys repelled both the Yorkers and the British.

As more homesteaders trudged into the state in the last two decades of the eighteenth century, when the danger of armed conflict had passed, the towns to the north of Bennington grew in size and influence, each with a distinctive atmosphere. Manchester, for example, has been a resort for the affluent for more than a century. Rutland, Vermont's Second City, prospered because of marble and railroading. Education flowered in Middlebury. At the delta of the broad, fertile Lake Champlain Valley lies Burlington, the state's only official metropolis. And somewhere between the head of Lake Champlain near Whitehall and its foot at the Canadian border may swim "Champ," Vermonters' beloved own Loch Ness monster, whose existence, like that of U.F.Os, has been documented by witnesses.

Pownal

In April 1789, the Rev. Nathan Perkins, the stocky, opinionated pastor of the Third Congregational Church in West Hartford, Connecticut, left his comfortable home and set off by horseback on an evangelical tour of Vermont from Pownal to Burlington and back along the rudimentary roads roughly paralleling what is now Route 7. Rev. Perkins was not thrilled by his first impression: "Friday entered ye State of Vermont — a bad appearance at ye entrance, Pawnal ye first town, poor land — very unpleasant — very uneven — miserable set of inhabitants — no religion, Rhode Island haters of religion — baptists, quakers, & some presbyterians — no meeting house."

One hundred and sixty-four years later, Dorothy Canfield Fisher described the spot rather differently in her book, *Vermont Tradition: The Biography of an Outlook on Life:* "Have you by chance ever driven over Route U.S. 7 north from

Williamstown? If you have, and if the day was fine, you have, no doubt, like other motorists, stopped your car to admire the view at the Pownal Turn. Nobody who has seen it can forget the complex, harmonious composition of its two green and smiling valleys, diverging in a V from below where you stand at the look-out place. For those with old Vermont memories in their bloodstream, the spot has an added touch of poetry. For, so tradition has it, the pioneer trail also passed this way and this very spot was an accepted overnight halting place. Eight to ten rough miles ahead was Bennington, already something of a settlement even before the full flood of northbound homesteaders. In his private journal, James Duane, the New York City lawyer, on his scouting trip to look over the country he confidently expected to rule as Lord of the Manor, noted with satisfaction his admiration of the pleasant village homes of Bennington, and that it had 'a genteel church' — the adjective being natural to a genteel New Yorker."

But there was nothing "genteel" about the hardy settlers from Connecticut and Massachusetts who were making their homes on land for which they did not intend to pay rent to Duane or any other 'Yorker, because they had already bought it from New Hampshire Governor Benning Wentworth.

Bennington

By 1789, even the skeptical Rev. Perkins was favorably impressed: "Friday came to Bennington 6 miles — Capitol at present of Vermont — a good town of land, people, proud — scornful — conceited & somewhat polished — small meeting house — considerably thick-settled, as many, as can possibly get a living; — no stone; — no fencing timber; — some elegant building; — a Country town; — a tolerable Court-house & jail; — a good grammar school."

The people of Bennington had good reasons to be "proud, scornful, conceited & somewhat polished." It was the first town to be chartered (1749) west of the Connecticut River in the New Hampshire Grants, and as the frontier flash-point for the decades of territorial conflict with New York, the townspeople became the human crucible from which Vermont's independence was forged.

Governor Wentworth's brazen challenge to New York's claims to everything west of the Connecticut River led King George to

Vermont's "Godfather," Ethan Allen, presumably looked like his statue on the Capitol portico; no contemporaneous portrait exists. —Vermont Historical Society

declare in 1764 that all Wentworth grants were invalid. New York did offer holders of the New Hampshire patents a way out: for a fee, the state would confirm the earlier titles. A settler with only a few acres might have found the cost manageable, but for the speculators with thousands of acres, the cost was prohibitive. Yorkers also started surveying disputed lands and ejecting settlers living on property claimed by the purchasers of New York grants. The "ejectment suits" to be tried in Albany in 1770 could decide once and for all the status of the New Hampshire titles.

The desperate New Hampshire grantees began to organize their resistance. Into this festering cause without a leader strode Ethan Allen, the thirty-year-old, one-man spectacle from Salisbury, Connecticut. He knew all about what was happening in the Grants from traveling land salesmen who were peddling lots to people in Connecticut and Massachusetts, and his cousin Remember Baker had been living in Arlington since 1763. By the time he was chosen to represent the defendants in the Albany trials, Ethan had demonstrated his solidarity by purchasing a thousand acres of wilderness in Poultney and Castleton for fifty Spanish dollars. More extensive investments followed. In 1773, with brothers Ira, Hemen, and Zimri, plus Baker, Ethan formed the Onion River Land Company which came to hold rights to more than seventy thousand acres of the Onion (Winooski) River Valley — on the water route to the great trading center of Montreal.

Ethan Allen has fascinated historians and biographers. In his *Reluctant Republic: Vermont 1724-1791*, Frederic Van De Water characterized him in language as colorful as Ethan's personality as "a more rugged Quixote, tilting at obstacles infinitely more dangerous than windmills; a coarser-fibered Cyrano, a less fantastic Munchausen....He was worshipped and extolled, hated and feared. If he shocked the old, he fired the young. He was anethema to the pious and mature. To the youthful, whom the land and spirit abroad in the land were molding into a special people, he was the tribal hero, the champion, the myth-maker....In a gray, grim pioneer way of life, he was a blazer of color and a great sound....He was not an American; he was a Vermonter."

Charles A. Jellison, author of *Ethan Allen: Frontier Rebel*, conveyed another facet of his character: "Although history remembers him mainly as a soldier and frontier strong man who specialized in bluster and violence, Ethan preferred to think of himself as a scholar — a sort of backwoods Aristotle who in writing to friends and relatives often signed his letter, 'The Philosopher.' " Jellison was referring to Ethan's authorship of *Reason the Only Oracle of Man*, the book that mocked the Puritan religion and shocked the pious.

Commenced in Salisbury with his friend Dr.Thomas Young, Ethan's book was finally published by the Bennington printers Hasswell and Russell in 1785. In it he shredded the Old Testament, calling Moses a colossal fraud, and ridiculed much of the New Testament as well. As a substitute for the "priest-ridden way of things," Ethan proposed what he called his "compendous system of natural religion" — harmony with nature as the essence of Godliness, a principle that animated the later New England transcendentalists.

The Green Mountain Boys mixed rum and rebellion in Bennington's Catamount Tavern. —Vermont Historical Society

As expected, the New Hampshire Grantees' claims were disallowed in Albany in 1770. When the Attorney General suggested that greater rewards would come his way if he deserted the cause, Ethan uttered his famous but rather enigmatic shout of defiance: "The gods of the hills are not the gods of the valleys." If the stodgy representatives of the Royal Province of New York did not understand what he meant, "Come up the hill in Bennington and find out," Ethan advised.

The embattled settlers thereupon resolved to defend their rights by arms, if necessary, meeting at Stephen Fay's tavern in Bennington, outside of which a stuffed catamount snarled toward New York from its twenty-foot perch, to organize the Green Mountain Boys guerilla force. Ethan was elected Colonel Commandant; others at the center of action included his brothers, cousins Baker and Seth Warner, Robert Cochran and Dr. Jonas Fay. For five years, the controversy simmered, causing schism between the Eastside and Westside settlers, and sporadic incidents of violence, but no fatalities. Ethan's subsequent exploits are cited below, as the action moved northward. He missed, however, as a British prisoner of war in England, the Battle of Bennington.

In July 1777, more than eight thousand British regulars, Hessians, Indians and Tories commanded by General John Burgoyne were advancing southward through the Champlain Valley toward General Howe's army of the Hudson. Settlers in the north were fleeing, but "Gentleman Johnny" Burgoyne found it increasingly difficult to feed his army. Strategically delayed by the Boys' sacrificial stand in the Battle of Hubbardton, Burgoyne ordered Lt.Col. Freidrich Baum, commander of the Brunswick dragoons, to take the supply depot at Bennington. But Ira Allen and others had called for reinforcements; militia from neighboring states responded, notably New Hampshire's Colonel John Stark. When Baum first encountered the defenders just short of the Vermont border on August 14, he found himself outnumbered more than two to one.

In the heat of the ensuing battle on Saturday, August 16, across the Wallomsac River in New York, Colonel Stark shouted to his men, "We'll beat them before night, or Molly Stark will be a widow!" There was no Widow Stark, but there was a Widow Baum by the time the fighting ended and the Germans had retreated in disorder. American losses were thirty dead and forty wounded; the invaders left two hundred dead and seven hundred prisoners.

Revolutionary War veterans in Bennington (1848); the gentleman seated on the left was the first boy born in Bennington.

*The Bennington
Battle Monument was
dedicated in 1891.
Vermont's centennial
of statehood.* —Vermont
Travel Division

The Battle of Bennington was the prelude to Burgoyne's disastrous defeat at Saratoga. The plan to split the colonies collapsed with his surrender in October, and with this decisive victory the French government agreed to the crucial alliance Benjamin Franklin had been negotiating.

The first Stars and Stripes flag, carried in the battle, is displayed in the Bennington Museum along with two oversized paintings of the aftermath of the engagement by Leroy Williams of Weston. On the site of the supply depot Baum sought to capture on the crest of the knoll in Old Bennington, towers the 306-foot bluish limestone monument to the battle, completed in 1889 at a cost of about $120,000 contributed by Congress, the states of Vermont, New Hampshire and Massachusetts, and countless individuals. The Egyptian obelisk design by J. Philipp Rinn of Boston was finally adopted after

16

several smaller versions were rejected. Dedication ceremonies waited until 1891, the centennial of Vermont's admission to the Union. On January 6, 1791, a convention in Bennington had ratified the Federal Constitution by a vote of 105-4 and officially applied to Congress for admission, becoming the fourteenth state on March 4.

Elaborate decorations, including a triumphal arch, awaited President Benjamin Harrison's official visit. Accompanied by Secretary of War Redfield Proctor, the Vermont marble king, and a special trainfull of other dignitaries, the President was entertained by John G. McCullough, whose wife's grandfather, Hiland Hall, had argued against a less impressive design for the memorial. A parade of nearly five thousand soldiers and veterans wound its way through town to the monument, surrounded by a crowd of thirty thousand.

Edward J. Phelps of Middlebury, orator of the day, declared that "Bennington may well be reckoned among the memorable battles of the world....Gazing forward, in the light of the afterglow of the dying century, we discern with the eye of faith and of hope, what this sentinel pile shall look out upon...Vermont: on whose valleys and hillsides the seed time and the harvest shall never fail; a land to which its people shall cling with an affection not felt for the surface of the physical earth, by any but those who are born among the hills, hallowed to them as to us by its noble traditions, sacred for the dead who rest in its bosom. The beautiful name which the mountains have given it will abide upon the land forever, Vermont, always Vermont!"

President Harrison responded in kind: "Vermont took a conspicuous, unselfish and glorious part in the independence of the United Colonies, trusting to the justice of her cause for the ultimate security of the homes of her people.

"She has kept the faith unfalteringly from Bennington to this day...Her representation in the National Congress...has been conspicuous for its influence...We have occasionally come to Vermont with a call that did not originate with her people, and those have been answered with the same, pure high public consecration to public duty as has been the case with those who have been chosen by your suffrages to represent the State, and I found when the difficult task of arranging a Cabinet was devolved upon me that I could not get along without a Vermont stick in it."

President Harrison spent the night in the nearby Walloom-sac Inn, built in 1766 by Elijah Dewey, the son of Bennington's first minister. He was not the first chief executive to do so. Thomas Jefferson's journal indicates that he and James Madison stopped at Dewey's, as it was then called, in 1791 while on a horseback tour of battle grounds and forts for George Washington; and in 1877, President Rutherford B. Hayes gave a reception there. Owned by the Berry family for many years, the inn continues to offer simple accommodations. Across from it is the graceful Old First Church, in whose burying ground repose five Vermont governors and Robert Frost. On this Monument Avenue, too, the site of Fay's Tavern is marked.

John G. McCullough, who entertained the President, was the third figure of the Hall-Park-McCullough triad whose mansion in North Bennington is now a historical museum and community center, and was elected governor of Vermont in 1902. Born in Delaware in 1835, McCullough, like Hall and Park, had been prominent in California. For fourteen years he had been vice-president and president of the Panama Railroad, a director of the Erie, president of the Chicago & Erie, and of the Bennington & Rutland line.

Trenor Park built this mansion in 1865; it's now a museum and community cultural center. —Vermont Historical Society

McCullough's father-in-law, Trenor Park, had made a fortune in gold-rush California as a lawyer — one of the partners in the early San Francisco firm formed in 1849 by Frederick Billings of Woodstock, Vermont — and built the thirty-five room house in 1865 on part of the farm owned by Hiland Hall, his father-in-law.

Admitted to the bar in 1819, Hall represented Bennington in the General Assembly, and was elected to Congress as a Whig in 1833. He served ten years, and returned to Vermont as a justice of the Supreme Court before being appointed comptroller of the United States Treasury by President Fillmore. Then, as chairman of the land commission in California, which was adjudicating claims for former Mexican land, he got involved with Billings and Park in the controversial settlement of John C. Frémont's Mariposa Ranch.

Hall was a member of the convention that met in Philadelphia in 1856 to establish the Republican party, and was elected governor of Vermont two years later. In retirement, he was the first president of the Vermont Historical Society, and in 1868 finished his *Early History of Vermont*, which stood for many years as one of the most comprehensive records, but which was later criticized for its dogmatic partiality.

The grand Victorian house was occupied by members of the McCullough family until 1965. Listed in the National Register of Historic Sites, it is open to the public for tours in the summer months.

William Lloyd Garrison's brief residence in Bennington in the late 1820s as editor of the anti-Jackson *Journal of the Times* galvanized the state's anti-slavery sentiments. Within three years, Garrison mobilized local anti-slavery societies that peppered Congress with resolutions and petitions for years afterward. Vermonters also supported repatriation, and by 1860 had collected $31,000 to send six hundred freed slaves back to Liberia.

Early Bennington pottery has long been eagerly sought by collectors. Its fame stems from 1793, when John Norton, a war veteran, built the first kiln on his large farm south of Bennington and produced simple redware pieces from local clay. The Norton pottery grew with the demand for salt-glazed objects. For several years in the mid-nineteenth century, the Nortons were joined by the Fentons of Dorset, but they eventually split up, and Christopher Fenton established a partnership with Alanson Lyman. The Lyman & Fenton pottery expanded in variety, with Parian, Rockingham and flint enamel pieces, and Daniel Greatbach, an English designer, created the fancy animal designs that won wide critical acclaim. Fenton's renamed United States Pottery Company was responsible for the extraordinary, ten-foot "Monumental Piece" exhibited at the Crystal Palace Exposition in New York in 1853. Now on permanent display in the Bennington Museum, this extravaganza demonstrates most of the known processes for which Bennington ceramics became celebrated. The Madonna at the summit and the bust of Fenton are of unglazed white Parian ware; pedestals and pillars are of multi-colored glazed flint enamel; the molded columns are in the mottled brown glaze properly called Rockingham rather than Bennington; and the base is of scrodded ware worked to resemble marble.

Fenton's pottery shut down in 1858, and Norton's in 1894. Work in ceramics was resumed after the Second World War when David and Gloria Gil formed the Bennington Potters in 1948, specializing in fabricated mat-glazed stoneware fired at high temperatures. Their Potters Yard continues to be one of the area's prime tourist attractions.

Soon after the first World War, Vermont's first — and only — automobile manufacturer began its brief life. Karl Martin, a thirty-two-year-old custom body designer from Buffalo, settled in Bennington and crafted the first of his spectacular Wasps in time for the 1920 New York Automobile Salon. "Buy a Wasp and get stung," jeered competitors in the luxury car market, but the purchasers of the eighteen models produced in six years were enthusiastic about their distinctive motor cars, which closely resembled the Rolls-Royce. The first six Wasps were built on 136-inch chassis; one of them was purchased by Douglas Fairbanks. The Wasp Six on a 144-inch chassis made its debut in 1924, costing around $7,000 depending on the custom body selected. Production halted in 1925; Karl Martin's dream faded, but the elegance of his designs influenced the later classic Packards, Pierce-Arrows, Lincolns, and Cadillacs.

Bennington's higher education star rose when Bennington College was chartered in 1925, conceived by the Rev. Vincent Rahvi Booth, pastor of the Old First Church. Robert D. Leigh, named president in 1928, developed an innovative plan for the

Karl Martin poses proudly with his elegant 1920 Wasp.
—Vermont Historical Society

women's liberal arts college and drew enough national support to open its doors at the depth of the Depression in 1932. The college was not located in Old Bennington, as Dr.Booth hoped, but North Bennington, on a 140-acre farm donated by Mrs. Frederick B. Jennings, a member of the McCullough family. A handsome commons and neat student houses were built; the barn, henhouse, brooder, and farm manager's house were adapted to educational use. By 1968 when men were admitted, Bennington was enrolling five hundred students, and was noted for its programs in art, music, dance, literature and independent studies. Twenty years later, it also had the doubtful distinction of being the most expensive — nearly $20,000 per year — private college in the country.

Founded in 1926 by the Catholic Sisters of St.Joseph as a business college, Southern Vermont College offers career-oriented instruction to students mostly within commuting distance. In 1974, the trustees acquired a magnificent campus of 371 acres on Mt. Anthony at the southwest edge of Old Bennington, the estate of Edward H. Everett, who used his $50 million Ohio glass-blowing fortune to build a huge English-

Norman stone mansion there in 1911. Everett imported thirty-two stone masons from Italy, who worked ten hours a day, seven days a week to complete the edifice in one season. Stone came from nearby quarries and each piece was hand-cut and fitted. Everett also built a mansion in Washington, D.C., that houses the Turkish embassy, and gave a million dollars for the construction of the Bennington Museum in 1927.

The museum's notable collection of southwestern Vermont memorabilia is complemented by a gallery of paintings by "Granda Moses," Anna Mary Robertson (1860-1961), who lived in Bennington for eight years from 1927 to 1935. Her famous "primitives," particularly lauded by another amateur painter, Dwight D. Eisenhower, are shown in the old schoolhouse she had attended in Eagle Bridge, New York, which was moved here in 1972.

Arlington

In the early years, both Thomas Chittenden and the ill-fated Remember Baker farmed their land in Arlington, the appealing village on Route 7A that should not be overlooked by motorists speeding along the limited-access Route 7 from Bennington to Manchester. First settled in 1763, Arlington was called Tory Hollow because so many of the first families remained loyal to the Crown during the Revolution. The Green Mountain Boys subjected a local physician, Dr. Samuel Adams, "tainted with devotion for the King," to the indignity of being hauled up the Fay Tavern's Catamount signpost and suspended in a chair over the heads of a jeering throng. Baker, who had built a grist mill, was taken from his home by a band of Yorkers, but were intercepted by a patriot posse before they could get their prize to Albany.

As the residence of Governor Chittenden, Arlington was the de facto capital of the young republic, and on an unseasonably chilly day in July 1780, when Ethan Allen was walking along the highroad, he was approached by a British agent disguised as a frontier farmer. This fateful encounter ignited the bizarre chain of events called the Haldimand Affair. Vermont may not have wanted to be a sovereign nation for the fourteen years between 1777 and 1791, but it acted like one. It minted coins, codified laws, organized a postal service, annexed neighboring territory, and was about to plunge into diplomatic negotiations with a foreign power. To the rest of the world, Vermont was still officially part of New York, and although the Continental Congress repeatedly rebuffed Vermont's overtures for statehood, Seth Warner's Vermont regiment was a unit of the Continental Army.

From the moment of Ethan's meeting with the British courier until the astonishing American victory at Yorktown in October 1781, Ethan, Ira, and the other leaders of the *junto* engaged in negotiations with the British through their governor of Quebec, Sr. Frederick Haldimand. For years, their motives for these Machiavellian maneuvers have been debated. As H. Nicholas Muller wrote in his introduction to the reprint edition of *The Reluctant Republic*, "generations of historians have agreed that the negotiations were not sinister but instead amounted to nothing more than a cunning, if extremely dangerous, form of Vermont and American patriotism. By seizing the opportunity to tantalize the British with their return to the fold, these backwoods Talleyrands cleverly neutralized the military threat to Vermont's unprotected frontiers and at the same time attempted to pressure the Congress for recognition of independence and a grant of statehood...This charitable interpretation stemmed from the Allens themselves, who began to prepare a defense even as negotiations proceeded by deliberate duplicity and the fabrication of several versions of the same document.

"The question came to a head," Muller continued, "in the session of the Vermont Assembly that met in Bennington in June 1781. The dour legislators demanded an explanation of the secret negotiations, and Ira Allen, with British spies looking on from the gallery, had to concoct a cunning story of half-truths to leave, in his own words, the 'opposite parties perfectly satisfied with one statement, and each believing what they wished to believe, and thereby deceiving themselves.' "

Defenders of the plot argued that what the Allens were hatching could not by definition have been treason, for since Vermont was not part of the United States, it owed the United States no allegiance, and, owing none, it could betray none. Refuting this assertion, Charles Jellison, Ethan's biographer, pointed out "Ethan's own personal involvement in the American cause was the somewhat embarassing fact that throughout his dealings with the British he continued to hold his brevet commission in the Continental Service."

It seems much more likely that Ethan was moved to act as he did mainly by a genuine concern for the future of Vermont...Pressured from all sides and harassed by enemies from within, Vermont seemed headed for disaster, and a detente with the British appeared to offer a chance to ward off the worst of it — possibly the only chance. This, rather than narrow self-interest [as a major land-holder near the border], was most likely what moved Ethan to put aside his hatred of the British and engage in a shamefully underhanded bit of skullduggery that was completely alien to his open nature.

Although the proposed treaty making all the territory claimed by Vermont into a British province controlled by the Crown was mooted by the British defeat in 1781, a second round of clandestine talks took place in 1782-83 on Haldimand's initiative. The governor was encouraged by a letter from Ethan in which he wrote, "I shall do everything in my power to render this State a British Province," a statement that seems to clinch the argument that his motives were, to put it mildly, confused. The frustrated British government called a halt to the affair, however, and Ethan was directed to suppress the rebellious Eastsiders.

Arlington today remains a shrine to the memory of two, more contemporary personifications of Americana, Dorothy Canfield Fisher and Norman Rockwell.

"I have lived in Vermont ever since 1763," Mrs. Fisher, then in her seventies, wrote in the opening paragraph of her delightful book, *Vermont Tradition, The Biography of an Outlook on Life*, published in 1953. Mrs. Fisher's literary achievements as prolific novelist and essayist were significant, but she regarded them with characteristic modesty. For twenty-five years after its inception, she was widely recognized as a judge of the Book-of-the-Month Club, which inaugurated an annual award to small public libraries after her death in 1958. Mrs. Fisher also demonstrated her passion for raising the standards of public education by serving on the state board of education. During the Second World War, she helped find homes for refugee children.

The marrow of the "Vermont Tradition" she treasured is deftly revealed in her book:

To those of us who live here it is as familiar and life-giving as air or water, and as difficult to define in terms of

Norman Rockwell portrayed his friends and neighbors, Dorothy Canfield Fisher and her husband. —Vermont Historical Society

human satisfaction. Can any words bring home to a reader in New Orleans or Singapore the tang of an upland October morning, the taste of a drink from a cold mountain spring? Certainly it is nothing fixed. Vermonters are fiercely unregimented....They will argue with each other and with the Road Commissioner hour after Town Meeting hour, about where to put a culvert. They disagree with one another more often than they seem to agree. Yet, although you can't predict exactly what they will do in any situation, you can always make a close guess as to the *sort* of thing they will do, and — more or less — what they will say while doing it. And what they will refrain from saying.

.... Travel through Vermont — north, south, east, west, from Pownal to Canaan, Guilford to Highgate — nowhere will you find a township where overwhelming majority opinion does not support this unwritten law: that, except where the safety of others is in danger, everyone must be allowed to do, think, believe whatever seems best to him;

that equality before the law is only the first step. Equality must extend to the protection of everybody's personal dignity within the community, for the backroad farmer and his wife bringing butter and eggs to the kitchen door, no less and no more than for the owner of the plywood factory. And this not by anyone's enlightened suffrance. By unquestioned right. By a right so taken for granted that nobody talks or thinks about it. Is this obligation honored in practice? Yes and no. What ideal is ever completely realized? But it is the bull's-eye which Vermont tradition all over the state holds up for us to shoot at. We miss sometimes. But when we do we are ashamed.

Norman Rockwell, her friend and neighbor in West Arlington from 1939 to 1953, used many townspeople as models for his homey *Saturday Evening Post* cover art that celebrated small-town America; an Arlington Town meeting is depicted in "Freedom of Speech," one of his World War II "Four Freedoms" series of poster paintings. Most of the originals of Rockwell's work are displayed in a museum in Williamstown, Massachusetts, where he lived for the last years of his life, but his fans crowd the Norman Rockwell Exhibition in a carpenter-Gothic former church on the main street of Arlington, and can even spend the night in his former home, the Inn on Covered Bridge Green, off Route 313, which was where Ethan Allen often mustered the Green Mountain Boys.

Arlington's reputation as an artists' colony also owed much to the presence of Carl Ruggles (1876-1971), the abstract painter and "disintegral" composer. In 1921, he shared a house in Sunderland with Rockwell Kent, and posed for Kent's illustration of Captain Ahab in the special Random House edition of *Moby Dick*.

Ruggles later bought an old schoolhouse in Arlington, and worked at Bennington College with Otto Leuning, the composer who pioneered electronic music.

Dr. George A. Russell, the country practitioner immortalized by Rockwell, collected Vermontiana for most of his long life. This third largest such collection can be consulted by researchers in a building behind the Martha Canfield Memorial Library.

The Arlington Inn occupies a beautiful Greek Revival mansion, built in 1848 by railroad-rich Martin Deming, and used as an inn off and on since 1899.

Manchester

In 1797, John Graham, the Rutland lawyer, visited Manchester and described it for his London friends in *A Descriptive Sketch of the Present State of Vermont:* "The best hotel in the place is kept by Dr. Allis; and this, however odd it may sound to a European ear, is the custom nearly all over New England, where the most respectable part of the Community are the inn-keepers, and where it not infrequently happens that the landlords are men of erudition, independent fortunes, and magistrates....In Summer there is such an equal serenity of weather, at Manchester, that one has scarce the power of wishing for a change: it is neither too hot nor too cold; and even in July and August, which are here the most sultry months in the year, the kind breezes, which whisper among the trees, and press between the mountains, refresh the weary traveller, and render this place, if I may venture to use such an expression, the habitation of the Zephyrs."

Graham had a glimmer of prescience: the "Gods of the West Wind" and Dr. Allis's successors collaborated to create Vermont's most glamorous resort town, exploiting, in turn, the annual fall of "white gold" to lure skiers to the slopes of Bromley and nearby Stratton. Framed by 3,816-foot Mt. Equinox, the highest promontory of the Taconics, the famous Equinox House has, for more than a century, been the centerpiece of the town's hospitality industry. Franklin Orvis, born in 1824, was largely responsible for the growth of Manchester as a summer retreat for affluent city folk. In 1850 he began making the Equinox House among the most fashionable watering places of the East, annexing older taverns and stores on Manchester Village's green that had been known as Marsh's Tavern, Munson's, Widow Black's Inn, and Vanderlip's, and the Taconic — and remains surrounded by marble sidewalks.

"The Hotel Equinox is generally called the finest in the state, and one of the most beautiful hotels in New England, with its high-studded porches supported by columns that would do credit to Monticello or Mount Vernon," Charles Edward Crane wrote in his book, *Let Me Show You Vermont*, published in 1937. "But the hotel is distinguished not alone for its beautiful white building in the spotless village of Manchester but for the quality of its four hundred guests. The Orvises have built up a

The stately Equinox House, restored to its glory as the queen of the 19th-century resorts. —Vermont Travel Division

clientele which comes year after year to enjoy the atmosphere, two picturesque eighteen-hole golf courses, mountain bridle paths and the generally beautiful Vermont scenery in a town notable for its many costly estates." The Equinox survived the Depression and the Second World War, but by 1974 it had not only deteriorated but lost its older generation of faithful upper-crust guests, and had to be shut down. Even during the Depression they had arrived in Lincoln limousines and Packard phaetons to be greeted at the portals by liveried, white-gloved, usually black servants, but the younger, monied professionals who came to ski preferred the modern amenities and atmosphere of the smaller inns and lodges. For ten years, the Equinox loomed over the village, a ghostly Titanic. In 1984, a several million-dollar restoration was launched, and, plushly redecorated, the Equinox reopened with considerable fanfare the following year.

Mt. Equinox itself is mostly owned by the Carthusian monks who occupy a large monastery at its peak. A five-mile toll road is open in the summer months.

Franklin Orvis's brother Charles also added to Manchester's siren song by starting a business in the 1850s that still bears the family name. The company grew from his own passion for fly fishing in the Batten Kill, the state's most famous trout stream, accessible from several places off Route 8. His internationally-known split bamboo rods, reels, and flies are made in the factory, sold in a store on Route 7A, and demonstrated in the company's fly-casting school. Nearby is the American Museum of Fly Fishing, which displays hundreds of rods and reels owned by such luminaries as Daniel Webster, Bing Crosby, Ernest Hemingway and Presidents Hoover and Eisenhower.

Bromley's ski area, eight miles east of Manchester on Route 30, was created in 1937 by Fred Pabst of the Milwaukee brewing family. One of the oldest — sunniest — ski areas in the country, it was the first to have snow making, snow farming, and condos. There are thirty-five trails along its 1,334-foot vertical drop.

Of the "many costly estates" that Crane mentioned, three are open to the public.

"Hildene," the splendid Manchester summer residence of Robert Todd Lincoln, the President's only surviving son, would not be a major tourist attraction without the energetic intervention of local preservationists headed by Oscar Johnson. The four-hundred-acre estate and twenty-four-room Georgian Revival mansion remained in the Lincoln family from 1904

Robert Todd Lincoln's summer mansion is now open to the public as a community center. —Vermont Travel Division

until the death of Mary Lincoln Beckwith in 1975. Mrs. Beckwith willed the estate to the Christian Science Church, which put it up for sale. To keep it out of the hands of real estate developers, the Friends of Hildene was formed in 1976 and, with the help of an anonymous donor, bought the place.

Robert Todd Lincoln had stayed with his mother at the Equinox House in 1863 and 1864 and returned in retirement after a successful career as attorney, business executive, diplomat and Cabinet member. He had served as Ambassador to the Court of St. James's, as Secretary of War, and as president of the Pullman Company. Nearly half a million has been spent on the restoration of the mansion and magnificent gardens and on the expansion of the nature and groomed ski trails. Besides summer tours of "Hildene" itself, the Friends sponsor craft, flower, antique and horse shows; polo matches and concerts by the Vermont Symphony Orchestra.

For many years, Manchester has attracted artists, among them the pioneering photographer Clara Sipprell, and the noted painter of realistic landscapes, Luigi Lucione, who once remarked, "Vermont is beautiful but not romantic. You have to go to it, it won't come to you." Many other painters and sculptors have lived in the vicinity, and their work can be viewed in the Southern Vermont Arts Center, handsomely housed on the three-hundred-seventy-five-acre former Webster estate on West Road.

The Wilburton Inn, a turn-of-the-century Tudor mansion on River Road below "Hildene," was built in 1909 by James Benjamin Wilbur, a wealthy book collector, who wrote *Ira Allen: Founder of Vermont, 1751-1814*, a definitive, two-volume biography published by Houghton Mifflin in 1928. He credits Ira as the man who had done more than any other individual in creating the state: "Although of a gentle disposition and humorous on all occasions, he fostered a fear of the Vermonters, not only in the British establishment, but in the leaders in the States surrounding Vermont, and caused Washington to doubt whether he could induce his army to subdue her."

Wilbur, who was born in Ohio and made his fortune in Chicago and Colorado, paid for the construction of the Ira Allen Chapel at the University of Vermont in 1927 and gave his notable collection of Vermontiana to the university library.

Manchester has also harbored other writers, notably the novelist and poet Sarah N. Cleghorn, and Walter Hard, whose narrative poems about Vermont life resemble a *Spoon River Anthology*.

Sarah Cleghorn was born in Norfolk, Virginia, in 1876, returned with her family and was educated at Manchester's Burr and Burton Seminary. An avowed pacifist, socialist and anti-vivisectionist, she startled her more genteel Manchester neighbors with her proletarian views, including the often-quoted quatrain about the Factory Point section of the town:

> The golf links lie so near the mill
>
> That almost every day
>
> The laboring children can look out
>
> And see the men at play.

Many of Walter Hard's slices-of-life were equally mordant. From *A Matter of Fifty Houses* (Vermont Books, Middlebury, 1952) comes "Contrast at the County Seat":

> The road drops quickly to the village.
>
> There the Green spreads out on either side.
>
> On the left stands the County House
>
> Offering hospitality to the traveler,
>
> While on the end of the hostelry
>
> Are the barred windows of the county jail.
>
> The County House is old and sedate in spite of the row
>
> Of gayly painted chairs on its long porch.
>
> There is the store still showing the simple lines
>
> Of its ancient architecture in spite of the shining windows
>
> Which reflect the row of red gas pumps
>
> Where the hitching posts used to stand.
>
> On the right the rambling tavern
>
> Remains true to its pristine dignity,
>
> Spotless in its white paint.
>
> Beyond there is the house built for worship.
>
> Between it and the tavern stands the court house,
>
> Whose tall fluted pillars cast shadows on its white

front.—A classic monument to the ancient dignity of the
Law.

On the hills, plows are turning long straight furrows

And harrows are making fields smooth for planting.

Along the street women bend over flower beds

Behind white picket fences.

Joyful children race around the school yard

Free for a moment from life's drudgeries.

The south wind stirs the new green leaves on the maples.

...

Inside the classic court house

A man is on trial for his life,

Accused of murdering a Chinaman.

Hard was born in Manchester in 1882, the fifth generation of
Hards in the Battenkill valley. After running his family's
drugstore, he and his wife, Margaret, also a writer, took over
the Johnny Appleseed Bookshop in 1935 and later moved it into
the 1830s brick bank building next to the Equinox House. Hard
published seven collections of his well-seasoned poems. His son
Walter, Jr., was editor of *Vermont Life* for many years after the
Second World War.

Dorset

The town of Dorset — North, South, and East — straddles
Routes 30 and 7, a few miles north of Manchester Center. The
community could fairly challenge Windsor's status as the
birthplace of Vermont, because the leaders of the Grants
assembled at Cephas Kent's tavern here twice in the summer
of 1776 to proclaim their independence of New York, allegiance
to the Continental Congress, and adopt Articles of Association.

With only one dissenting voice at the first convention in July,
the Grants were declared "a separate district." Furthermore,
the committee of safety representatives agreed:

We the subscribers, inhabitants of the District of Land
commonly called and known by the name of The New
Hampshire Grants do voluntarily and solemnly engage
under all the ties held sacred amongst mankind, at the

risque of our lives and fortunes to defend by arms the United American States against the hostile attempts of the British fleets and armies until the present unhappy controversy between the two countries shall be settled.

Ira and Hemen Allen, Jonas Fay, and Thomas Chittenden were delegated to take further measures.

In September, representatives of forty-four towns gathered at Kent's Tavern; for the first time, delegates from Eastside and Westside met in concert, endorsing the Articles of Association. Such unity was rare for several years thereafter, when, as we shall discover in Chapter Two, Eastsiders asserted their own independence.

The first commercial marble quarry in America was opened here by Isaac Underhill in 1785. From it came the marble for the New York Public Library. The quarry is a popular swimming hole today. An uncommonly pristine village, with affluent summer and year-round residents and a summer theater playhouse cobbled together from two barns in 1929, Dorset visibly proves the theorem that it takes money to prevent future shock. The Dorset Inn, a National Historic Site, is the collateral descendant of Kent's Tavern.

Ten miles northwest of Dorset on Route 315 is the town of Rupert, site of Vermont's mint. In 1785, the legislature, assuming the powers of an independent government, granted to Ruben Harmon the exclusive right to coin copper money. Harmon built his primitive mint on Mill Brook, a tributary of the Mettowee River. At the east end of the structure was the furnace for melting the copper and machinery for rolling and cutting it. Stamping was done by means of an iron screw attached to timbers and moved by hand-held ropes. Between thirty and sixty coppers per minute were turned out.

Danby

Danby children still get Christmas presents from the legacy of Silas Lapham Griffith, said to be Vermont's first millionaire because of the fortune he made in the mid-nineteenth century as a lumber baron. Born here in 1837, Griffith first made a success of a general store in Danby, then sold out to produce charcoal. Eventually, he owned fifty-five thousand acres of timberland in Vermont, with twelve sawmills cutting fifty million feet of lumber a year; extensive properties in Kansas and the state of Washington; and a fruit ranch in California. Griffith built a new house in Danby for his second wife, an actress and dancer from New York. The mansion is now an inn.

In the early 1970s, Pearl Buck, the Nobel prize novelist, invested substantially in the restoration of several Danby buildings after the village was bypassed by Route 7. This adaptive preservation and restoration effort languished after her death, but was renewed by Annie Rothman, also an author who had a vacation home in town before moving there for good.

Wallingford/Tinmouth

The Old Stone Shop on Route 7, which is open in the summer, was built by Lyman Batcheller in 1848 as a mill for the pitchfork company he founded in 1836, from which grew the True Temper Tool factory.

Paul Harris (1868-1947), founder of Rotary International while he was working in Chicago in 1905, was born here and went to school in the small brick building on Main Street where the local club meets Monday evenings.

Five miles west on Route 140 is Tinmouth, once the Rutland County seat and site of Nathaniel Chipman's 1781 bar iron forge. Chipman, a Yale graduate, was the principal architect of the state's fundamental Code of Laws, adopted in 1791, and served three times as the state's Chief Justice, as Federal District Judge, and as U.S. Senator for six years. That his farm became the property of the forebears of Vermont's contemporary senator, Robert T. Stafford, is historically and politically serendipitous. During the Revolution, not all Vermonters embraced the American cause with as much enthusiasm as the Green Mountain Boys. The Tory loyalists, a scorned minority, were subjected to the confiscation of their property in 1777. The victims included Ethan Allen's "Goddam devilish Tory" brother, Levi, who was actually more of a profiteer than a turncoat and who, at the time, was trying to swindle Ethan and Ira out of a sizable parcel of land in northern Vermont. Tinmouth was the scene of a fatal encounter that year when a squad of Rangers — Captain Ebenezer Allen, Lieutenant Isaac Clark, and Privates Train and Clough rode into the village to check up on the Irish brothers, William and John.

Both brothers were reportedly on the verge of accepting the protection being offered by General Burgoyne to those settlers who did not oppose his army. When the scouting party reached one of the adjoining Irish farms, Clough, a Tinmouth man, began asking the tough questions. Captain Allen, afraid that John Irish was about to attack Clough, shot him in the hand, whereupon Lt. Clark killed him with a rifle shot. Clark admitted later that he got the wrong man: he had intended to kill William Irish, who had a price on his head and escaped after learning of his brother's fate.

Rutland

Vermont's Second City is to Burlington what Chicago, with its physical energy, is to New York and its nervous energy. A growing metropolis with a population of nineteen thousand and a trading area of another fifty thousand or more, Rutland has always been a crossroads city: once a railroad hub and still the congested intersection of Routes 7 and 4 with their stretches of strip development road rash. Although the Rutland Railroad and the marble mills created a few rich men in the nineteenth century, Rutland has always been mostly a working class community with strong ethnic and family ties.

The first land grants were made around 1761; its name was probably borrowed from Rutland, England, and John Murray of Rutland, Massachusetts, a land speculator whose name appeared at the top of the list of original proprietors. James Mead was the first to build a permanent log home for his wife and ten children in 1770.

The history of Rutland can be traced through that of the *Rutland Herald*, the state's best daily newspaper, whose Federalist origins lie in the hands of the Rev. Samuel Williams, undoubtedly the most learned immigrant to venture into this near-wilderness in 1789. The pastor of the Rutland Congregational Church arrived from Massachusetts with remarkable scholarly credentials — and trailing a cloud of scandal. Graduating from Harvard College at the age of eighteen, Williams studied science and theology and was appointed Hollis Professor of Mathematics and Natural Philosophy at Harvard in 1780. In recognition of his scholarship, he was awarded honorary degrees by the University of Edinburgh and by Yale. He was a member of the American Academy of Arts and Sciences, and of the Meteorological Society of Mannheim, Germany, indicating that his attainments were recognized in Europe at a time when few such honors were extended to Americans. His brilliant career at Harvard came to an abrupt end in 1788, however, when the Overseers passed a resolution: "Whereas sundry reports [of financial irregularities] greatly to the disadvantage of Professor Williams have been circulated through the State, which, if true, will reflect a great dishonor on the University..." A committee of inquiry was appointed, but Dr. Williams submitted his resignation and moved to the frontier village of Rutland.

The itinerant and condescending preacher, Nathan Perkins, met him in the spring of 1789: "Went to Rutland on ye Otter Creek, a County town, considerably settled, called on Mr. Williams Esq., and was introduced to Dr. Williams from Cambridge, Massachusetts, late professor of philosophy there, but was guilty of forgery & resigned,— a well looking & a learned man — a good speaker, lofty & haughty in his air — & preaching there, to my surprise, elevated with ye idea of having a College there.— Lodged at Mr. Flints in Brandon,— meanest of all lodgings,— dirty,— fleas without number."

Samuel Williams, the layman referred to, was a member of the Council of State and a judge of the Court of Common Pleas as well as the pastor's partner in publishing the newspaper, *The Farmers' Library*, which they had purchased from Matthew Lyon's son and renamed. Along with helping Ira Allen found the University of Vermont, which he hoped to see located in Rutland, Dr. Williams wrote *The Natural and Civil History of Vermont*, published in 1794 in Walpole, New Hampshire, by the great New England printer Isaiah Thomas. A second volume followed in 1808.

Dr. Williams and his partner might well have joined the legendary celebration of Vermont's statehood on March 8, 1791, when the justices of the Vermont Supreme Court, the state's attorney general and other dignitaries slopped through the slush to Williams' Inn, where food and drink awaited them. In his *Reluctant Republic*, Frederic Van de Water recreated the bibulous scene: "Glasses were filled and filled again. Faces grew pinkly radiant with patriotic fervor. The assemblage drank to 'The union of Vermont with the United States' — May it Flourish Like our Pines and Continue as Unshaken as our

Mountains'... Strong men visibly were moved by the historic significance of the occasion. They drank with intervening bursts of impassioned cheering to 'May the Patriotism of America Secure it from Venality'...'The Clergy — May They Dispel the Clouds of Ignorance and Superstition'...'The Memorable Sixteenth of August on Which was Fought the Glorious Battle of Bennington'... and with immense emotion to 'May We Never Experience a Less Happy Moment than the Present under the Federal Government.'

"Here a pause intruded. An ode, specially composed for the occasion, was sung to 'Washington's Birthday,' a familiar tune. A select choir of singers had been provided to guide the assemblage's voices, which, otherwise, might just possibly have been inclined to stray. It was a long ode. The following is a sample verse:

> Come each Green Mountain Boy;
> Swell every breast with joy;
>> Hail our good land.
> As our pines climb the air,
> Firm as our mountains are,
> Federal without compare,
>> Proudly we stand.

"One more toast was drunk, so that parched throats might be eased — 'May the Vermonters Become as Eminent in the Arts of Peace as They Have Become Glorious in Those of War.' This was followed by 'continued demonstrations of joy.' "

For his British readers of his 1797 *Descriptive Sketch*, the Rutland lawyer John A. Graham called Dr. Williams "the most enlightened man in the state in every branch of philosophy and polite learning, and it is doing him no more than justice to say there are very few in the United States possessed of greater abilities or more extensive information; added to which, he is a most excellent orator....In politeness, ease and elegance of manners, Doctor Williams is not inferior to the most polished English gentleman." Williams died in 1817. His son Charles K. Williams served the state as Chief Justice of the Supreme Court and as governor 1850-52.

The purpose of Graham's travelogue was not only to impress potential British investors in his Vermont Mining and Smelting scheme, but to support the campaign he was vainly waging in England to persuade the Archbishop of Canterbury to consecrate his cousin, the Rev. Samuel Peters, a Connecticut Tory then living in exile in London, as Bishop of Vermont. The minister had claimed, in 1763, that he had climbed "Mount Pisgah" (Killington) near Rutland and with the aid of a bottle of rum christened the Grants "Verd Mont — in token that her mountains and hills shall ever green and shall never die." Later disputing the name adopted in Windsor in 1777, Peters wrote in 1807: "Since Verd Mont became a state, its General Assembly have seen proper to change the spelling of Verdmont, Green Mountain, to that of Vermont, Mountain of Maggots."

Quite a different clergyman ornamented early Rutland, the Rev. Lemuel Haynes, who, as the first Black in America to serve as pastor for a white congregation, ministered to the town's West Parish for thirty years after 1783. The illegitimate child of a Negro and the daughter of a socially-prominent white family in Hartford, Connecticut, the five-month-old baby was abandoned by his parents and adopted or indentured to a white family in Massachusetts. In 1775 he enlisted in the Minutemen, and marched north with Benedict Arnold to join Ethan Allen in the attack on Fort Ticonderoga. In his twenties, Haynes studied Latin, Greek, and theology, and was licensed to preach in 1780. He fell in love with a young white woman in his Connecticut congregation; she proposed to him, and they were married in 1783, producing, over the years, ten children. At its second commencement in 1804, Middlebury College gave him an honorary degree — another unprecedented event. Haynes filled other pulpits, in Bennington, Manchester, and Granville, New York, before his death in 1836 at the age of eighty.

John Deere, maker of the "Plow that Broke the Plains" and founder in 1868 of the farm machinery company in Moline, Illinois, that bears his name, was born on a farm in Rutland town. After apprenticeship to a blacksmith in Middlebury and still in his twenties, he headed West to the prairie village of Grand Detour, Illinois. There he designed and built a highly polished, properly shaped steel plow that cut cleanly through the fertile, sticky, heavy soil and proved to be the prairie-tamer.

Portrait of Lemuel Haynes by Eugene Bischoff, commissioned for the Bennington Museum in 1940. —Vermont Historical Solciety

Ownership of the *Rutland Herald* was in several hands until the 1850s, when it was bought by the George Tuttle & Sons printing company. Between 1887 and 1927, it was owned by Percival W. Clement, one of the state's railroad barons and governor 1919-21.

Born in Rutland in 1846, Clement used the fortune from the sale of his family's marble company to start a bank and to buy control of the Rutland Railroad in 1882. Five years later he sold it to the Delaware and Hudson, retaining the presidency of the Hudson Canal Company, which he leased to the Central Vermont Railroad in 1891. Clement then built the Rutland-Canadian Railroad through Grand Isle county, creating a new scenic route from New York to Montreal. He also bought up the Ogdensburg and Lake Champlain, the Bennington and Rutland and the Chatham short lines and consolidated them with the Rutland-Canada; built a million-dollar freight terminal in Chicago, and acquired the Dunmore and Woodstock Hotels in New York City.

Clement's son-in-law, William Field, associated with the *Chicago Tribune* and *New York Daily News*, ran the paper until his son took over in 1935. The present publisher, Robert W. Mitchell, has owned it since 1947.

John A. Mead, president of the Howe Scale Company, Rutland's major industrial plant for nearly a century after 1888, bank president, and an officer and director of the Rutland Railroad, was another native Rutland worthy to combine business and politics. A graduate of Middlebury College in 1864, he enlisted in the 12th Vermont Volunteers in his senior year. Mead then received his medical degree from the College of Physicians and Surgeons in New York City, and returned to a successful practice in Rutland. He was elected lieutenant governor in 1908, and occupied the governor's office in 1910-12. Among his benefactions was the Mead Chapel at Middlebury College.

Solomon Foot, an outstanding nineteenth-century figure on the national political landscape, represented Rutland in the legislature in the 1830s and was elected to Congress in 1842. Born in Cornwall and a graduate of Middlebury College, Foot first embraced education as a career, founding in 1827 the institution that later became Castleton State College. An ardent Whig in Washington, he opposed the admission of Texas and the Mexican War. In the U.S. Senate from 1850 to 1866, he was an advocate of transcontinental railroad legislation, but argued strongly against the annexation of Cuba and all forms of military intervention in Central America, schemes that he suspected were Southern plots to extend slavery. During the Civil War he was President Pro Tem of the Senate, and died in office.

Many of the substantial Victorian mansions built by Rutland's nineteenth-century Establishment can still be found, but several landmarks of the era were razed in the spectacular fire which broke out on an early Sunday morning in February 1906 and destroyed many of the businesses on Merchants Row and Center Street, including Dr. Mead's building, the former Bates House. This opulent, dome-topped old hotel, swankiest in the

Rutland's marble and railroad barons lived lavishly, as the Baxter mansion attested. —Vermont Historical Society

region, had burned once before, ten years after it opened in 1866.

Rutland's political influence was reasserted in 1958 when Robert Stafford, the Attorney General, was narrowly elected governor, defeating his Democratic opponent by only eight hundred votes. After his first term, Stafford climbed another rung of the political ladder and spent ten years in Washington as the state's lone Representative. In 1972 he was sent to the Senate, where, until his retirement in 1988, he personified the legacy of integrity and independent-mindedness that has characterized nearly every member of Vermont's Congressional delegation for almost two hundred years. In the spirit of Theodore Roosevelt's progressive Republicanism, he staunchly supported environmental protection and federal aid to education; and in the Reagan years defied the administration's policy of military aid to the Nicaraguan contras.

Just before his retirement from the Senate, Stafford turned back to the Treasury more than $200,000 in office expense funds. Such annual refunds were a Stafford hallmark; he gave back more than $2.7 million over the years since his Senate career began.

In 1974, another Rutland native, James Jeffords, challenged more conservative Republicans and won election to the House of Representatives, where he perpetuated the state's maverick tradition through his seven terms before succeeding Stafford as Senator in 1988.

Pittsford

Originally called Pitt's Ford in honor of Prime Minister William Pitt, who sympathized with the American colonists. The town is where Samuel Hopkins was awarded the first U.S. patent, signed by George Washington in 1790, for his pearl-ash formula for making soap.

The New England Maple Museum, north of town on Route 7, has an attractive display of the history, production, and consumption of maple syrup, once called "sweet water," one of Vermont's principal exports. The Danforth Collection of antique sap buckets, taps and evaporators is featured, along with a slide show of old and new methods of sap gathering.

Brandon

The town was first settled in 1773 under the Indian name Neshobe, but changed to Brandon in 1784 after the refugees from the war returned to their land and rebuilt cabins burned in an Indian raid. Deposits of bog iron discovered in 1810 fueled John Conant's thriving furnace, from which was manufactured the first cooking stoves made in Vermont. The iron industry flourished; by 1845, two hundred workers were producing twelve hundred tons of iron. In 1857 the Howe Scale Company was founded by F.M. Strong and Thomas Ross; the company moved to Rutland a decade later.

In the nearby hamlet of Forest Dale lies Thomas Davenport, the blacksmith who invented the electric motor in 1834. The windings of the armature of his experimental model were made from the threads from his wife's wedding dress. Potential investors from New York who wished to exhibit the model showed it to Samuel F. B. Morse. After the famous inventor examined it, he would say only, "It is certainly worthy of careful consideration and the subject is one in which I feel a lively interest." Davenport continued his experiments, developing a twenty-four-wire telegraph for long-distance communications.

Although Morse had not thought of a single wire until this time, he refined Davenport's idea into one.

In 1840, Davenport began the publication of a newspaper in New York City whose printing press was driven by one of his electric motors. In an editorial he compared the cost of steam generated by the burning of wood with power from electric batteries, and predicted that electricity "must and will triumphantly succeed," a prophecy fifty years before its time. On the verge of inventing a phonograph, but disheartened by public indifference, he returned to his forge and anvil in Brandon.

One of Vermont's most eminent sons, Stephen A. Douglas, was born here in 1813, in a small cottage where a marble monument now stands. His father died soon after his birth; the lad moved with his mother to a farm, and later to Middlebury as apprentice to a cabinet maker. His mother remarried, and he went with her to New York state before heading West to Illinois.

The "Little Giant" visited his home state in 1851 to receive an honorary degree from Middlebury College and again during his presidential campaign in the summer of 1860. At forty-seven, Douglas was the best-known candidate in the field, and the most influential Democrat in Congress, where he had served for thirteen years. When Southern Democrats caused the repeal of the Missouri Compromise in 1854, Senator Douglas embodied in the Kansas-Nebraska Act the doctrine of popular sovereignty, whereby people in the territories would decide whether to permit slavery. Even Abraham Lincoln conceded, on the eve of his senatorial debates with Douglas in 1858, that his opponent "is of world-wide renown," and regarded as a potential president. "On the contrary, nobody has ever expected me to be President," Lincoln said sadly.

Douglas was the first presidential candidate to stump the country during a campaign. Quixotically, he chose to spend four days in Vermont, the most Republican state in the nation. Since visits of famous men were rarities, they turned into great public celebrations, with parades, salutes, band concerts, and fireworks. In Brandon, he addressed several thousand people for more than an hour from the park across from the Brandon House. Here he repeated what he had said at Middlebury: "I love the old Green Mountains and valleys...Vermont is the most glorious spot on the face of the globe for a man to be born in — provided he emigrates when he is very young." Many listeners were shocked by this wry reference to the decimating Westward migration from the state that was under way, but Douglas knew that he would probably not have made such a national reputation had he remained. "It does a man good to emigrate," he added. "I once thought that within this circle of hills and mountains was the great center of civilization; that outside it all was little better than barbarians. But I have found other communities and other people, and we are all brethren and kindred."

At the Burlington railroad station, Douglas found some five thousand people to greet and escort him to the town hall. Among the reception committee were George Perkins Marsh, the Congressman, ecologist and diplomat, who supported Lincoln but had known Douglas in Congress; and John Godfrey Saxe, the poet who twice ran vainly for governor as a Democrat.

Stephen A. Douglas, the "Little Giant," was born in Brandon. —

44

Douglas told the throng that he had told his wife — the granddaughter of Dolly Madison's sister — he was coming to Burlington to show her the most beautiful town site in the world. Here and in Montpelier he appealed for moderation in the controversy over slavery, defending popular sovereignty as nothing more nor less than minding one's own business and letting one's neighbor alone. He also implied that Vermonters would not be such extreme abolitionists if they had closer and more frequent contact with Southerners.

In Vermont, Douglas polled only nineteen percent of the votes, and in the nation, only the electoral votes of Missouri and some of New Jersey's. He died not long after the election, in June 1861.

Lincoln carried every Vermont county by large majorities. On the eve of the election, the *Montpelier Watchman* expressed popular reaction to Southern states' threats of secession: "Let them go if they are bent upon it. Let them go, bag and baggage, with all they are entitled to. Let them go unharmed, unwhipt, unhung; and joy go with them if this is possible."

Middlebury

Gamaliel Painter, surveyor, industrialist, political leader, was one of the first settlers here when the village began to take shape in the 1780s. His vision of an institution of higher education was encouraged by a visit from Timothy Dwight, president of Yale College and son of the first white child to have been born on Vermont soil. Dwight promoted Middlebury College, chartered in 1800, as a religious antidote to Ira Allen's "ungodly" University of Vermont. Indeed influenced by a procession of nineteenth-century divines, non-sectarian Middlebury is now firmly established as a respected liberal arts college renowned for its foreign language schools and Bread Loaf School of English.

Painter's immortality was insured when in 1916 a cane said to be carried by the college's principal founder was dusted off and put to symbolic uses. "A song was written about him and his cane," W. Storrs Lee, former dean of the college wrote, "football teams conquered in its courage; under emotional stress students pledged themselves 'to do as Painter did'; in their choruses the fraternity boys interspersed rappings and tappings to simulate Painter's hobbling with his staff; the

Gamaliel Painter's gracious residence now houses the Vermont Folk Life Center. —Vermont Historical Society

senior women came out with replicas of the cane and introduced a commencement ceremony as colorful as a West Point wedding; grown alumni reverently rose to their feet, doffed their hats and held them over their hearts while they sang of Gamaliel." Here is a partial version of this anthem:

> When Gamaliel Painter died,
> He was Middlebury's pride,
> A sturdy pioneer without a stain.
> And he left it all by will
> To the college on the hill,
> And included in his codicil a cane.
> Oh, it's rap, rap, rap,
> And it's tap, tap, tap —
> You can hear it sounding plain!
> As a helper true and tried
> As the generations glide,
> There is nothing like Gamaliel Painter's cane!

During the second decade of the 1800s, Middlebury developed into the largest and most substantial community west of the Green Mountains. The graceful Federal Painter House on Court Square, now used by the college and the Vermont Folk Life Center, was finished in 1807. Perhaps the finest Congregational church in Vermont was completed in 1809. The brick mansion built in 1816 by Horatio Seymour, who served in the United States Senate from 1821 to 1833, has been the community house for many years. With a population in 1820 of 2,535, it exceeded Bennington, Rutland and Burlington. The Otter Creek Falls powered grist, woolen, and marble mills, where Isaac Markham rediscovered the means of sawing marble with sand, water and multiple toothless saws.

Women were not admitted to Middlebury College until 1883, but Emma Hart Willard (1787-1870) pioneered American education for women when she came here in 1807 to take charge of the Middlebury Female Academy. When Dr. Willard, her husband, was compelled to give up his practice, she opened her own seminary and wrote her widely-circulated and influential book, *Plan for The Improvement of Female Education*. In

Middlebury College students of the 1880s rally on the steps of Old Chapel. —Vermont Historical Society

the spring of 1819 she moved her school to Waterford, New York, and became internationally acclaimed for the Emma Willard School in Troy.

Another Middlebury College benefactor was Joseph Battell, who left it thirty thousand acres of mountain land when he died in 1915. Battell was the unusually hospitable proprietor of the Bread Loaf Inn, an upland hotel colony on the mountain pass between East Middlebury and Hancock. He had inherited the means to support this avocation, publish a county weekly newspaper, develop his Morgan horse farm, and buy most of the lofty wilderness he could see from the inn. For as little as twenty-five cents an acre, he added to his Bread Loaf holdings most of Worth Peak, Monastery Mountain, Boyce Peak, Roosevelt, Grant, Lincoln, and Camels Hump until he owned more territory than any other individual in the state.

Battell's Morgan Horse Farm, on the edge of Middlebury toward Weybridge, is now a breeding and training center operated by the University of Vermont and open to visitors. The stylish, sturdy, alert Morgans, exceptional for their endurance, plucky disposition, and cheerful understanding, are lineal descendants of "Figure," brought to Randolph, Vermont, by

A spirited Morgan mare with foal at the Morgan Horse Farm, in Weybridge. —Vermont Travel Division

Justin Morgan from Massachusetts in 1795 in payment for a debt. The young psalmodist, composer, and singing-master, suffering from tuberculosis, rented the two-year-old colt to a farmer, Robert Evans, who used the undersized — fourteen hands — horse for all kinds of farm work, and discovered that despite his short legs he was a high-stepper and fast mover.

Morgan himself died three years later, unaware that he was godfather to a new breed that would become famous. The horse "Justin Morgan" changed hands several times, sired many sons and daughters, and died on a farm in Chelsea in 1821 at the age of thirty-two. Plucky Morgans distinguished themselves in the Civil War as mounts for the First Vermont Cavalry. A Confederate captured by this unit was heard to exclaim, "It was your hawses that done licked us." When the tide of Vermonters swept West, Morgans took them. Typically Morgans were not bred for speed, but at least forty of "Figure's" progeny established records as trotters.

Battell loved his horses and hated automobiles, which he tried to ban from his Bread Loaf road. In his little book, *Shall Autombiles Have Their Own Roads?*, he protested, "With what more lethal weapon can man be assaulted than the terrible and destructive motor car trespassing on the highway? Sooner or later it will come to this — the automobiles will be driven from the highways or the horses will be driven from the highways."

John W. Stewart, a lawyer, was speaker of the house for four terms, governor of Vermont in 1870-72, elected to Congress in 1882 and was appointed to fill out the term of Senator Redfield Proctor. In December 1883, Edward Phelps, a distinguished Burlington lawyer, friend, and Democrat wrote Republican Stewart: "As you are now fairly installed in the Great American Beer Garden, and as I am anxious you should emerge from your present unfortunate situation with as little discredit as possible, I have concluded to inscribe a few maxims for your guidance. Paste them in the top of your hat for ready reference. And pursue them rigidly....Vote steadily against all propositions whatsoever [except motions to adjourn]. There is already legislation enough for the next five hundred years....Make no speeches. Nobody attends to Congressional oratory when delivered. When printed, nobody reads it, and it is a nuisance to the mails....Cultivate assiduously all newspaper correspondents. All there is of public life is what the papers say. And they will

Greater Downtown Middlebury soon after the major fire in 1891.
—Vermont Historical Society

say anything that is made worth their while....Do not become a candidate for the Presidency. There are enough in the field already....Beware of statesmen with Great Moral ideas. You will find immoral ideas more honest as well as more interesting...."

Phelps' wit matched his enviable reputation as a practicing lawyer and professor of law. Originally a Whig, he became one of the few prominent Democrats in the state when the Whig Party disbanded. Born in Middlebury in 1822, the man who was nearly named Chief Justice of the United States Supreme Court graduated from Middlebury College at the age of eighteen and attended the Yale Law School. He moved to Burlington in 1845. His abilities as a lawyer were recognized outside the state when he was elected president of the American Bar Association in 1881, after running unsuccessfully for governor of Vermont. Phelps then taught at the Yale Law School and lectured at Boston University.

Upon taking office, President Cleveland appointed him Minister to Great Britain, a choice praised by the *Burlington*

Free Press: "It is certainly an honor to our State that a Vermonter should be selected for the highest diplomatic appointment in the gift of the President, and it will be highly gratifying to our readers, and to Vermonters generally of both parties. In ability, cultivation, courtesy and high breeding, he is equal to the place, and will fill it, we are sure, with dignity, capacity and success, though it has been occupied by such men as Charles Francis Adams, Hamilton Fish, John Lothrop Motley and James Russell Lowell." When Cleveland won the popular vote but Harrison the electoral vote, and the Republicans recaptured the White House, Phelps had to leave London. At a testimonial dinner, Lord Chief Justice Coleridge remarked that America had sent great men to represent it, "But I venture to say that no one of Mr. Phelps' predecessors has ever been the recipient of such unanimous and cordial expressions of regard, and I am sure that no American Minister has ever left our shores amid more universal regret."

The Vermont historian Walter Hill Crockett observed, wryly: "Mr. Phelps would have adorned any public station to which he

E. J. Phelps.
—Special Collections,
University of Vermont Library

might have been called, but as a result of his political affili-
ations, in a State which more steadfastly than any other had
given its adherence to another party, he had been shut out from
the more important official positions which Vermont had to
bestow. But he missed by a very narrow margin appointment
to one of the greatest and most responsible positions in America, and one for which he was eminently qualified, that of Chief
Justice of the United States Supreme Court."

Cleveland had decided to appoint Phelps, but was deterred
from submitting his name for confirmation by Irish Democratic
leaders in Boston and New York who distrusted his cordial
relationships with the British, and who threatened to withold
their support of Cleveland's re-election. Ironically, in spite of
yielding in the Phelps appointment, Cleveland was defeated in
1888. Five years later, President Harrison appointed Phelps
senior counsel for the United States in the international tribu-
nal for the Behring Sea case in Paris, where he delivered an
eleven-day closing argument.

After leaving public life, Phelps resumed his lectures at Yale,
where he died in 1900. He was buried in Burlington near the
grave of his friend, Senator George F. Edmunds — who might
have been President. "Vermont has contributed to the service
of the Nation," Crockett wrote, "none greater than these neighbors who lived and labored together and now sleep on the same
fair hillside which looks out upon the serene and majestic
beauty of the Green Mountains which both loved so well."

Robert Frost, cited by the legislature as Poet Laureate of
Vermont in 1961, summered for the last twenty-two years of his
life in a farmhouse on the slopes of Bread Loaf in Ripton.
Although born in San Francisco, the gifted and sagacious poet
spent more than half his life in or near Vermont. "The attach-
ment between Frost and Vermont reflects mutual admiration,"
wrote his friend Reginald L. Cook, Middlebury professor of
American Literature, in 1976. Cook described Frost's years in
Ripton, living in a rustic cabin on a rise above the house:

> At the farm, the poet with his rugged features—strong
> mouth, stubborn chin, wide-set dreamy eyes, thick eyebrows,
> fine broad, wrinkled forehead, and shock of rumpled white
> hair—would be found. Sometimes he would be seen outside
> the cabin returning from the woods with a white ash,
> heavy-duty pack basket strapped on his back in which were

forest seedlings for transplantation, or trimming back alders in the pasture with long-handled pruning shears, or patiently grazing Morgan horses on tether on the back lawn. More often he would be found stretched at ease in an old Morris chair before an open fireplace in the cabin, a writing board propped against the chair, a gnarled walking stick close by. Off the farm, he was glimpsed marketing in the local grocery stores, greeted at the post office, and viewed more formally while "saying" his poems in the Little Theatre before enthusiastic audiences at the School of English (from 1921 through 1962) on the mountain campus...

In acknowledging the legislature's resolution, Frost wrote a quatrain that appeared in his last published collection, *In the Clearing* (1962):

Vermont's Poet Laureate, Robert Frost, at his Bread Loaf retreat. —Vermont Historical Society

53

Breathes there a bard who isn't moved

When he finds his verse is understood

And not entirely disapproved

By his country and his neighborhood.

In 1964, the year following Frost's death, Senator George Aiken successfully sponsored a bill empowering the Secretary of the Interior to acquire up to a thousand acres of land around the farm, and the Vermont Division of Historic Sites created the Robert Frost Wayside Area and trail. In 1972, a sixteen-mile stretch of Route 125 was dedicated as the Robert Frost Memorial Drive.

From Shoreham, southwest of Middlebury on Route 22A, sprang two notable political figures, Governor Silas Jenison and Levi P. Morton, Vice President of the United States.

Jenison (also spelled Jennison) was the first native-born governor, propelled into office in 1835 when no gubernatorial candidate could gain a majority. After three days of wrangling and sixty-three ballots, the unicameral legislature authorized Lieutenant Governor Jenison to continue to perform the duties of governor. The acting governor headed the Anti-Masonic state ticket the following year, and was elected by a small majority. Born in 1791, Jenison worked on his family farm, represented Shoreham in the legislature, and sat as judge of the Addison County Court. He held the office of governor until 1841. In 1837 he had to deal with the consequences of the uprising in Canada, led by L.J. Papineau, that aroused much sympathy along the Vermont border. After a battle in November in which the rebels were defeated, many of them fled across the border to refuge in Swanton and Highgate before mounting another raid with arms supplied by Vermont sympathizers. Governor Jenison issued a proclamation calling for the preservation of order along the border. The United States was at peace with Great Britain, he said, and aid to the rebels constituted a breach of neutrality. He sternly cautioned the people of Vermont "against all acts that may subject you to penalties, or in any way compromise the Government." The governor's firm stand was largely ignored, and despite the presence of federal troops ordered to the frontier by President Van Buren, the disturbances continued for another two years. The governor conceded that he had lost support while performing his duty. In his 1838 message to the legislature, he expressed his own mixed emotions: "Men of the best feelings and much moral worth participated largely in their sympathies with those whom they deem oppressed. This state of things was to be expected. Our institutions, habits and education lead to that result." After two more terms, Jenison retired in 1841. One of his chief legislative achievements was repeal of the law that required the imprisonment of debtors.

Levi P. Morton was born in Shoreham in 1824 and named for his grandfather, Rev. Levi Parsons, the first Protestant missionary sent from America to Palestine. As a lad, Morton grew up in eastern Massachusetts and southern New Hampshire, where his clergyman father served Congregational churches. After several years of experience in retailing, he founded in 1854 the dry goods firm of Morton and Grinell in New York City. Financial losses during the Civil War caused the store to fail. Morton then organized the investment banking house of L.P.Morton & Company, which became so profitable that all the creditors of the bankrupt store were invited to a banquet, where each guest found under his plate a check for the amount due with interest. He served one term in Congress and as Minister to France before being elected Benjamin Harrison's Vice President in 1888. Later, he was governor of New York and an unsuccessful candidate for President in 1896.

Vergennes

With 2,300 residents, Vergennes is the smallest, and almost the oldest, *city* in the country. First settled by a Scotsman in 1764, the townspeople were evicted by Ethan Allen, who named the town after Count de Vergenne, the French Minister of Foreign Affairs, a strong supporter of the American Revolution.

In 1814, Thomas McDonough used the basin below the Otter Creek Falls here to build, in record time, three ships, including the 734-ton, 26-gun *Saratoga*, and equipped nine gunboats with which he defeated the British fleet in Lake Champlain off Valcour Island.

The Basin Harbor Maritime Museum, at the entrance to the Basin Harbor Club — a classic lake resort— off Panton Road, west of the intersection of Routes 23 and 22A, is an early nineteenth-century stone schoolhouse displaying objects from Lake Champlain's ten-thousand-year history. The Museum is the center for current marine archaeological explorations; demonstrations in early boat building techniques are scheduled in the summer months.

Three miles north of Vergennes on Route 7 in Ferrisburg is the Rokeby Museum, the home of Rowland E. Robinson, the nineteenth-century author, illustrator, and naturalist. The eight rooms of exhibits, open June to October, contain furnishings and personal items from four generations of the Robinson family, who were active in the anti-slavery cause in the 1840s, when Rokeby became a well-known stop on the underground railway. When the local sheriff got word of a runaway slave in the vicinity, he would start out for Rokeby. His first stop, however, was a local tavern, where, over refreshments, he

Otter Creek Falls at Vergennes, where Commodore Thomas McDonough built the fleet that defeated the British in the Battle of Plattsburgh in 1814.
—Vermont Historical Society

56

announced loudly that he was on his way to search the house. News of his impending visit always reached the Robinsons' before the sheriff.

Shelburne

Shelburne was settled in 1768 by two German loggers, reportedly murdered for their money by soldiers sent from Montreal presumably to protect them from the Indians. A decade later, two more settlers were killed by raiding Indians and Tories, who torched the cabins. The settlement might have gone up in smoke except for a handy hogshead of home brew that was used to douse the flames.

Shelburne's fame today rests on the legacy of Dr. W. Seward and Lila Vanderbilt Webb, who created one of America's grandest country estates in the 1880s and '90s. Webb first traveled to Vermont in 1880, eyeing the Rutland Railroad as a potential acquisition for William Henry Vanderbilt, whose daughter he married the following year. Webb had left the medical profession, and proved his managerial skills by reviving the failing Wagner Palace Car Company. Enthusiastic about the Burlington area, he and his bride decided to make it their summer home instead of following their wealthy friends and relatives to Newport, Rhode Island. They rented a house and began building a relatively modest cottage at Oakledge, on a lakeshore bluff south of the center of Burlington.

In 1886, armed with Lila's $10 million bequest from her father, and impelled by atavistic instincts, Webb began to assemble the land for a much larger estate in Shelburne. Among the thirty farms he acquired was property on Lone Tree Hill that had been granted to his grandfather, General Samuel B. Webb, who had fought at Bunker Hill, and served as an aide-de-camp to George Washington. To make the best use of his four thousand acres, the doctor retained the famous landscape architect Frederick Law Olmsted, who had designed not only Central Park in New York but was laying out the the grounds of "Biltmore," the Ashville, North Carolina, chateau built by Lila's brother George Vanderbilt on a hundred-thousand-acre spread. To achieve his vision of a model agricultural estate, Webb also brought in Gifford Pinchot, the noted forester and conservationist.

The House at Shelburne Farms.

58

Webb's passion for horses, especially the all-purpose Hackneys, was realized in a tremendous breeding barn that had stables for three hundred and an indoor polo field. Even larger was the farm barn, an immense, five-story stone and timber building with two wings enclosing a two-acre courtyard. A large coach barn held stalls for forty-eight horses and an elevator for lifting carriages to the second floor.

A temporary, Shingle Style cottage, designed by Robert H. Robertson, was built for the Webbs in 1887-88, and then converted into the rambling, free-style Queen Anne mansion with one hundred and ten rooms that was completed in 1899 and is now open summers to the public as an inn.

Turn-of-the-century life here has been colorfully portrayed in *The House at Shelburne Farms: The Story of One of America's Great Country Estates* by Joe Sherman, published in 1986. The Webbs lived on a grand scale, with a private railroad car and a 117-foot steam yacht, and a 40,000 acre "camp" in the Adirondacks.

Webb hoped to become governor and assiduously courted all the Republican nabobs, inviting them to dinner whenever he entertained Presidents. In 1901, Vice President Theodore

The legendary lake steamer Ticonderoga *in its Shelburne Museum permanent berth.* —Vermont Travel Division

Roosevelt, a house guest, sailed from Shelburne to Isle La Motte aboard the *Elfrieda* to address the Vermont Fish and Game League. Leaving the rostrum, he was informed that President McKinley had been shot in Buffalo, New York. As President, Roosevelt was again a guest of the Webbs during his official tour of the state in 1902, when he said in a speech at Windsor, that Vermont "has shown that healthy sanity of public sentiment which has so prominently distinguished it, because Vermont had understood that while it was a mighty good thing to produce material prosperity, it was a better thing to produce men and women fit to enjoy it."

For Shelburne Farms the 1920s marked the start of a long decline, Sherman wrote. "So promising of great things in the 1890s, this pace-setter in agricultural experimentation and breeding seemed to come to a standstill after the first decade of the new century. Farmers bought cars and tractors, not hackneys, so that venture failed...Cash flowed out in support of the estate, the Adirondack game park Nehasne, the mansion in New York and a new winter place in Florida." Dr.Webb's health continued to decline, and his Wagner Palace Car Company had ended up in the hands of George Pullman. Seward Webb died in 1926 and Lila followed him ten years later. The Vanderbilt Webb side of the family continued to live in the house at various times, and in 1972, the members of the present generation transformed the estate into Shelburne Farms Resources, a non-profit center for conferences, concerts, crafts shows, and educational programs for children. Marilyn Webb and her husband began a major restoration of the mansion in 1985, and two years later Shelburne House opened as Vermont's most distinctive place to stay, a "back to the future" recreation of Edwardian country house life.

Begun in 1947 by Electra Havemeyer and J. Watson Webb originally to house his father's collection of carriages and sleighs in the Horseshoe Barn, the Shelburne Museum and Heritage Park has absorbed a major share of the Webb family fortune as well as Mrs. Webb's sugar refining inheritance. J. Watson Webb, the eldest of Seward and Lila's three sons, had been given Southern Acres, about half of the total property, in 1910. The Museum is situated on forty-five acres of that property along Route 7. To it were moved thirty-five historic buildings, including a stage coach inn, general store, one-room schoolhouse, a covered bridge, the Colchester Reef Lighthouse, all exhibiting distinguished collections of Americana.

From its most recent acquisition, the round barn transported to the site by helicopter to become the visitors' center, one can stroll or ride a tram through beautiful landscaping, stopping at will to visit, for example, the Greek Revival Webb Memorial House, in which rooms from the Webbs' New York apartment have been installed, with Rembrandt, Monet and Degas paintings on the wall. The former Shelburne Depot is a gallery of railroad mementos; beside it sit a Rutland Railroad locomotive and the "Grand Isle," the luxurious private car that Dr. Webb gave Governor E.C.Smith in 1890.

The most outstanding feature is the sidewheeler *Ticonderoga*, retired in 1950 after forty-four years of plying the waters of Lake Champlain. To preserve "The Ti" for posterity, the historian Ralph Nading Hill persuaded Electra Webb to buy it and move it overland to a permanent berth in the Museum. To accomplish the monumental task of moving the 220-foot, 900-ton ship two miles overland from Shelburne Bay was an engineering feat. A special cradle with sixty-four railroad wheels was constructed, onto which the vessel was floated from a flooded basin like a canal lock. Once in position, the ship was slowly winched along a set of railroad tracks to the dry dock on the Museum grounds. The ship's main salon and several cabins have been restored; paintings, broadsides, and photographs recall the heyday of steamboating on the lake.

The Museum is open daily from mid-May to late October.

Richard Snelling, a Shelburne industrialist, recaptured the governor's chair for the Republicans in 1976. His re-election to a fourth term was unprecedented: only three prior chief executives had served more than six years. During his terms, Snelling took the lead in amending Vermont's constitution to include the Equal Rights Amendment, and to acquire low-cost Canadian power. In his last formal message to the legislature, he said:

> Vermonters love the past, but they love the future far more. We have never sacrificed the future. We shall not do it. We do not sacrifice it for the comfort of the moment; we cannot do it. Vermont is moving. Our people rightfully have a sense that we here have the best combination of any people of this country of a wholesome place in which to live

and a decent access to the financial circumstances which permit us to enjoy our natural surroundings.

In 1984, Democrat Madeleine Kunin's election to the governorship and a Democratic majority in the senate for the first time proved again that Vermont is a two-party state, with a probable balance of independent voters.

Burlington

The state's only metropolis was born in modest circumstances but with ambitious godparents. On June 7, 1763, Samuel Willis and sixty-six other Connecticut proprietors received seventy-two shares of 320 acres of Burlington from Benning Wentworth. The group met the following year, elected Thomas Chittenden moderator and Ira Allen clerk, and agreed that the Allens' Onion River Land Company should be rewarded by choice river lots for their enterprise in cutting a seventy-mile trail through the forest to the Onion (later Winooski) River from Castleton.

A decade went by before the first few settlers arrived, and they were forced to retreat from the undefended frontier until the Revolution ended. The first census, in 1791, recorded 332 inhabitants, living in clusters from the lakeshore to the Winooski Falls, where Ira Allen had constructed his large two-story house, saw mill and iron forge. In this setting, the last chapter of Ethan Allen's life was acted out, far more serene than his earlier years, but ending with characteristic drama. In the spring of 1787, he moved to his farm in Burlington on land along the Winooski he had swapped with his brother for several hundred acres of woodland adjacent to Ira's sawmill at the falls. "I have lately arrived at my new farm of 1,400 acres," he wrote a friend, "in which there are 350 acres of choice river intervale, rich upland meadow interspersed with the finest of wheat land and pasture land, well-watered and by its nature equal to any tract of the same number of acres that I ever saw. I have about forty acres under improvement." He also built a one-and-a-half-story, post and beam house, twenty-four feet wide, sheathed with clapboard from wood sawn at Ira's mill. The house was small, far more modest than Ira's, but more substantial than most others in the vicinity. Here Ethan settled down with his wife, Fanny, the five surving children of his two marriages — and a sixth on the way — plus three freed Negro hired hands.

While he, Ira, and their unreconstructed Tory brother Levi were shipping beef and lumber to Canada, Ethan returned to his writing and completed a somewhat tedious tract called *An Essay on the Universal Plenitude of Being*, in which he stressed the importance of intuition as a way of creating closer harmony with the universe. On February 11, 1789, Ethan and Newport, one of his hired men, crossed the frozen lake to South Hero with an ox-drawn hayrack. It had been a poor summer for farmers, and Ethan needed the hay that his cousin Ebenezer offered him. Ethan, Ebenezer, and a few neighbors probably spent the night drinking; Ethan had to be carted home the next day. Whether or not he had a monumental hangover, Ethan indeed suffered a stroke or seizure, and died at home that afternoon. He was fifty-two.

In his biography of Allen, Charles Jellison records his demise: "Stories aplenty have also been told about the death scene in Ethan's front bedroom. One of these has Ethan recanting his sins and omissions in the presence of the local minister, and then begging for and receiving Communion with Christ. Another has him remaining defiant and unbelieving to the end. 'The angels are waiting for you, General Allen,' the minister is supposed to have said. Whereupon, with his last ounce of strength, Ethan raised himself up in bed and shouted: 'They are, are they? Well, Goddam 'em, let 'em wait.' Actually, he neither said nor did anything. He lingered in a coma until late that afternoon, when, after being bled and physicked, he died without ever having regained consciousness. That night they moved his body across the river to Ira's place where it was packed in ice and laid out for viewing."

Ethan was buried with full military honors in an elaborate ceremony that drew a huge crowd of mourners, despite the bitter cold. Not long afterward, the sanctimonious Rev. Nathan Perkins visited Ethan's grave and noted, with a shudder, "one of the wickedest men that ever walked this guilty globe...I stopped and looked at his grave with pious horror." By the time the state legislature got around to commissioning an appropriate memorial monument in 1858, no trace could be found of Allen's body.

In 1988, the Ethan Allen Homestead Trust opened the restored house on the grounds of the Winooski Valley inter-municipal park. A multi-media dramatization of Allen's life is presented in the visitors center, a memorial to Ralph Nading Hill, the historian who identified the long-overlooked site and raised the funds to insure that the father of Vermont was recognized in an authentic and tangible fashion.

The condescending Reverend Perkins was miserly with his compliments. He paid a visit to Governor Chittenden, noting: "A low poor house — a plain family — low, vulgar man, clownish, excessively parsimonious, — made me welcome, — hard fare, a very great farm, — 1000 acres...a shrewd cunning man—skilled in human nature & in agriculture — understands extremely well ye mysteries of Vermont, aparently and professedly serious. Williston a fine township of land...And all ye towns upon ye lake Champlain & for three teer back ye best sort of land."

"One-eyed Tom" Chittenden, Vermont's first governor. —Vermont Historical Society

64

"One-eyed Tom" — as he was called by his critics — Chittenden had settled in Williston in 1774 when he was forty-four, but when the war broke out, he and his wife and ten children walked back to Castleton. He had been elected the state's first governor in 1778, but at the time of Perkins' sojourn, he was temporarily out of office and under a cloud of suspicion because of the Haldimand negotiations and for having signed over some public land to Ira Allen. Chittenden proved that this conveyance was legitimate compensation for a loan Ira had made to the state, and was re-elected in 1790. In his last message to the General Assembly in October 1791, he said: "Suffer me then as a father, as a friend, and as a lover of this people, and as one whose voice cannot much longer be heard here, to instruct you in all your appointments, to have regard for none but those who maintain a good moral character — men of integrity, and distinguished for wisdom and abilities." He died August 25, 1799, at the age of sixty-nine. Over his grave in the old cemetery in Williston, the state erected a monument, on which is suitably etched, "Out of the storm and manifold perils rose an enduring state, the home of freedom and unity."

Even before Burlington had established itself as the state's principal mercantile center, Ira Allen had the vision and the means to found the University of Vermont, chartered in 1791; the first class of four graduated in 1804.

In the same year, Ira's wealthy partner Thaddeus Tuttle, who was deviously conspiring to put him in debtors' prison, started building Grasse Mount, the finest Federal house in the state. Financially overextended in 1824, Tuttle had to sell the mansion to Cornelius Van Ness, a Dutchman from New York who had come to Burlington to practice law and won the governorship in time to give a glittering state dinner for the Marquis de Lafayette. During his triumphant tour of the Northeast, General Lafayette arrived in Burlington from Montpelier in an open barouche to lay the cornerstone of a new building at the university, to which Grasse Mount was eventually sold. When the Cornelius Van Ness and his family moved out, to take up his post as Minister to Spain, Heman Allen, Ira's nephew, moved in, having served as Minister to Chile.

With the opening of the Champlain Canal in 1823, the balance of trade shifted to New York from Montreal, thanks to the all-water route that reduced travel time to the port of New

York from the lake towns. In less than two weeks, the sloop-rigged canal boat, *Gleaner*, carried a thousand bushels of wheat, thirty-five barrels of potash and ten passengers from St. Albans Bay to New York City. In the decade from 1823 to 1833, shipments of wool escalated from ten thousand tons to more than four hundred thousand tons. Exports of butter, cheese, beef and pork grew comparably. Burlington merchants benefitted accordingly, especially Timothy Follett, Guy Catlin, and Samuel Hickock, who exported livestock, wool, and other products and imported consumer goods.

The dramatically colorful history of the Champlain Transportation Company's steamboats in the nineteenth century, and Burlington's fame as a lumber port, have been marvelously recreated in Ralph Nading Hill's panoramic book, *Lake Champlain: Key to Liberty*, published in 1977. "Of the 40 million board feet Burlington was handling by 1860 a lumberman wrote that no one dreamed the port would be 'lumbered up with boards and planks on their distant voyage to Europe, South America, California, and the far isles of the Pacific, but such is the fact.'

"By 1868," Hill continued, "thirty acres around the wharves were stacked with lumber brought there by some 400 vessels, American and Canadian...At the height of the boom 1,021 steamers, ships, and canal boats, manned by crews numbering 3300 were registered in the Champlain district.

"In the vintage year of 1873 when it was the third largest lumber port in the United States, Burlington received 170 million board feet; a decade later the mill of one firm alone was planing 40 million feet a year. The mills spawned a host of satellite industries and as many fortunes, spent by lumber barons on opulent mansions on the hill. Cheap immigrant labor abounded..."

One of these splendid houses, a red stone chateau, belonged to LeGrand B. Cannon, who combined the Lake Champlain steamboat line with the Delaware and Hudson Railroad and provided fashionable and lucrative passenger and freight service to New York City. In 1895, James Roosevelt replaced Cannon as president; during his six-year tenure, his young son Franklin D. Roosevelt took frequent trips on the steamers, and later boasted that he was one of two amateurs who could steer the *Maquam* through "The Gut" into St.Albans Bay.

John Dewey, the great philosopher of progressive education, was born in Burlington. —Special collections, University of Vermont Library

Once lauded as "the second Confucius" by the rector of the National University at Peking, John Dewey, the distinguished philosopher and educator, was born in Burlington in 1859. From the city's public schools, he entered the University of Vermont, graduated in 1879, and after three years as a classroom teacher, went to graduate school at Johns Hopkins. From 1886 on, he taught at the University of Michigan, the University of Minnesota, and as chairman of the Department of Philosophy, Psychology and Education in the newly-founded University of Chicago. Here, in 1903, he published his seminal work, *Studies in Logical Theory*, in which he introduced his doctrine of instrumentalism—logic as an art of adjustment and control—and instituted one of the first experimental schools in the country. From Columbia University after 1904, he published other books advancing his guiding principle that experience is life, and life is change and growth. In 1931 Dewey was named William James Lecturer in Philosophy at Harvard.

Writing of his early life in Vermont, Dewey declared his gratitude "that I was born at a time and place where the earlier idea of liberty and the self-governing community of citizens still sufficiently prevailed....In Vermont, perhaps even more than elsewhere, there was embodied in the spirit of the people the conviction that governments were like houses we live in, made to contribute to human welfare, and that those who live in them were free to change and extend the one as they were the other, when developing needs of the human family called for such alterations and modifications."

Professor Dewey's seventieth birthday was the occasion for a two-day celebration in New York, attended by more than two thousand scholars, who paid tribute to his eminence in education, social policy, and philosophy, among them James R. Angell, president of Yale, another native Burlingtonian. Internationally honored, Dewey died in 1952 at ninety-three.

Speaking in 1909 at Burlington's Tercentenary Celebration of the discovery of Lake Champlain, Lord Bryce, the British historian and former ambassador to Washington, warned, prophetically, of what could happen to Vermont, "the Switzerland of America":

> As wealth increases in other parts of the country, as the gigantic cities of the Eastern States grow still vaster, as population thickens in the agricultural and manufacturing parts of Ohio and Pennsylvania, and Indiana and Illinois, one may foresee a time when the love of nature and that love of recreation and health will draw more and more of the population of those overcrowded cities and States to see the delights of nature in these spots where nature shows at her loveliest. I would need the imagination of a poet or the pen of a real estate agent to figure out what the value of property will become on the shores here half a century hence, but this I can say, that I do believe that all eastern America will come more and more to value this region of mountains and lakes, as the place in which relief will have to be sought from the constantly growing strain and stress of our modern life...
>
> Save your woods, not only because they are one of your great natural resources that ought to be conserved, but also

President Taft debarks from Seward Webb's yacht to open the Lake Champlain Tercentenary in 1909. —Vermont Historical Society

because they are a source of beauty which can never be recovered if they are lost. Do not permit any unsightly buildings to deform beautiful scenery which is a joy to those who visit you. Preserve the purity of your streams and your lakes, not merely for the sake of the angler, although I have a great deal of sympathy with him, but also for the sake of those who live on the banks, and those who come to seek the joy of an unspoiled nature by the riversides. Keep open the summits of your mountains. Let no man debar you from free access to the top of your mountains and from the pleasure of wandering along their sides...Keep open for the enjoyment of all of the people, for the humblest of people, as well as for those who can enjoy villas and yachts of their own, the beauties with which Providence has blessed you.

President Taft also addressed the Tercentenary celebrations, which attracted as many as sixty thousand people. Taft, whose grandfather, Alphonso, was born in West Townshend, referred to his Vermont roots wherever he spoke during his tour of the state: in Burlington, he said "...I did not wish to miss the honor of being present on this occasion to testify to the pride I have in showing three generations of my ancestors as Ver-

The graceful Unitarian Church at the head of the Church Street Market was built in 1816 from plans by Bulfinch. —Vermont Travel Division

mont men. I am proud of it because it means that they lived among people of rugged honesty, with the spirit of true liberty, with faith in God, and with ability to help themselves." At a banquet he added: "If I were to describe the Vermonter in one word I would say he was a safe man, safe for himself, safe for his family, safe for his State and safe for the Nation. His experience was not unlike and his standing in our community is not unlike that of the canny Scot in Great Britain."

Describing the celebration in his memoirs, Henry Holt, the New York book publisher who summered in Burlington, wrote: "When they got to Burlington, the Bryces were put in my charge and spent the night with us. As we drove up from the boat, one of the crowd on the sidewalk shouted the name of the borough Bryce had represented in Parliament, and he and his wife were immensely pleased. Shortly before noon the big guns of the party fired off speeches in the public square, and I was impressed with the quietness of Bryce's....The visitors were given a good lunch at the Ethan Allen Club, an historic pageant on the lake shore, in the afternoon, and an abominable dinner, by a Boston caterer who got drunk, at the University gymnasium."

Three years later, in Woodstock enjoying the fall foliage, President Taft said, "I think all Vermonters stand together. There is a sort of freemasonry to it...and when they stand together, they generally come out ahead. Delighting his audience of community boosters, he added: "I am glad to hear that so many come to Vermont to spend their money. You should get out of them all you can get. And they should make these landscapes beautiful with their homes."

Contemporary Burlington, the urban center for more than 100,000 people, is a junior Boston, the financial, cultural, medical and educational capital of the state, with 10,000 students enrolled in U.V.M and three other colleges, and an expanding medical center. Among its architectural landmarks stand the Greek Revival mansion built by Timothy Follett, designed by Ammi B. Young; the Unitarian Church, built in 1816 from plans by Charles Bulfinch; and three buildings by the renowned firm of McKim, Mead & White — the City Hall(1926), the Robert Hull Fleming Museum (1931), and the Ira Allen Chapel (1927) on the university campus next to H.H. Richardson's last work, the romanesque Billings Library (1885). An ambitious urban renewal program has transformed much of the downtown shopping area, and is being extended to the waterfront.

Cultural resources abound: the summer Champlain Shakespeare Festival in U.V.M.'s Royall Tyler Theater; the Vermont Mozart Festival performances; the George Bishop Lane Series of concerts and lectures in the restored art-deco Flynn Theater for the Performing Arts; and the Vermont Symphony Orchestra.

Usually Democratic, Chittenden County sent the party's first governor, Philip Hoff, to Montpelier for three terms after 1962, produced the state's first Democratic Senator, Patrick Leahy, the son of a Barre printer, who was re-elected for a third term in 1986; and kept Madeleine Kunin in the governor's chair for three terms.

The once rather stodgy city acquired such a yeasty atmosphere that a Socialist mayor, Bernard Sanders, a Brooklynite, was elected by ten votes in 1981 by what a *New Republic* writer called "the 'hipboisie,' the granola-chewing exemplars of backpack chic who have come here for the university and the mountains." Mayor Sanders was re-elected three times by a substantial plurality, and nearly outpolled Republican Peter P. Smith for the state's lone Congressional seat in 1988.

Despite the evidence of its pastoral past, Burlington is not immune to symptoms of urban blight — traffic congestion, parasitic strip development along Routes 7 and 2, smog and polluted beaches in the summer of 1988, and a housing shortage. One merchant on the Church Street pedestrian shopping mall, vexed by the rowdiness of a few of the street-people, formed Westward Ho! and gave one-way bus tickets to Oregon to the most threatening. He was loudly denounced by civil libertarians, but other storekeepers contributed to the cause.

But in an imperfect world, Burlington is, comparatively, an oasis of urban civility and unusually attractive natural endowments.

Winooski

This small city, now an integral part of Burlington's sprawling suburbia, detached itself from the surrounding town of Colchester in 1922. When Ira Allen owned most of the land along the river here, he leased a parcel by the falls to a weaver "for as long as water runs, timber grows, or the sun shines," and for more than a century and a half thereafter, the Burlington Woolen Company and later the American Woolen Company's mills employed nearly everybody — some two thousand during World War II. In the early 1970s, after they had been closed down and an urban renewal project was underway, one innovative city planner boldly proposed that the downtown core be enclosed in a massive plexiglass dome. Less dramatic adaptive preservation measures transformed one mill into an indoor shopping center, and another into low-cost housing.

Two Roman Catholic institutions reflect the French-Canadian tradition: St.Michael's College was established here in 1904, and the Fanny Allen Hospital was named for Ethan's daughter, who, ironically, became a Catholic in 1811 and Vermont's first nun.

Colchester

Before he was forty, Ira Allen owned most of this township and, indeed, was the largest landholder in Vermont and one of the richest men in America at the time. Propserous, influential,

Ira Allen, pioneering land speculator and the republic's crafty statesman, founded the University of Vermont.
—Vermont Historical Society

respected and resented, he blundered into misadventure, and landed in a foreign prison, as had Ethan.

In 1795, land-poor and risking imprisonment for debt, Ira boldly decided to go to Europe to buy muskets for the Vermont militia, of which he had been appointed Major General. He would use what cash he had left and resell the arms to the state for a profit. In England, he found the British unwilling to sell guns to an American who lived on the Canadian border. He was greeted more cordially in Paris, where the Directory's president Carnot agreed to sell him 20,000 muskets and twenty-four field pieces for $50,000 — $10,000 down and the balance over seven years. By September 1796, Ira had chartered the British ship *Olive Branch* to pick up the arms at Ostend. Delayed by a month, the ninety-foot ship finally slipped secretly out of port,

73

but was intercepted by a British warship and escorted to port because its log showed it had recently carried contraband from London to Dunkirk. In May 1797, the Admiralty Court released the ship but not the muskets. For another year, Ira appealed, but his enemies at home and in England conspired to frustrate him. "They knew his finances were strained to the breaking point," Ralph Hill wrote in *The Winooski: Heartway of Vermont*, "and that he was forced to sell some of his Onion River lands to pay the staggering costs of his case. They knew that his best friend, Chittenden, the governor, had died the previous summer, that his old enemy, Isaac Tichenor had replaced Chittenden, and that the legislature of Vermont had levied a tax of a cent an acre on all the land in the state. The British Foreign Office, in league with the captors...was intent upon destroying the man who had played a dominant role in wrecking one of its campaigns of the Revolutionary War."

Two and a half years after leaving Colchester, Ira was beset by problems at home, too, where his holdings were disintegrating, raided by unscrupulous real estate operators and loaded with taxes and mortgages. Nevertheless, in quest of documentation that would clear his title to the arms, he optimistically returned to France — and was promptly jailed by French authorities bribed by the British. Helped by Talleyrand and Thomas Paine, he was bailed out and arrived in Paris only to find that Carnot had absconded to Switzerland with Ira's down payment. Carnot's enemies threw Ira into the Temple, with the worst criminals in France. In poor health and deeply depressed, Ira used his time to write, entirely from memory, his *History of Vermont*, published in 1798. Talleyrand worked for months to secure his release, which did not occur until September 1799. Ira convalesced in Paris, where Napolean and Talleyrand now reigned, and finally set sail for home in November 1800.

Ira's troubles had not ended. He could not afford to hire lawyers to regain his property; his English bankers failed; his appeals to the state and federal governments were ignored. His creditors put him in debtors' prison. Raising bail by mortgaging all of his remaining lands, Ira departed his beloved state in 1803 for Philadelphia, where he died in 1814.

There is no record that the legislature ever recognized his death, and for many years his descendants did not acknowledge their patrimony.

Fort Ethan Allen, whose campus, former barracks, officers' quarters, and stables spread over some six hundred acres between Winooski and Essex Junction, was one of Redfield Proctor's pet projects when he was Secretary of War in 1889 and later Senator. Proctor was determined to establish a regular army garrison in his home state of Vermont as part of a string of military posts along the border with Canada that might be strategically important in the event of future hostilities with Great Britain. The project was not universally popular: the St. Johnsbury *Republican*, for example, commented, "Vermont wants a military post as much as a toad wants a tail." After spirited games of legislative ping-pong, however, and arguments over its placement, the base was approved by Congress in 1892.

W. Seward Webb of Shelburne was one of the major contributors of private funds to purchase the land. Construction of its facilities for four troops of cavalry was completed in 1894. The 3rd Cavalry moved here from Illinois and Kansas. The 10th, a black regiment, was stationed at the Fort between 1909 and 1913. It was decommissioned after World War II, and the buildings used mainly by St. Michael's College.

Essex Junction

Routes 2A, 117, and 16 converge here with the Central Vermont Railroad, which never connected with the Rutland Railroad in Burlington because of their builders' bitter rivalry. Thirty trains a day once stopped here, stranding their passengers. Their frustration was immortalized in an 1865 poem, "The Lay of the Lost Traveller," by the talented Edward J. Phelps, which ended:

> I hope in hell
> Their souls may dwell
> Who first invented Essex Junction

After World War II, Thomas J. Watson, who enjoyed skiing at Stowe and Smugglers' Notch, decided to build an International Business Machine plant here. The electronic giant has been largely responsible for the rapid growth in Chittenden County's population and economic prosperity.

The Islands

Traveling north between Burlington and the Canadian border, motorists have the choice of staying on Route 7 or Interstate 89 or branching off westerly on Routes 2 and 129 through the sparsely settled chain of four islands that extends thirty miles south from the border. Originally owned by Ethan and Ira Allen and called the Isle of the Two Heros, Grand Isle County embraces Isle la Motte, North Hero, Grand Isle and South Hero, homesteaded by Ebenezer Allen, Ethan's cousin, in 1783. On Grand Isle, the Vermont Board of Historic Sites restored the log cabin that was built in that year by Jedidiah Hyde, a veteran of Bunker Hill, Bennington, Germantown and Valley Forge, and owner of Hyde Park. Accessible also by ferry from Cumberland Head, New York, to Grand Isle, this tidy archipelago remains one of the most pastoral parts of Vermont, with its fertile farms, thriving orchards, and simple hamlets, punctuated by sailing marinas and fishing camps.

Samuel de Champlain's discovery of the lake is commemmorated by an impressive granite statue adjacent to St. Anne's Shrine on the shore of Isle La Motte, the site of the French settlement in 1666. There are daily outdoor masses in the pine grove chapel during the summer.

Benedict Arnold anchored off this shore before the battle of Valcour Island on October 11, 1776. Arnold's flotilla consisted of three schooners, one sloop, seven gondolas, and one galley, armed with thirty-two guns and manned by more than five hundred men. That the timbers for these vessels had been growing in the woods earlier the same year testifies to Arnold's extraordinary feat of ship construction at the primitive shipyard at Skenesborough (Whitehall). He planned to intercept Sir Guy Carleton's British fleet of fifty-three ships and boats, which passed to the east side of Valcour Island without knowing that Arnold's ships were lying in wait on the west side, between the island and the New York shore. In the first American naval battle, Arnold's vessels were badly damaged by the superior fire power of the British, but he managed to evade capture. But he had frustrated the enemy's strategy; by the time Carleton reached the heavily-defended Ticonderoga and Mount Independence, it was so late in the season that he returned to Canada for the winter, blunting the British advance for a year.

Benedict Arnold (right) prepares for the Battle of Valcour Island, in October 1776. —Vermont Historical Society

Sunk by the British during the battle, Arnold's gondola *Philadelpha* was salvaged one hundred and fifty-nine years later, her mast and cannon still in place, and placed on permanent exhibit in the Smithsonian Institution.

St. Albans

This one-time railroad capital and Franklin County seat, originally located around a bay on Lake Champlain, has been the scene of more violent incidents than any other town in the state. Jesse Welden, a half-Indian from Connecticut, moved here before the Revolution, but there was no permanent settlement until 1785. Levi Allen, Ethan's Tory brother, claimed the town soon after it was organized, brazenly addressing his wife as "the Duchess of St. Albans." Altercations followed, and he retreated in disorder.

Between 1807 and 1814, a local merchant financed a large gang of smugglers, who transported potash and other contraband to Canada on their *Black Snake*. Three federal officials were shot and killed when they tried to stop the boat at the border. The crew was arrested, tried and convicted. One of them, Cyrus Dean, was hanged in Burlington in November 1808, attracting a crowd of some ten thousand morbid onlookers.

With many French-Canadian settlers in Franklin County, anti-British sentiments ran high in support of the rebels across the border in 1837, and the army was called in to defend St.Albans and Swanton when raiders from Quebec threatend to burn both towns in retaliation.

The town's permanent place in American history was assured on October 19, 1864, when, in the northernmost engagement of the Civil War, fourteen armed Confederate soldiers, young Kentuckians led by Bennett H. Young, who had slouched into town in mufti several days earlier, held up the three banks, shot and killed a visiting carpenter,stole horses, and escaped back to Canada with their loot of $201,000.

They had evidently planned to set fire to the mansion of Governor J. Gregory Smith, who was in Montpelier at the time. Soon after the raid began, a maid from a neighbor's house

Some of the dashing Confederates who raided St. Albans in 1864, commanded by Lt. Bennett H. Young (seated at the right).
—Vermont Historical Society

rushed to Mrs. Smith, crying: "The rebels are in town, robbing the banks, burning the houses, and killing people. They are on the way up the hill to burn your house!" Mrs. Smith alerted the servants, drew the shades, closed the blinds, and bolted every door but the front entrance. Mrs. Smith's first impulse was to run up the flag, but instead looked for weapons. She found only a large horse pistol without ammunition, and with this in hand took her stand in front of the house. Just then, a horseman galloped up the hill, who turned out to be not one of the raiders, but her brother-in-law, a member of General Custer's staff, home on leave. Later that night, soldiers were stationed at the governor's house, and remained there for nine months.

In his four-volume history of Vermont published in 1921, Walter Crockett paid tribute to the governor's wife: "Mrs. Smith was one of the most remarkable women Vermont has produced, courageous in the face of danger, possessed of great executive ability, a brilliant mind and scholarly attainments. The daughter of one of Vermont's anti-slavery leaders [U.S.Senator Lawrence Brainerd], the wife of one of the ablest railroad presidents of his day and one of the foremost Civil War governors, the mother of one of the later Green Mountain Executives, she may well be taken as a noble type of Vermont womanhood; and her courage in taking her stand alone, re-volver in hand, to defend her home and her children against the expected attack of a band of desperadoes, is an inspiring example of heroism for all future generations."

One of the raiders was wounded and died shortly thereafter. The surviving Confederates were arrested in Montreal, tried, but never extradited, despite energetic efforts by Washington. Lt. Young, rose to the rank of General. When he visited Montreal again in 1911, a group of St. Albans dignitaries paid him a courtesy call at the Ritz-Carlton Hotel.

Two years after the raid, another international incident impended when a second guerilla force of several hundred Fenians, perhaps as many as 3,500, poured off special trains from Boston in June 1866. The Fenians were determined to liberate Canada from the British and establish an Irish Free State. After camping out on the green, they marched north until they were about six miles over the border. Martial law was declared in Canada for two weeks. The Fenians retreated to St. Albans, where they found the park occupied by U.S.

troops ordered there by President Johnson to enforce neutrality. The crestfallen Irishmen were escorted to the depot and shipped back to Boston, while St. Albans residents were entertained by army band concerts.

Governor Smith, widely lauded for his outstanding leadership during the Civil War, had left office by then, and was devoting his considerable entrepreneurial energies to the Vermont Central Railroad and his vision of extending railways to the West Coast. The rise and fall of the Smith family — a small-town "Dynasty" — is a cautionary American tragedy. John Gregory Smith was born in St. Albans in 1818; his father, John, had trekked into the northern wilderness from Barre, Massachusetts, and quickly became a successful lawyer, banker and politician. When John senior was defeated for reelection to Congress in 1841, he was a moving force in the construction of the Vermont and Canada Railroad and a connecting link to the Great Lakes area. J. Gregory graduated from the University of Vermont and the Yale Law School, joined his father's practice, and followed his political footsteps into the state legislature, where he was Speaker of the House in 1861-62 when he was elected governor. Following his father's death, he was made the trustee and managing director of the Vermont Central and Vermont and Canada railroads.

With Thomas Canfield of Burlington and Frederick Billings of Woodstock, he invested in the Northern Pacific Railroad, and as president, projected its route to Puget Sound. His vision and ambition outstripped his managerial skills in this national arena, however, and when Jay Cooke, the investment banker, took over the financing of the Northern Pacific, Smith was relieved of the presidency, for, according to George W. Cass, his successor, "prodigal disbursement of money funds for which no services were rendered." Smith had nevertheless made a fortune, and was living in considerable splendor in a grand, mansarded Victorian mansion on the crest of the hill overlooking the city — a landmark that was, unfortunately, razed during World War II. He died in 1891. His career, John T. Cushing later wrote in *Vermonters: A Book of Biographies* (1932), "should demonstrate to Vermonters that a man may live in the state, there perform the major part of his life's tasks, and at the same time exercise a potent influence on the political and economic affairs of his nation. Manhood is manhood

One of the last of the powerful Central Vermont locomotives pauses at the St. Albans headquarters of the railroad. —courtesy Vermont Historical Society

wherever it is found...John Gregory Smith recognized no boundaries to his talents and accomplishments."

Worthington C. Smith (1823-94), the governor's brother, served in the Vermont legislature and for three terms in Congress.

The family's politico-economic influence was carried into the twentieth century by Edward C. Smith, his son, born in 1854, educated at Yale and the Columbia Law School. He ruled the Central Vermont Railroad until its sale to the Canadian National in 1928, governed the state between 1898 and 1900, and built a munitions factory in Swanton just before the First World War. He, too, lived exceedingly well in a Georgian white brick mansion, Seven Acres, across the street from his father's; traveled on the private railroad car given him by Dr.Seward Webb to his salmon fishing camp in Madawaska, Maine; and drove around town in a chauffeured Packard town car.

E.C. Smith's three sons — Edward, Curtis, and J.Gregory— did not fare as well. The crash and the Depression depleted the family fortune. There were rumors of financial irregularities when their banks re-opened after Roosevelt's "holiday." The

Railroads, banks, and real estate contributed to Governor J. Gregory Smith's splendid mansion overlooking St. Albans. —Vermont Historical Society

sons had good war records, but due to the times and their temperaments, they could not achieve the success their fore-bears earned and enjoyed. J. Gregory's political aspirations faded when he lost the Republican primary for lieutenant-governor in 1924. In the 1960s, Seven Acres was sold for taxes; after a brief re-incarnation as The Governor Smith Inn, a fire reduced the house to a forlorn shell.

The saga of the Smith family ended in a sordid tragedy when J. Gregory's second wife, who had just been elected mayor of St. Albans, was murdered by his male nurse.

An amusing footnote to the history of presidential campaigns was created in 1896 when a hundred happy Vermont admirers of William McKinley took a special train from St. Albans to Canton, Ohio, to congratulate their hero. As the *Vermonter* magazine reported, "The St. Albans Glee Club was engaged to accompany the party and contribute to the pleasure and enthusiasm of the occasion." When the crowd reached the McKinley home, they presented Mrs. McKinley with a case of Vermont butter molded in the form of a cross, imprinted with the portraits of the candidate and his running mate. This buttery tribute was a rebuke to McKinley's opponent, William Jennings Bryan, who stood for the free coinage of silver and whose stump speeches rang with the warning that the Republicans must not "crucify mankind on a cross of gold."

During the presentation, the glee club sang "We Want Yer, McKinley, Yes, We Do," the chorus of which ran:

> We want yer, McKinley, yes we want yer mighty bad;
>
> Ten cents a pound for butter...well you bet it makes us mad.
>
> McKinley and Protection
>
> That is our selection,
>
> An' we want yer, McKinley, Yes we want yer, want yer,
>
> Want yer
>
> An' we want yer, McKinley, yes we DO.

East Fairfield

About twelve miles east of St. Albans off Route 36 is the secluded birthplace of Chester A. Arthur, the twenty-first President of the United States. The replicated farmhouse may have been where he was born: his itinerant clergyman father, an Irish Baptist, often preached in Canada; Arthur's political

Chester A. Arthur birthplace — long before its renovation as an historic site. —Vermont Historical Society

adversaries hinted he might, indeed, have first seen the light of day across the border, making him ineligible for the presidency. In any event, he was born on October 5, 1830, and was smart enough to enroll at Union College when he was fifteen, graduating with the class of 1848. When he left college, Arthur was determined to become a lawyer, and studied law while he was principal of a boy's school in North Pownal, Vermont. He had grown up instilled by his father with a hatred of slavery, and as an attorney obtained a landmark decision in the Superior Court of New York, later upheld by the United States Supreme Court, "that no human creature could be held in bondage in the state, except under the national law." Prominent in New York Republican politics after 1856, Arthur, as engineer-in-chief, quartermaster general and inspector general of the state militia with the rank of brigadier general, virtually commanded New York's 690,000 Union troops.

In 1871, President Grant appointed him Collector of the Port of New York, a post he held until fired by President Hayes in 1878. Two years later at the Republican National Convention, the Vermont delegation whipped up a boomlet for its native hero, Senator George F. Edmunds, but James A. Garfield was

President Arthur enjoys a picnic with a pal. —Vermont Historical Society

ultimately nominated as president and Arthur as vice president. When the President was assassinated by a disappointed office holder within nine months of his inauguration, Arthur succeeded to the White House. Something of a dandy, he was known as the best-dressed president, and probably the most honest to hold the office in that era of rampant political corruption. Reform of the civil service was his principal accomplishment. One pundit of the day said of him: "No man ever went into the White House under more unfavorable circumstances and no man ever left it with a cleaner record."

Failing to win renomination, Arthur outlived his term as president by less than a year, his death occuring in New York City in November 1886.

Fairfield Pond is also called "Dream Lake," because of an 1842 crime. A hired hand on the Stephen Marvin farm nearby, the story goes, took his wife and child out for a rowboat ride one afternoon. In the evening he returned alone, explaining that he and his wife had quarreled and that she had left him, taking the child with her. Several nights later, Mrs. Marvin had a dream, in which she saw the hired man kill his wife and child, throw their bodies into the lake, and bury their belongings under a tree on the shore. She told the authorities, who found the clothing. The murderer was arrested and convicted.

Swanton

Historically-speaking, Swanton is Vermont's oldest community, a camp site for Indians around 6,000 B.C., claimed for France in 1609 by Samuel de Champlain, occupied by Abenaki villagers in 1682, and colonized by a few Europeans in 1740 after the Abenakis— the People of the Dawn— returned from St. Francis to their village on the bank of the Missisquoi River.

According to one appealing legend, there might have been white visitors even earlier than Champlain. In 1835 a leaden tube was found on the bank of the Missisquoi River that contained a curious document: "Nov.29, A.D.1564—This is the solme day I must now die this is the 90th day since we lef the Ship all have perished and on the banks of this River I die to farewell my furure Posteritiye know our end — John Graye." One theory held that the unfortunate Graye might have been a survivor of one of Martin Frobisher's expeditions, but the message has never been authenticated.

Most of the French withdrew from the area after New France surrendered to Great Britian in 1759; conflicting land grants were issued by New Hampshire and New York; Ira Allen bought up several parcels; but not until 1786 did the first permanent white settler appear in Franklin County, John Hilliker. Once New York gave up its claim in 1790, town government was organized for the seventy-four inhabitants.

Two hundred years later, Swanton was the geographical and tribal center for the nearly three thousand Abenakis in Vermont, officially ignored, but living testimony that, contrary to many historians, their nation had ceased to exist after 1783. Demanding tribal recognition by the state and federal governments, aboriginal hunting and fishing rights, and the return of such lands as the federally-owned Missisquoi Wildlife Refuge, Chief Homer St. Francis set off a fuse of legal actions and tribal controversies that were still unresolved by the end of 1988.

For many nineteenth-century years, marble was the backbone of Swanton's expanding economy. With the area dotted with quarries—notably black marble from Isle La Motte and a light chocolate colored stone — six marble mills were operating by 1837, when the industry went into a decline because of the importation of less expensive marble from Italy. The Barney Marble Company continued producing, and supplied flooring for the State, War and Navy Departments Building in Washington, D.C., in 1877. A flourishing limestone quarry and plant was started by Charles Rich in 1847.

Ammunition was the other economic mainstay after 1898, when Governor Edward C. Smith of St. Albans, N.P. Leach of Swanton, and two Montreal financiers opened the Robin Hood Powder Company. Bulk shotgun powder for reloading shells was its first product, followed by ten and twelve-gauge shotgun shells. By 1914, the renamed Robin Hood Ammunition Company's payroll had grown from thirteen to about three hundred, and warehouses had been established in seven cities across the country. At the start of World War I, the French government ordered fifty million cartridges for its Lebel rifle — and soon reordered. Remington U.M.C. bought the company in 1915 and constructed more buildings. The plant, employing about a thousand workers, ran twenty-four hours a day, many coming by special train from St. Albans.

"In order to prevent sabotage," Robert Ledoux wrote in *The*

History of Swanton (1988), "a large fence was built around the plant and guards with German Shepherd dogs patrolled the plant's grounds. The plant came under military protection on March 25, 1917, when Company B, local unit of the Vermont National Guard, was activated to stand guard duty...The plant was never sabotaged, but one soldier was accidentally killed by his own firearm."

Smith and his associates formed the International Explosives Company, which manufactured primers, detonators and time fuse exploders for, among others, the Russian government. "The first American casualty of World War One," Ledoux wrote, "was said to have been at the International Explosives Company when its general manager, Dr. E.M. Funk, was fatally injured in an explosion on March 15, 1917." The plant itself blew up on March 28, 1918, killing two Swanton women, and was never rebuilt. The Remington plant closed down a year later.

Swanton was served by four railroads in the nineteenth century. A dock at nearby Maquam Bay on Lake Champlain was used to transfer lumber and marble from rail to sloops or canal boats. In 1881, the 145-foot steamboat *Maquam* was built there by the St. Johnsbury and Lake Champlain Railroad to transport passengers and freight to railroad connections in Burlington and Plattsburgh.

Among some notable Swantonians was Agnes Elizabeth Joy, born here in 1844, who achieved fleeting fame as the Princess Salm-Salm who tried to save the life of Emperor Maximilian of Mexico in 1867. After her family moved to Phillipsburgh, Quebec, she ran away to join the circus and performed as an equestrienne. As Agnes LeClerq, an actress and dancer, she met the Prussian Prince Felix zu Salm-Salm in Washington, D.C.,in the summer of 1861 when he was fighting in Virginia as a volunteer with the Army of the Potomac. After the Civil War, they went to Mexico. The prince and his friend, Maximilian, were captured and sentenced to death by revolutionaries. The princess attempted to save them both, but rescued only her husband.

Swanton's green, scene of an annual festival, is graced by a pair of swans — domestic replacements for Betty and Sam, given to the village in 1961 by Queen Elizabeth and flown by jet from Norfolk, England.

Highgate

From this small border village sprang two eminent Vermonters, the nineteenth-century poet-politician John Godfrey Saxe, and the twentieth-century politician-statesman Senator Warren R. Austin, the first United States Ambassador to the United Nations.

The township of Highgate, which includes the villages of Highgate Falls and Highgate Springs, was settled in 1787 by a group of Hessian soldiers, British mercenaries who decided to stay in the New World and thought they were taking up residence in Canada.

They were preceded by a German youth, John Saxe, who built a grist and saw mill. John Godfrey, born in 1816, worked on his father's farm until he was seventeen, and then graduated from Middlebury College in 1839 after a spell at Wesleyan University. He was admitted to the bar in 1843, and while he was Chittenden County school superintendent in 1847-48, he published his first work of poetry, *Progress*. In 1850, Saxe became editor of the Burlington *Sentinel*, published *Poems*, a collection which was to go through thirty-eight editions in the next twenty-three years, and served as state's attorney for the county. An enthusiastic Democrat, very much in the minority, Saxe ran for governor in 1859 and 1860.

He treated his defeats sardonically:

> When John was contending (though sure to be beat)
>
> In the annual race for the Governor's seat,
>
> And a crusty old fellow remarked, to his face,
>
> He was clearly too young for so lofty a place,—
>
> "Perhaps so," said John; "but consider a minute;
>
> The objection will cease by the time I am in it!"

Other collections of his frankly romantic or satirical works followed. His amusing light verse captivated the nation. Among his most popular works was "The Proud Miss MacBride, a Legend of Gotham." Here are two of its thirty-eight stanzas:

> O, terribly proud was Miss MacBride,
>
> The very personification of Pride,
>
> As she minced along in Fashion's tide,
>
> Adown Broadway,— on the proper side,—

When the golden sun was setting;
There was pride in the head she carried so high,
Pride in her lip, and pride in her eye,
And a world of pride in every sigh
    That her stately bosom was fretting;

        * * *

Depend upon it, my snobbish friend,
Your family thread you can't ascend,
Without good reason to apprehend
You may find it waxed at the farther end
    By some plebeian vocation;
Or, worse than that, your boasted Line
May end in the loop of stronger twine
    That plagued some worthy relation!

In 1872, Saxe moved to Albany and the editorship of the *Evening Journal*, becoming widely known as a lecturer, and familiar habitue of Saratoga Springs summer hotel piazzas, where he held court, dressed in white linen suits and sometimes mistaken for Mark Twain. But profound melancholia overcame his wit and sociability; he never recovered from a train wreck while he was on a lecture tour in the West, when he was pulled unconscious from a burning car, nor from the death of his wife and all but one of their five children. Saxe became a bitter recluse, and died at his surviving son's house in Albany in 1887.

John Godfrey Saxe, the popular poet, was a lawyer, newspaper editor, and Democratic candidate for governor. —Special collections, University of Vermont Library

Warren Austin's rise to national prominence began when he, too, started law practice, joining his father's firm in St. Albans after his graduation from the University of Vermont in 1899. By 1909, he had become a Republican power broker in the state and mayor of St. Albans. His skill as a trial and corporation lawyer attracted the attention of the National City Bank in New York, whose American International subsidiary retained him in 1915 to go to China to negotiate a $130 million loan for railroad and canal construction.

During the 1920s, in Burlington, he made a reputation as a spellbinder before juries, winning the notorious alienation of affection suit known as Woodhouse v. Woodhouse. For his client, the impressionable daughter of a soap salesman, wooed, won and spurned by the scion of a wealthy and influential family, Austin wangled the record jury award of $465,000 — subsequently whittled down to $125,000 by the judge.

Following the death of Senator Luther Greene in 1931, Austin, asserting his "young guard" posture, won a bitter primary and special election for the unexpired term. Although he was an ardent opponent of Roosevelt's New Deal, Austin was also a burr under the saddle of the Republican isolationists in the Senate. As the Nazi threat to peace grew more apparent, Austin voted to repeal the Neutrality Act, and supported Lend-Lease. He was never given a seat on the Senate Foreign Relations Committee, but Secretary of State Hull nevertheless appointed him a member of the semi-secret Committee of Eight that was planning a post-war international organization. In 1946, President Truman appointed him as the first United States Ambassador to the United Nations.

At seventy-three, stout and courtly, "Austin sallies into U.N.'s polemic fray with certain granitelike inner qualities," *Time* reported in its 1951 cover story: "tenacity, common sense... and a God-fearing faith in the cause of freedom and collective security." At times, he bumbled, as he did during the Arab-Israeli crisis in 1948 when he proposed that their representatives sit down together "like Christian gentlemen."

When the Korean war broke out in 1950, he was constantly in the limelight. "Once more excited to battle, septugenarian Austin went forth to smite the foe," noted *Time*. "All summer long, deftly seconded by Britain's Jebb, the U.S. Ambassador denounced the Big Lie of Russia's Jacob Malik — that the U.S., and not Communism, had committed aggression in the Far East. The free world had no champion quite like the portly, pince-nezed American. His voice had the range and righteousness of an Old Testament prophet as he flailed Communism's 'shameless travesties of the realities.' " A dramatic moment came on September 18, when he rebutted Malik's claim that the Russians had supplied no weapons to their Korean comrades, by waving aloft in the Security Council a Russian-made Tommy gun captured from the North Koreans.

Austin summed up his feelings about his native state in a letter to a Swanton girl: "I love Vermont because it was there I was born and...prepared for...the opportunity to qualify to humbly serve in the greatest cause mankind has ever know— in the relations of nations, to hasten the day when 'men shall beat their swords into plowshares' and live in security and peace."

When the Truman administration ended, Austin retired and returned with his wife to their Georgian brick house in Burlington, surrounded by an old-fashioned "international" apple orchard. He died there in 1962 at the age of eighty-five, praised as another memorable figure in Vermont's Pantheon of uncommon Congressmen who had far more influence on the national and international stage than the state's size seemed to warrant.

Affable U.N. Ambassador Warren Austin wins a faint smile from the Soviets 'nyet-man' Molotov. —Vermont Historical Society

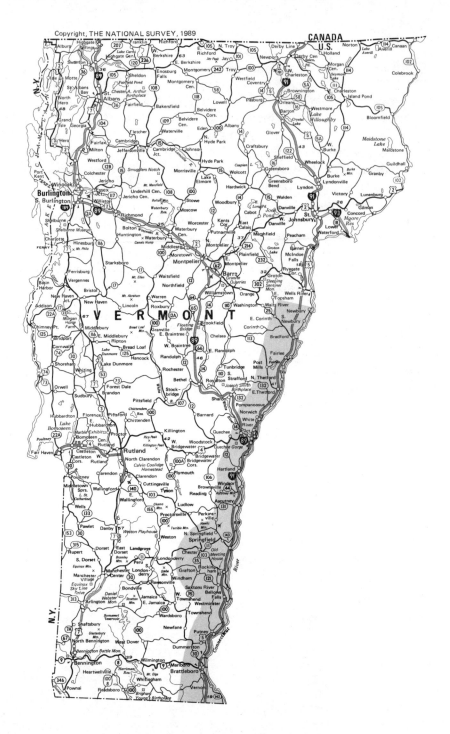

Copyright, THE NATIONAL SURVEY, 1989

Route 5 : The Connecticut River Corridor

92

Chapter Two

Route 5—
The Connecticut River Corridor

"The ideal of early Vermonters was liberalism. Even for those early days they may have appeared wild and undisciplined. The Constitution of Vermont [1777] must have been the most radical document of its day. It prohibited slavery in any form, it extended the right of suffrage to all men, regardless of property ownership; it recognized the subservience of private property to public need; it specifically permitted freedom of speech and of the press."

— Governor George D. Aiken,
Speaking from Vermont, 1938.

Before the completion of Interstate 91 in the 1960s, which links the university centers of New Haven, Northampton, Amherst, and Hanover, well-travelled Route 5 was called "The College Highway." In Vermont, paralleling I-91, it still snakes along the west bank of the sinuous, largely unspoiled Connecticut River, to which Atlantic salmon have been induced to return via fish ladders at the periodic dams. From its humble origins in the northeast wilderness to its union with the sea at Old Saybrook, the Connecticut has served itinerant Indians, the early up-country settlers, small-scale traders, massive log drives, and to generate hydroelectric power.

If some scholars' theses were to prevail, the river may indeed have been ascended by ancient Celts from the Iberian Peninsula. In 1975, interest in Vermont's odd stone structures reached a peak when Professor Barry Fell, a retired marine biologist from Harvard, took the position that he had identified inscriptions on some of these slab-roofed stone chambers as an early form of Ogam script dating from 1000 to 300 B.C. To Fell, it was clear that the Celts had fashioned these megalithic chambers, rocks carved into the shape of male and female genitals, deity and animal figures; and he and others, notably Professor Warren Cook of Castleton College, came up with archaeoastronomical data suggesting the deliberate placement of several structures. These Celtic settlements in the uplands off the Ottauquechee River—mostly in Windsor and Orange Counties— had been colonized from the mouth of the Connecticut. "In the secluded valleys and on the hilltops," Fell wrote, "the priests (or Druids) erected the temples and circles of standing stones required by their religious beliefs, using, like their European cousins, the great stone boulders left upon the land by the retreating glaciers at the end of the Ice Age."

Not so, argued Giovanna Neudorfer, Vermont State Archaeologist, who maintains that most of Vermont's stone chambers were built as root cellars or chimney supports. "While there appears to be no evidence of ancient pre-Columbian European settlement in Vermont," she wrote in *Vermont History* in 1979, "it does not mean that evidence of ancient European settlements may not be identified in the future. In Vermont and elsewhere, there are features which are presently unexplained. For example, the 'Memphremagog stone' on the Vermont-Quebec border exhibits markings which appear to be neither

weathering, dragging or glacial scoriations, nor plowmarks
....While there are still many archeological puzzles in Vermont,
the stone chambers are not among them."

In recent years the Connecticut River has been the benefici-
ary of several protectionist groups, notably the Connecticut
River Watershed Council and the Nature Conservancy, which
aims to preserve a hundred or more ecologically significant
habitats along the four-hundred-mile corridor from Norton
Pool at the northwestern tip of New Hampshire to Selden Neck
in southern Connecticut.

Oddly, the center of the river does not constitute the border
between New Hampshire and Vermont: after a century or more
of wrangling by the two states, the United States Supreme
Court ruled in 1933 that the New Hampshire border extended
to the low-water mark of the west bank — a blow to the Granite
State's tax collectors who had been trying to levy taxes on the
paper mills along the west bank in Bellows Falls.

Brattleboro

Resembling a movie lot for *The Magnificent Ambersons* or
another Victorian family saga, Brattleboro is a lively, rather
cosmopolitan town of 12,000 people, and serves as the state's
southeast foyer for travellers from New Hampshire and Massachusetts, Connecticut and New York City. Here, past and
present are tangibly linked, from the first permanent Colonial
settlement in 1724 at Fort Dummer to Vermont Yankee, in
Vernon, the state's only nuclear power plant, which has been
producing electricity since 1972.

The land that became Brattleboro was bought at auction in
1718 for a farthing an acre by a group of Bay Colony swells from
Cambridge, including Lieutenant Governor William Dummer
and William Brattle, who never saw the place that bears his
name. The small settlement was first called Dummerston,
after Fort Dummer, the blockhouse erected to protect the
settlers in the valleys to the south from marauding Indians.
The remains of Fort Dummer lie beneath the waters of the
Connecticut backed up by the Vernon Dam. Later, Benning
Wentworth, the avaricious governor of New Hampshire, issued
a royal grant for the same land, naming it Brattleborough. In
1766, the grantees secured a confirming patent from New York,
which claimed the area as Cumberland County. In 1778,

residents rejected by a 165-1 vote accession to "the pretended State of Vermont"; Ethan Allen and his militia brought them to heel in 1782.

Many of the residents of Guilford, Brattleborough and Marlborough belonged to the *contras* of the day, a loose alliance of Connecticut River valley dwellers who opposed the Allen brothers' Westside *junta*. Some favored annexation by New Hampshire, others a separate state of their own, and the rest remained loyal to New York. For example, Charles Phelps of Marlborough and his sons were violently antagonistic to Vermont's jurisdiction over what had been New York's Cumberland County. He has been described by Frederick Van de Water as a man "six feet three, with a peaked bald head, snub nose, [and] a little mouth — an inadequate orifice for the amount of speech with which his fat body seemed crammed." Phelps and his New York Party were clearly in the minority, but he was commissioned by New York to set up a *de facto* civil government. The General Assembly of Vermont promptly responded with an act "for the punishment of conspiracies against the peace, liberty, and independence" of the infant state, setting the stage for the Allens to recruit armed militia to quell the insurrection. In Guilford, Ethan roared: "I, Ethan Allen, do declare that I will give no quarter to the man, woman, or child who shall oppose me, and unless the inhabitants of Guilford peacefully submit to the authority of Vermont, I swear that I will lay it as desolate as Sodom and Gomorrah, by God." The terrified Guilfordites fled.

Timothy Phelps, Cumberland County sheriff, was arrested and jailed, but Charles, his father, eluded the posse despatched to arrest him, and managed to make his way to Philadelphia, where he pelted Congress with petitions supporting New York's claim to Cumberland County. The Continental Congress, still preoccupied with winning the war with the British, equivocated by passing a resolution that, in effect, ordered the New York Party to cease claiming jurisdiction, but directed the Vermont authorities to make restitution to the rebels. Charles Phelps soon realized that further resistance was futile. In 1784 he asked for and received a pardon from Vermont's General Assembly. Still nursing his allegiance to New York, he died in 1789, at seventy-three, two years before Vermont finally wrung statehood from an exasperated Congress.

Meanwhile, Brattleborough was growing, sprouting mills, meeting house, post office, and general store. Pitch, tar, lumber, turpentine and pearl ash where shipped downstream; flatboats offloaded salt, sugar, molasses, codfish, cloth, glass, black powder and cigars. By 1850, when the town's population reached 3,816, Brattleboro (as its name was simplified) was firmly on the map, noted for its therapeutic water cure.

The hydropathic system of physical rehabilitation introduced by Dr. Robert Wesselhoef drew well-heeled convalescents from New England. His spartan Brattleboro Hydropathic Institution, opened in 1845, offered America's most expensive ($10 a week, $11 in summer) cure, and was patronized by such literary luminaries as Harriet Beecher Stowe, Henry Wadsworth Longfellow, Francis Parkman, James Russell Lowell and William Dean Howells.

Howells was attracted by more than cold water and stale bread: he married a Brattleboro belle named Elinor Mead, the daughter of Larkin G. Mead, an attorney, whose second son, Larkin, Jr., became one of America's best-known sculptors. A fourth son, Rutherford, was a partner in the notable architectural firm of McKim, Mead & White.

Equally accomplished were the Hunt brothers. William Morris Hunt was born in Brattleboro in 1824, studied art in Paris, and pursued a successful career in Boston until he drowned in 1879. His much-admired "Prodigal Son" painting hangs in the Brooks Library. Richard Morris Hunt, his younger brother, designed a series of architectural landmarks, including the base of the Statue of Liberty, and palatial houses for the Vanderbilts, "The Breakers" in Newport, Rhode Island, and "Biltmore" in Ashville, North Carolina.

Notorious for less scrupulous achievements was "Jubilee Jim" Fisk, who moved to Brattleboro from Pownal as a lad, the son of an itinerant pedlar who built the graciously proportioned brick Revere House in 1849 and ran it as a temperance hotel. There was nothing temperate about Jim, Junior, the greedy financier who first profiteered in blockaded Southern cotton during the Civil War and the sale of worthless Confederate bonds to gullible Britishers. On Wall Street after the war, he and his fellow piratical corporate raiders, Daniel Drew and Jay Gould, wrested control of the Erie Railroad from Commodore Vanderbilt, and milked millions from the unfortunate line.

Fisk and Gould then tried to corner the gold market, ruining enough investors to cause the "Black Friday" panic of September 24, 1869. The thirty-seven-year-old Fisk's gargantuan appetites for wine, women, and song fatally betrayed him. For his mistress, the actress Josie Mansfield, he built an opera house on 23rd Street in New York, but on January 7, 1872, he was shot to death by Ed Stokes, a rival for her affections. His corpulent remains lay in state in the Revere House; the entire town turned out for his obsequies; and Larkin Mead, Jr.,was commissioned to create an appropriate monument, which may be admired in the Prospect Park Cemetery.

Along with native artists and architects, Brattleboro nourished an enduring literary scene. To nearby Guilford in 1791 came the clever lawyer and droll playwright, Royall Tyler, whose *The Contrast* was the first American comedy regularly acted by professionals when it opened in New York in March 1787, followed shortly by a two-act comic opera, *May Day in Town*. Boston-born and Harvard-educated, Tyler moved in a cosmopolitan world, reading law with Francis Dana and wooing but not winning Abigail Adams. Law was his vocation, writing his recreation (rather like today's prolific novelist Louis Auchincloss). Within a few years of his arrival in Vermont, Tyler was State's Attorney of Windham County, moving up to the Supreme Court in 1801 and the Chief Justice's seat in 1807. By then, he had also published in 1797, anonymously, *The Algerine Captive*, a novel which won international recognition and the first American work of fiction to be published in England. In this tale, "Updike Underhill," the archetypical Yankee, relates the story of New England life as a prelude to the hero's captivity on Algerian shores. Tyler was a law professor and trustee of the University of Vermont in Burlington, where the campus theater bears his name. He died in 1826.

Brattleboro has provided many footnotes to literary history over the years. T.P. James, an itinerant printer, arrived in town the year that Charles Dickens died in England, leaving unfinished his latest novel, *The Mystery of Edwin Drood*. Possessed by the spirit of Dickens, James secluded himself and went to work. Although he had never before written anything, James finished the last half of Dickens' tale as if in a trance. The press took up the story; Sir Arthur Conan Doyle began probing the strange case, and to everyone's astonishment,

Rudyard Kipling's vermont feud was played out in and around his "Naulahka" home in Dummerston. —Vermont Historical Society

James' style of writing duplicated the famous author's so that it was impossible to tell where Dickens' stopped and James' took over. The book was published in 1873 with the approval of Dickens scholars.

Had it not been for a stubbornly proud and profane Vermonter named Beatty Balestier, Rudyard Kipling might have lived out his life in Dummerston and added his name to the galaxy of American authors. As explained in *Rudyard Kipling's Vermont Feud* by Frederic F. Van de Water, it was Kipling's "odd fate to find wife and friend and most vindictive foe in a single family. He had left India with the dawn of his amazing fame in his face. Its full sunrise found him in England [in the late 1880s]...In London he met Wolcott Balestier." Wolcott, whose father had moved to Brattleboro before the Civil War, was in London representing a Boston book publisher, with his "scapegrace" younger brother, Beatty. When Wolcott died of typhus in Dresden in 1891, Kipling mourned him almost as if they had been lovers — but married his sister Caroline and brought her back to Dummerston in March 1892.

With Beatty's guidance, Kipling built his ark-like country house called "Naulakha." The Kiplings dressed for dinner every night; Caroline, according to Van de Water, had been reared and schooled in America; her sojourn in England had been brief but she had returned to her native land with heavy Mayfair graces and clung to British ways more stoutly than her husband did. "She insisted upon English house servants and an English coachman. No Vermonter, while conscious, could have been cajoled into the top-boots, doeskin breeches, blue coat and top hat that Matthew Howard wore. The progress of Mrs. Kipling down Main Street in a basket phaeton, drawn by horses in tandem, was one of Brattleboro's major spectacles."

With neighbors respecting his privacy, Kipling finished *Captains Courageous* and *The First and Second Jungle Books*. Fame brought so much mail that a private post office was lodged in the home of his neighbors, the Waites. Kipling despatched hundreds of postcards, reading:

Please note change of address from
Brattleboro, Vt., to WAITE, Windham County, Vermont. Be careful not to omit name of county.

"Thus Vermont remembers him, " Van de Water writes, "a swarthy and sturdy little man, with thick eyeglasses and a great bunch of black mustache, who, like the cat of the *Just So Stories*, went his own way and reveled in his loneliness. He was cold and sometimes deliberately uncivil to adults who sought him out, but he had a fondness for and a way with children. Youth could reach him where maturity could not."

The simmering feud between the brothers-in-law erupted over a property dispute in 1896. Van de Water describes their final confrontation: "Beatty Balestier swung his team across the road and Rudyard Kipling fell off his bicycle to avoid collision. He cut his wrist, but bodily hurt was forgotten in the shock of greater mental injury. Beatty bawled: 'See here, I want to talk to you,' and Kipling answered primly, freeing himself from his machine: 'If you have anything to say, say it to my lawyers.'

"It was not the wisest retort he could have made. Beatty glared down from the buckboard at his sister's husband. Beatty's voice was shrill with long-cherished rage and more recent drink. His words bit deep into the memory of Kipling who repeated them thereafter on the witness stand:

"'By Jesus, this is no case for lawyers. You've got to retract the Goddamned lies you've been telling about me. You've got to retract them in a week or by Christ I'll punch the Goddamned soul out of you.'"

Reporters from the metropolitan press swarmed over the ensuing court hearings of Kipling's assault charges against Balestier. His seclusion blown, Kipling and his wife left town forever.

Van de Water has been quoted here at some length as a sampler of his supple prose. Van de Water's farm in West Dummerston, where he lived for many years after 1934, was not far from Kipling's. While still a newspaperman, he had published several mystery stories, but his career as a serious author of more than thirty books began with his move to Vermont. At heart a historian, Van de Water's most significant and enduring work was *The Reluctant Republic*, a perceptive, lively account of Vermont between 1724 and 1791, first published in 1941 and reissued in 1974. In the concluding lines of his description of the protean Allen brothers, he wrote that "among the lank and shabby statesmen who talked through their noses and, ill-advisedly, were derided by their more worldly adversaries, the Allen brothers stand first — Ethan the whirlwind, the earthquake and the fire; Ira the small voice; Ethan who stamped an impression of himself deep upon the state he served; Ira who is the very substance of the state itself."

Twentieth-century political leadership has been personified by three generations of Brattleboro's Gibson family. Ernest W. Gibson represented the Progressive movement in the 1912 Republican Convention as a Roosevelt delegate, and served in Congress as Representative and Senator from 1923 to 1940, when he was succeeded by George Aiken. Opposition to the Proctor family's control of Vermont politics has been called the Aiken-Gibson wing, and the showdown came in 1946 when Ernest W. Gibson, Jr., unseated the incumbent Governor Mortimer Proctor.

"For nearly twenty years," Gibson declared, "the rule of succession has dominated the Vermont politics. Under this rule a relatively small clique of people choose governors nearly ten years in advance, supporting them up a series of political steps to the highest office...To stop this unwholesome practice, to promote a greater democracy and to make economic security march hand in hand with political liberties in Vermont is the challenging reason for my candidacy." Gibson served until 1950, when he was appointed a federal district judge by President Truman. His son, Ernest W. Gibson, III, was elected to the legislature, and sits as a justice of the Vermont Supreme Court.

For over a hundred years, the fortress-like Brooks House has dominated Brattleboro's Main Street. Built at a cost of $150,000 on the site of the catastrophic fire of 1869, George J. Brooks's five-story, eighty-room hotel rivaled its metropolitan counterparts in luxurious accommodations. When first constructed, it sported a forty-foot, two-story verandah with Corinthian columns and iron railings, surmounted by a Mansard roof and strands of iron grillwork. In 1872, the *Vermont Phoenix* described its interior:

"The new hotel is most elegantly and thoroughly furnished. The carpets, bedding and linen are from Stewart's [the fashionable New York department store]. The hall carpet is a Wilton with a rich, handsome figure; the parlor carpet is a magnificent Marquette procured at a cost of about $800. The furniture is of black walnut.....Everything is arranged with taste and an eye to the convenience and comfort of guests, and the entire expense of furnishing will fall little if anything short of $30,000."

Until its renovations in 1928, the Brooks House remained more or less intact; but it lost its faithful clientele and closed down in 1963. After an interim as the Yankee Doodle Motel, the Brooks House was transformed in 1970 by Norman B. Chase into offices, apartments, retail stores and restaurants. Adaptive preservation also saved the downtown railroad depot, which was remodeled into a museum and art center a few years later.

Another landmark, the Latchis Memorial Theater, is now on the National Register of Historic Places and the National Trust for Historic Preservation. The Latchis building on Main Street, with its art deco facade of poured concrete, was opened in 1938 by the four sons of Demetrius P. Latchis, a Greek immigrant whose original fruit stand in Brattleboro grew into a chain of fifteen movie houses and three hotels. The gala September 22 opening, featuring Sonja Henie in *My Lucky Star* and a stage show with Felix Ferdinando and His Hotel Montclair Orchestra from New York, was threatened by the hurricane that swept New England, but residents filled the 900-seat auditorium and 300-seat balcony, decorated with classic Grecian architectural details and mythological murals and statues. The Latchis family scored a coup in 1940 when they screened *Gone With the Wind* shortly after it opened in Atlanta, New York and Boston, giving Brattleboro the distinction of being the first small town in America to see the film classic.

J.Estey & Company, makers of parlor or "cottage" organs, was the most important commercial enterprise in Brattleboro from 1855 until the 1920s. At its nineteenth-century zenith, Estey's sprawling factory could use four carloads a week of black walnut lumber for cases.

Another local institution, known today as the Brattleboro Retreat, opened in 1836 as the Vermont Lunatic Asylum, one of the first hospitals in America designed especially for the scientific treatment of mental illness. Its facilities now include drug and alcohol abuse rehabilitation centers.

Ski jumping was a popular winter sport long before the commercialization of downhill skiing, and Fred Harris of Brattleboro popularized it. At Dartmouth College in 1908-10, Harris promoted the formation of a ski and snowshoe club and the first ski jumping contest. Subsequently, his seventy-meter hill outside Brattleboro was a celebrated site for many years.

Among Brattleboro's cultural assets are Rudolf Serkin's summer Marlboro Music Festival, held at the small college seven miles west on Route 9, where Pablo Casals was for many years the maestro; and the distinguished New England Bach Festival Orchestra and chorus, directed by Blanche Moyse, which presents a fall concert tour in Vermont and elsewhere.

Putney

A few miles north of Brattleboro, the once serene, now touristy village of Putney claims several human landmarks, notably George D. Aiken, nurseryman, governor, dean of the United States Senate, and author of what has come to be acccepted as "the Aiken Solution" (his formula for liberating the United States from the Vietnam War: "Declare we've won and get out"). Long before the Age of Aiken, however, Putney was the home of quite a different independent spirit, John Humphrey Noyes, the guru for a group of high-minded hippies who scandalized their neighbors in the 1840s. Indeed, Windham County was especially attractive to religious cultists of the period. Around 1800, the Dorrilites appeared, recruited by a refugee from Burgoyne's army who claimed supernatural powers. He and his disciples were vegetarians and refused to wear any clothes that came from animals. One follower, a blacksmith, had to use linen instead of leather in his bellows. They defied civil laws and celebrated Dorril's divine revelations with unrepressed revelry. And on October 20, 1844, a large band of Millerites (the faithful followers of William Miller), having disposed of all their worldly goods and donned white robes for "going up," climbed the hills of Jamaica to await the Second Coming of Christ.

Noyes's "Bible Communism," however, outlived the Millerites. A native of Brattleboro and a graduate of Yale, Noyes was the son of a Congressman and cousin of President-to-be Rutherford B. Hayes. He and his Perfectionists dwelt in Putney for several years after 1838, creating the original American commune, devoted to social, economic, and religious equality. But the serpent of wife-swapping shattered this Eden: in 1847 shocked neighbors caused Noyes to be charged with adultery. Noyes posted bond and fled with his followers to Oneida, New York, where the community was re-established— along with the plated silverware company for which Oneida is renowned.

George D. Aiken, who died in 1986, is revered by Vermonters of every political persuasion for his probity, wisdom and wit. When the author once asked him if he had been born in Putney, the "Governor" (as he preferred to be called even after 36 years in the United States Senate) replied, "No, Dummerston. And you know what? There's the most expensive historic marker in the country over my birthplace — three million dollars' worth of I-91."

Aiken always made his home in Putney, however, and before running for office made an enviable reputation there as a nurseryman and author of *Pioneering with Wildflowers*, self-published in 1933 and subsequently reprinted in various editions for another forty years. The book, an oustanding work on the preservation and cultivation of endangered wild flowers, is dedicated to "Peter Rabbit in the hope that flattery will accomplish what traps and guns have failed to do and that the little rascal will let our plants alone from this time on." At an

Governor George D. Aiken was the universally-admired "Dean" of the United States Senate for many years. —Special Collections, University of Vermont Library

autographing appearance for the fourth edition in 1976, an elderly admirer leaned across the table and asked, "Governor, do you still go tramping around in the woods looking for those wildflowers?"

"No," the 84-year-old Aiken replied serenely, "they come to me, now."

Elected to the legislature in 1931, Aiken moved up to be Speaker of the House and lieutenant governor before running successfully for the governorship in 1936. As one of only four Republicans elected as governors in the Democratic landslide, Aiken soon found himself in the national spotlight. While attacking the New Deal as "that visible and invisible government in Washington whose thoughts and actions are so alien to the free-thinking people of Vermont and the nation," he exhorted the Republican party to reform itself. An Aiken-for-

President boomlet swelled, and in his nationally broadcast Lincoln Day Dinner to the National Republican Club in 1938, he was characteristically blunt: "The greatest praise I can give Lincoln...is to say he would be ashamed of his party's leadership today."

Aiken's book, *Speaking from Vermont*, published in 1938 in his first term as governor, drew national praise for its commonsense treatment of economic problems, and became part of his platform to recast the Republican Party in a more responsive and progressive mold as an antidote to the "centralized paternalism" of the New Deal Democrats.

Underscoring the self-sufficiency of Vermonters, Aiken wrote: "When depressions and recessions land upon us today, this inherited facility of being able to do without things which people accustomed to more cash feel they must have, stands us in good stead. Particularly at the present time we keep faith in New England and in the nation, because we know that in spite of the increasingly small amount of cash in circulation, happiness and real living are not wholly a matter of dollars and cents....We are proving the value of a life more slowly paced and more highly productive of returns in living values. Whereas the people of the densely populated centers used to laugh at our apparent frugality of income and enjoyment, they are now looking earnestly and a little enviously at the New England habits of living....And in seeing all these things there is intensified in the hearts of all Americans a hope that a return to more of the New England ways of doing things may prove to be the best way out for America."

In 1940, Wendell Wilkie won the G.O.P's nomination, and Aiken was elected to the United States Senate. In many ways, he "typified the Republican rule that had held sway in Vermont for a century," William Doyle writes in *The Vermont Political Tradition*.

Toward the end of his thirty-four years in Congress, he was acknowledged as "the Dean" of the Senate.

Neither a hawk nor a dove during the Vietnam War, Aiken was called the "wise old owl" after he proposed in 1966 that the war be ended by declaring victory and withdrawing American troops, the solution followed seven years later by the Nixon administration. His lifetime campaign expenditures were only a minute fraction of what most candidates spent in a single election, and his Senate staff— headed by his wife Lola— was always the leanest in Washington. From the time he married his former secretary, Lola Pierotti, in 1967 she served without pay as his chief administrative assistant and press secretary, positions then normally paying $50,000 a year. When he finally retired in 1974, he was one of the most respected men in the Senate, the ranking Republican on the Agriculture and Foreign Relations Committees. One of his enduring achievements was his fight for the St. Lawrence Seaway and its related power project, which brought inexpensive hydroelectric power to Vermont just when the state's post-World War II economic expansion needed it most. "Aiken's popularity was so great," Doyle writes, "that he claimed he never had to ask for a vote. 'Get into the community and find out what the problems are. That's the best politics,' he said. When Aiken retired at eighty-two, he said he would miss his friends in the capital [particularly his pal, Senator Mike Mansfield], but not Washington. 'I've never been at home in Washington...Home's up on the mountains in Vermont where I always lived.' "

"George Aiken's retirement to his Vermont orchard left the Capitol's supply of agrarian morality sadly diminished," Ralph Nading Hill wrote in his foreword to *Aiken: Senate Diary*, published in 1976. "A ponderous government forged by pressure groups makes it unlikely that an old-fashioned populist with abiding faith, not in mobs but in individuals, will again achieve his kind of influence at home and abroad. He acquired this influence because he did not seek it. Since no posse ever conducted him into the Senate or pursued his power after he got there, he could be everybody's man because he was nobody's man but his own."

Aiken was succeeded in the Senate by the first Democrat in Vermont's history to hold that seat, Patrick J. Leahy, the Chittenden County prosecutor. Now in his third term, Leahy has proven once again that the state's Congressional incumbents have tenured positions.

Putney has been in the educational vanguard, too. The progressive and coed, secondary Putney School has been flourishing since 1935; Landmark College, the first one organized specifically for dyslexic students, has occupied the former Windham College campus designed by Edward Durrell Stone since 1985.

Westminster

Westminster, placidly occupying part of the mile-wide Connecticut River terrace north of Putney, is an historic hamlet that was once incorrectly called the site of the first armed engagement of the Revolutionary War. What actually happened there in 1775, however—"The Westminster Massacre"—crystallized the Vermonters' guerilla campaign against the incursions of New York land grabbers.

Originally granted by Benning Wentworth in 1735, the land was divided into sixty-two allotments. A sawmill and at least one house were built, and the unusually wide, straight King's Highway laid out. The first settlement was abandoned in 1740, regranted in 1752, and then appropriated as part of Cumberland County by the state of New York. The County Court house was built in 1772 (and razed in 1806). In 1755, an armed party of local dissidents seized the courthouse, refusing admission to officials. They, in turn, summoned the sheriff with an armed posse, and on March 13 attacked the courthouse, killing twenty-two-year-old William French and another defender. Young French's emotionally-freighted martyrdom at the hands of "Cruel Ministereal Tools of Georg ye 3rd" and his Tory crew aroused a wave of popular loathing toward the British as well as the Yorkers, and led to a convention in Westminster on January 15, 1777, where Vermonters declared their independence from everyone. A replica of French's headstone in the Westminster burying ground still attracts epitaph hunters and gravestone rubbers.

In 1778, Judah Paddock Spooner and Timothy Green set up a press and began publishing the territory's first newspaper, *The Vermont Gazette* or *The Green Mountain Post Boy*. The venerable press now reposes in the museum of the Vermont Historical Society in Montpelier. Some historians contend that it is, indeed, the original 17th-century Stephan Daye Press, established in Cambridge, Massachusetts, the first in North America.

Another of the town's influentials was Stephen R. Bradley, a graduate of Yale, who was admitted to the bar in May 1779, served as state's attorney, and carried "Vermont's Appeal to the Candid and Impartial World" to the Continental Congress in 1780, one of the many White Papers Vermont submitted in its clamorous campaign to secure statehood. Bradley later served as one of Vermont's first United States Senators from 1791 until 1813.

From Westminster, too, came Augustus Willard, an ambitious youth who worked in Chase's Hotel in Brattleboro and on Hudson River steamboats before opening the famous Willard Hotel in Washington in pre-Civil War days.

Westminster's multi-purpose brick Community Hall today includes a small museum of various artifacts from those yeasty years.

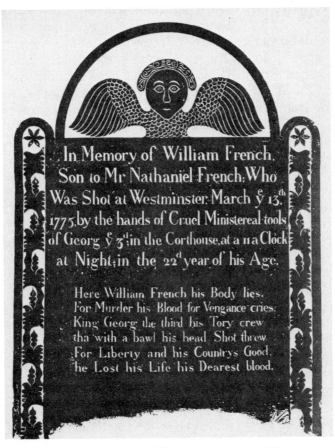

Headstone over the grave of William French in the Westminster burying ground. —Reprinted from *The 1976-77 Official Vermont Bicentennial Guide*. Rubbing by Don Nute, 1975

Bellows Falls/Rockingham

Rockingham, the tiny hill-cloistered village off Route 103 overlooking the Williams River, gave its name to the township which includes the much larger community of Bellows Falls, and is remarkable for the preservation of the Rockingham Meeting House on the knoll, a beautifully spartan church built in 1797. The township also includes Saxtons River on Route 121, site of Vermont Academy, a secondary boarding school established in 1876. Its headmaster in 1911, James P. Taylor, founded the Green Mountain Club that laid out the Long Trail. Vermont Academy pioneered in winter sports programs that grew into the Dartmouth Winter Carnival.

Once Vermont's (and the nation's) principal paper mill center, Bellows Falls' rather dreary nineteenth-century buildings cascade down hill to the biggest natural falls on the Connecticut River. The township of Rockingham was settled about 1753 and the largest village was named for Col.Benjamin Bellows from Walpole, across the river in New Hampshire. The Great Falls' barrier to northward navigation caused the construction between 1792 and 1802 of the first canal in America upon which work was commenced, though not the first completed. Nine locks were required to raise barges, rafts and small steamers. One side-wheeler proved too wide and had to be drawn through the village streets before continuing its trial voyage upriver to Hartland. The canal slipped into disuse after the 1840s and the arrival of the railroads. The rag-paper mills grew up after 1802, and William A. Russell, later first president of the International Paper Company, operated one of the first pulp-paper mills here after 1869.

Hetty Green, "the witch of Wall Street," remains Bellows Falls' most legendary figurine. Heiress of a tidy New Bedford whaling fortune, Hetty Robinson, born in 1835, grew up in dour surroundings, adhering to her millionaire father's admonition, "never owe anyone anything, not even a kindness." She was no stranger to New York society, however: her most intimate friend was Annie Leary, who became a Papal countess, and at a ball in 1860 Hetty danced—twice—with the Prince of Wales, later King Edward VII. After getting her hands on a second fortune (perhaps fraudulently) from her Aunt Sylvia, Hetty married a third, in the oversized person of Edward Henry

Hetty Robinson Green, "the witch of Wall Street" and America's richest woman, on the porch of her Bellows Falls home in 1913.
—Vermont Historical Society

Green, a native of Bellows Falls, who had struck it rich as a merchant-trader in Asia. The couple had two children, Ned, and Sylvia.

In a lifetime characterized by paranoia and litigation, Hetty nevertheless amassed a fortune estimated at $100 million by the time she died in 1916. Tales of her eccentricities were legion. When she was not in Bellows Falls, the richest woman in America stayed in $7-per week lodgings in Brooklyn, travelling there by day coach, looking like a bag-lady. In their 1930 biography, Boyden Sparkes and Samuel Taylor Morse describe her arrival at her Wall Street bankers during the panic of 1885: "In black cotton gloves Mrs. Green's hands were clasped about a worn black reticule held tightly against that spot where her paunchy abdomen pressed hardest against her shiny skirt. She never wore corsets. Her dress was a plain garment of black alpaca, the chief merit of which was that it would not easily betray the presence of dirt. The flounce of her petticoat hissed against striding legs in black ribbed cotton stockings and balbriggan underwear. It had been bitterly cold in Vermont, but now Mrs. Green permitted her cut-velvet dolman to float back from her shoulders as if it were a banner. Her brownish hair, streaked with gray, had been hastily twisted into a figure eight, on top of which rode a matronly bonnet without strings. A blue cotton veil tied under her determined chin held the unsightly millinery rigidly in position. Her face did much to offset these terrible garments....'I've come for what belongs to me,' began Mrs. Green, and clamped her lips."

Hetty was informed that she was merely one of eight hundred or so creditors of the bank; either she would pay off her husband's indebtedness or the bank would retain her securities. For days she besieged the bank, finally paying off Mr. Green's debt with a check for $422,143.22, and departing in a cab crammed with bundles of her securities which had a market value of $25 million. Edward Green, broke, went not long afterward to live at the Union League Club; for the information of tax assessors in Bellows Falls, he listed his posessions as $7 and a watch. Hetty had thrown him out because he had disobeyed her in a financial transaction. Among Hetty's holdings were real estate in Chicago's Loop and stock in several railroads. For Ned, she bought the Texas Central Railroad and the branch of the Houston & Texas that Collis P.

Huntington coveted. Ned reportedly once confessed, "I was born a Quaker, raised a Protestant, educated a Catholic, and by business I'm a Jew."

Villagers in Bellows Falls talked about Mrs.Green so much that when little Sylvia, a child of eleven, appeared on the streets with wads of cotton stuffed into her ears someone started the story that she did this to avoid hearing unpleasant gossip. Hetty loved her son Ned, but her parsimony cost him his leg. At fourteen, a coasting accident left him with a dislocated kneecap, which she treated with a poultice. Two or three years later, in New York, dressed as a beggar, she appeared with the lad at the office of a New York doctor who had Ned admitted to Bellevue Hospital's charity ward for treatment. Five years after the accident, Ned's leg had to be amputated. Hetty was always trying to get free advice from doctors and lawyers, pretending the information was for a friend or family too poor to pay for the consultation, and confessed to a friend in Bellows Falls that she had gone to a medical clinic under an assumed name.

Before she died in 1916, Hetty had the satisfaction of seeing her daughter married to the great-grandson of John Jacob Astor.

When Charles Doe of Bellows Falls was growing up in Milton, Massachusetts, before the First World War, his father and uncle were fascinated by Marconi's early radio. In 1921, the Vermont Farm Machinery Company hired him to come back to town and set up a radio station, the state's first. On September 4, 1922, WLAK, a 500-watt, 2500-volt, D.C., broadcasting outfit made its debut, featuring Bellows Falls' own Brazil's Orchestra. The sponsor sold kits to farmers and aired weather reports, how-to-farm-better tips, and light entertainment.

The first Civilian Conservation Corps camp in Vermont was opened near Bellows Falls in June 1933, setting the stage for what was probably the most productive and enduring C.C.C. program in the country. Initially, Vermont was allotted four camps for unemployed young men, but Perry Merrill, the state forester, had the foresight to plan for a much larger effort; by the time the war ended the program in 1942, Vermont had at least twenty-four camps. Vermont was authorized to enroll some two thousand men for six-month hitches, but there were many times that number through the years. It was a solid tribute to Merrill that in these years, the C.C.C. advanced the state's recreational objectives by fifty years. The state forests were improved by pruning and thinning, and by more than a hundred miles of new roads for management and fire protection. They did flood and pest control, constructed miles of trails and twenty miles of ski slopes.

Rockingham is the home of Thomas Salmon, an attorney who served as the second Democratic governor of Vermont for two terms after 1972. Salmon was identified with a property tax relief program, fiscal conservatism, and a "Keep Vermont for Vermonters" effort to put the brakes on development. Campaigning as a liberal, he has nevertheless been called the most conservative governor in modern Vermont history. Salmon could have been nominated for the United States Senate seat vacated by George Aiken in 1974, but he chose to wait; Aiken was, indeed, succeeded by a Democrat, Patrick Leahy of Burlington. Salmon was subsequently defeated by Senator Robert Stafford, the Republican incumbent in 1976.

Grafton

Grafton, ten miles northwest of Bellows Falls on Route 121, has been called Vermont's "Cinderella," because of its dramatic transformation into one of the most meticulously restored villages in New England. Smaller and less celebrated than Deerfield, Massachusetts, Grafton nevertheless has a similar aura, one that magnetizes antiquarians from far away places. Before the Civil War, Grafton was home to 1,480 people and 10,000 sheep. Wool was milled into 75,000 yards of Grafton cloth annually, and soapstone from thirteen local quarries left town as sinks, stoves, inkwells and footwarmers.

One in three Grafton men marched off to the Civil War, and few returned. An 1869 flood destroyed the village's six dams and its principal road. The now-famous Tavern, built in 1801, prospered, however, as innkeeper Marlan Phelps invested his Gold Rush fortune in adding a third floor and double porches, attracting such celebrities as Ralph Waldo Emerson, Henry David Thoreau, Rudyard Kipling, and, later, Theodore Roosevelt and Woodrow Wilson.

The meticulously restored Old Tavern in Grafton, which attracted many 19th-century luminaries. —Vermont Travel Division

By 1940, however, the tavern and its environs were deteriorating badly. Providence intervened in the person of Matthew Hall, a New York financier and descendant of the town's first pastor, who summered nearby. With money bequeathed by his aunt, Hall and Dean Mathey of Princeton, New Jersey, created the Windham Foundation in 1963 and set out to restore the tavern and the town. The Old Tavern, now an exquisite country inn, is the centerpiece for the vintage village.

One of Grafton's leading citizens was Samuel B. Pettengill, the outspoken Democratic Congressman from Indiana who made a widely-publicized break with Franklin D. Roosevelt over the President's Supreme Court "packing" attempt in the mid-thirties. Twelve of Pettengill's ancestors fought in the Revolution, a heritage he proudly proclaimed in his last book, *The Yankee Pioneers*, published in 1971. In it, he wrote that one reason Vermont was attractive to settlers from other New England states after the Revolution was its conservative monetary policy. " 'Not worth a continental' was the reproach attached to the so-called dollars of paper money. In Virginia, by 1781, this currency fell to one thousand for one dollar in hard money. Foreigners bought five thousand dollars' worth of Continental scrip for a single dollar of gold." But, Pettengill continued, "Old Tom Chittenden, Vermont's first governor, who served for seventeen years and had only one eye, could not see how a government could make its people affluent by printing dollar signs on pieces of paper and making them legal tender! He was a conservative in money matters. Vermont coined its own hard money and did not go head-over-heels in debt. Its legislature decreed that counterfeiters should 'suffer death'; nothing less. This was later softened to forfeiture of the counterfeiter's entire estate, cutting off his right ear, branding him with a hot iron with the letter 'C' and imprisoning him for life. This was strong medicine, but it created confidence in the new Republic and undoubtedly influenced migration to the state."

Large families were commonplace in Grafton as in most eighteenth-century farming communities. When Josiah White of Rockingham died at the age of ninety-six, he left three hundred and eighty-six children, grandchildren and great-grandchildren. Grafton's Noah Emery had twenty-one children. In the severe winters, church goers often brought little footstoves filled with hot coals or pieces of soapstone from the local quarry wrapped in a blanket to warm their feet. Eventually, the church would get a little more comfortable. When Noah Emery and his brood arrived, the church door had to be kept open longer than usual to allow the procession to enter, dropping the temperature perceptibly. Members of the congregation huddled down into their cloaks and muttered,

"Here comes Noah [pronounced Nore]
And twenty-two more."

Also according to Helen M. Pettengill's "Sidelights on Grafton History," a general practice in the early days was the "warning out," which meant that selectmen could order anyone to leave town upon arrival if the newcomer seemed likely to become a public charge. The selectmen had no power to enforce the law, but the luckless target could expect no public assistance from Grafton. "A case in point is that of a young physician who came to town in 1808 with no worldly goods except what was in his saddle bags, and a good name. The sleepless eyes of the guardians of the town were immediately upon him, and a paper was put into his hands reading as follows: 'To Caleb Hall, Constable: You are hereby directed to summons Dr. John Butterfield to depart this town forthwith; herof fail not, but make due return. [Signed] John Barrett, Barzillai Burgess, Selectmen.' Dr. Butterfield, who came from Rockingham, did not obey the mandate, and the first doctor in town, Dr.Amos Fisher, having just died, left Dr.Butterfield as the only doctor. He did so well that by 1811 he was able to build for himself and family the handsome house on Main Street" that became the public library.

Chester

A storied inn is also the centerpiece of Chester, seven miles north of Grafton, one of the most scenic drives in the state, at the the junction of Routes 35, 11, and 103. Settled in 1756, the town includes a remarkable cluster of "Stone Village" houses on North Street (Route 103), a double line of thirty, extremely rare, distinctive homes built by two brothers in the 1850s from gneiss, and rough-hewn mica schist quarried from nearby Flamstead Mountain.

On October 10, 1774, a group of Chester citizens anticipated other colonies' action by issuing a declaration of independence, stating that "all the acts of the British Parliament tending to take away Rights of Freedom ought not to be obeyed."

Since 1912, Chester has been the home of the National Survey Company, the famous mapmakers founded by Lawton V. and Henry F. Crocker, sons of the town's Baptist minister. It has produced millions of maps for states, foreign countries, and private industry. In the early years, salesmen made their rounds on bicycles.

In 1986, The Chester Inn, a three-story landmark built in 1920 when its predecessor burned, was bought and renamed The Inn at Long Last by Jack Coleman, the former president of Haverford College and New York City philanthropoid. Coleman got national publicity when, as a college president and later a foundation mandarin in disguise, he worked incognito as a garbage collector, ditch digger, homeless vagabond, and prison inmate, recording these sabbaticals in a book, *Blue Collar Journal*.

Springfield

Ever since William Lockwood built a dam and sawmill at the falls of the Black River in 1774, Springfield has been a busy town. But Lockwood was a late-comer: in 1730, James Coss with twelve Caughawaga Indians explored the trail from Fort Dummer to Lake Champlain and camped at the mouth of the river. Twenty years later, John and Ruth Nott built a log cabin there; he worked as a ferryman near the blockhouse serving the Crown Point military road.

For more than a century, Springfield's machine tools stamped Vermont indelibly on the world's industrial map, and as a byproduct, bred two distinguished public servants, James Hartness and his son-in-law, Ralph Flanders. The decline of the machine tool industry in Springfield in recent years makes an interesting if sobering study of what happens to home-grown, family-owned manufacturing companies when they are taken over by much larger, out-of-state firms, especially con-glomerates, and cease to be under local control. The once familiar names of Hartness, Fellows and Flanders have van-ished from the scene, replaced by Textron and other nationally known corporations. Jones & Lamson, once the employer of several thousand workers, has shrunk to a payroll of fewer than a hundred, and even they may be out of work by the time this book appears. "Absentee" ownership has not been the sole cause: American supremacy in machine tools, an industrial resource that helped win two World Wars, has been supplanted by post-industrial, hi-tech foreign competitors.

From the 1880s onward, however, "Precision Valley" boomed. In 1888, the new owners of Jones & Lamson, which had been born in Windsor, brought in a twenty-seven-year-old mechanic and designer, James Hartness, who trimmed the company of all products except his famous turret lathe. Hartness' protege Edwin R. Fellows left the firm in 1896 to start his pioneering gear shaper plant, which played a strategic role in the automo-bile industry. Fellows was succeded by W.J.Bryant, who in turn left the parent company in 1909 to form the Bryant Chucking Grinder Company. Ralph Flanders, the brilliant engineer who married the boss's daughter Helen Hartness (later widely known as the collector and preserver of early Vermont ballads), became president of Jones & Lamson in

Machine-tool maker and U.S. Senator Ralph Flanders (left) dared to oppose McCarthyism in the early 1950s. —Vermont Historical Society

1933 and was later made chairman of the Federal Reserve Bank of Boston. James Hartness, who patented 120 different machines, was an astronomer, aviation pioneer, and served as governor of Vermont in 1921-23. Visitors to the Hartness House inn, his former mansion, can play with the telescope he installed in his private observatory, reached through a tunnel.

Hartness built a small airport on the edge of town in 1919, where, in July 1927, thirty thousand people gathered to cheer Charles A. Lindbergh's triumphal visit.

Ralph Flanders, elected to the United States Senate in 1946, was one of the very few Republicans who dared challenge the dangerous demagogue, Senator Joseph R. McCarthy. In a speech to the Senate on June 1, 1954, Flanders said: "one of the characteristic elements of communist and fascist tyranny is at hand, as citizens are set to spy on each other. Established and responsible government is besmirched. Religion is set against religion, race against race...Were the junior senator from Wisconsin in the pay of the Communists, he could not have done a better job for them." Later, the dignified Flanders personally handed the glowering Wisconsin witch-hunter a subpoena during the televised "Army-McCarthy" hearings, summoning him to a Congressional accounting that resulted in censure. When asked by a television newsman why he had chosen to enter the hearing room, Flanders replied, "I had a compulsion."

Springfield was home to other men who created useful things: David Smith invented a combination lock, one of the first adding machines, a corn planter and a breech-loading rifle. Herbert Warren collected a fortune from his invention of gravel roofing. A.H. Ellis made a steam shovel in 1848, a mechanical wonder which helped construct railroads in Vermont and elsewhere, and invented the jointed doll! Luke Taylor introduced a superior mop, and his friend B.B. Choate patented the mop wringer.

Weathersfield

Vermont's early nineteenth-century agrarian economy was radically transformed when struggling, largely self-sufficient farmers turned to sheep raising as a remedy for their increasing hardships. The father of this movement was the crafty William Jarvis, who, as American consul in Lisbon, managed to smuggle 4,000 Merino sheep out of Spain and ship them home in 1810. He gave two each of Spain's finest woollies to President Madison and former President Jefferson, and herded 350 of them to his farm in Weathersfield. Merinos soon displaced the inferior native breeds and by the 1830s, the hills of the northcountry were alive with them. At the height of the woolgathering mania in 1840, there were more than 2,250,000 sheep in Vermont and New Hampshire, two-thirds of them in the valleys of the Green Mountains. One farmer refused an offer of $10,000 for his best ram, and another is said to have turned down $50,000—a fortune—for a flock of 200 Merinos. Vermont had shifted to a one-crop economy. In Addison County flocks averaged 373 to the square mile. But the depression after 1837 and the loss of tariff protection in 1841 and 1846 caused the boom to bust: prices fell to twenty-five cents a pound, and by 1849 flocks were being ruthlessly sold off for hides and mutton. In 1850 there were a third less sheep in the pastures, and the decline continued steadily for the next hundred years.

In the 1970s, however, sheep raising in several parts of the state began to revive at the hands of "the new farmer"— upper-middle-class refugees from the cities and suburbia.

Windsor

Vermont was born, everyone agrees, on July 8, 1777, around a table in Elijah West's tavern, as storm and war clouds swirled around the delegates. "Gentleman Johnny" Burgoyne's magnificently equipped new army was marching south from Canada to clear the waterways and link up with General Howe's forces at Albany and split the American rebellion in two. No one knew when or where Burgoyne would strike first; there was more dread than pride in the hearts of the men who gathered on July 2 to frame a constitution for the infant state. Without the British threat, agreement might not have been accomplished as quickly, and without a thunderstorm it might not have been achieved at all.

Before settling down to work, the delegates endured an interminable sermon from the Rev. Aaron Hutchinson, the long-winded evangelical preacher from Woodstock, leaving them thirsty for more than righteousness. The pace quickened on July 3 when a hastily scrawled letter from Col. Seth Warner sounded the alarm: the British army had been sighted. Its flotilla was moving up Lake Champlain with troops on either shore, aiming at Fort Ticonderoga. Warner called for all militia units to be sent to the fort at once. Bickering ceased. The delegates — especially those from the westside in the path of the invaders — rolled up their sleeves and addressed the latest missive from Dr. Thomas Young, a close friend of Ethan Allen's, who submitted the constitution of Pennsylvania as a model. Dr. Young is generally accepted as the originator of the name "Vermont," which had recently been substituted for the earlier "New Connecticut." Young reportedly arrived at his invention by the unholy alliance of the Gallic words for "green" and "mountain," but his French was obviously inadequate. Nevertheless, it had a nice ring and was accepted into general use between January and July 1777.

Young had already made a bootless appeal to the Continental Congress, asking that Vermont be "ranked among the free and independent states and be granted a seat," but in June Congress rejected the petition.

Using Pennsylvania's constitution as a draft, the delegates imprinted their own brand. With the British on their doorstep, the pattern of their hatred was not altered: one paragraph of the preamble was sufficient for an expression of grievances against George III, but *fourteen* were required to list the reasons for their loathing of New York.

The hardy young men around the tavern table demonstrated their passion for freedom by making Vermont the first state to abolish slavery. The document provided that no person — slave, apprentice, or servant— should be held in bondage after the age of eighteen if female, and twenty-one if male. The new republic was also the first American state to establish universal male suffrage. Pending election of a constitutional government, the republic was to be ruled by a Council of Safety: Thomas Chittenden, Heman and Ira Allen, Joseph and Jonas Fay, Moses Robinson, Jacob Bayley, and Paul Spooner were among its membership of twelve.

Word came on July 8 that Ticonderoga had fallen, that the frontier defenses had caved in, and that the British force was marching into Vermont as irresistibly as the black clouds were piling up behind Ascutney's ridge.

The Old Constitution House in Windsor, birthplace of "The Reluctant Republic" in 1777. —Vermont Travel Division

"There was no immediate outcry after the disheveled rider had bawled his tidings," Frederic Van de Water wrote in *The Reluctant Republic*. "Silence, magnified by a distant rumbling, lay on the convention hall, and delegates, peering about, saw only the white, stricken faces of other men. The great fortress had been captured. The citadel in which had lain all Vermont's strained hope for protection from invasion had been taken with incredible ease.

"The palsied moment passed. Feet scuffled, chairs clattered as the meeting rose. Voices babbled for immediate adjournment and then were smothered beneath explosive flashings as the storm broke...[and] went by like an advancing army, and men who would march with the last militia companies and men whose families were on the now defenseless frontier were forced to linger, waiting for its passage. One cleared his throat and addressed Joseph Bowker, the presiding officer...Since time was precious now and should not be frittered away, might it not be better if the convention, instead of just sitting here on its behind, occupied itself until the storm was over in approving the Constitution of the State of Vermont, just in case Johnny Burgoyne left anything to apply it to later?" Two more days passed before the final document was adopted and the worried delegates galloped home.

The Old Constitution House, where this drama was played out, was moved from its original location, renovated in 1914, and presented to the state as an historic site in 1961.

The new constitution was not universally popular. Ira Allen admitted in his *History of the State of Vermont* that "Had the constitution been then submitted to the consideration of the people for their revision, amendment, and ratification, it is very doubtful whether a majority would have confirmed it."[1]

---

[1] During Vermont's Bicentennial observance in 1976-77, rumors circulated that the state's constitution permitted Vermont to secede from the union at will, and some wags began urging it, pointing out that "we'd get more in foreign aid than from revenue sharing." In *Out! The Vermont Secession Book* published in 1987, Frank Bryan and William Mares confirm the absence of such an "escape clause," but claim that in a document called "The Moscow Covenant" (because it was found near the hamlet of Moscow, near Stowe), Ethan Allen and George Washington reached a secret accord in Hackensack, New Jersey, in January 1789, in which Washington in effect signed over the thirteen original colonies to Vermont! The Covenant provided that "As the conscience of the United

After the close of the October 1778 session of the second Vermont General Assembly, Ira Allen lingered in Windsor to attend to an important piece of state business, and entered in his expense account a charge of ten shillings for two days to draw a state seal and an equal amount to Reuben Dean, a local craftsman and silversmith, for etching it. The Great Seal of Vermont designed by Allen features a truncated, fourteen-branched pine tree, representing the United States with Vermont as the fourteenth state, a row of wooded hills, a cow, four sheaves of wheat, and the spear of a halberd, underscored by the motto, "Freedom & Unity."

Windsor's main street leading to the Old Constitution House is ideal for a stroll because it is lined with unusually handsome Federal houses, flanking the magnificent Old South Congregational Church designed by Asher Benjamin, built in 1798, and subsequently remodeled (without exterior degradations). St. Paul's Episcopal Church, a distinctive mix of Georgian Colonial and Greek Revival, consecrated in 1822, is the oldest Episcopal church still in regular use in the Diocese of Vermont. And Windsor House, considered the best public house between Boston and Montreal after it opened in 1840, was saved from the bulldozer in 1972 by a determined group of local preservationists. It now houses the Vermont Crafts Center, a showcase for artists and artisans.

As well as being the birthplace of the state of Vermont, Windsor was also the midwife for first machine tools that later grew to maturity in Springfield. One of the first and most versatile inventors of the 1800s was Lemuel Hedge, who began a notable career with a machine for ruling paper in 1815, dividing scales in 1827, and a band saw in 1849. Asahel Hubbard produced a revolving hydraulic pump in 1828, which formed the basis for the National Hydraulic Company. Appointed warden of the state prison in Windsor, Hubbard induced the state to install a stationary steam engine and

States, Vermont has an inalienable right to declare null and void and thereby ignore and avoid any law of the United States it wishes, and Second, if at any time the United States fails to satisfy Vermont's high standards of probity, generosity, morality, and sobriety, Vermont may banish the United States from its borders forever." The authors proceed to describe what happens when Vermont invokes its right of secession in 1991, two hundred years after it accepted statehood.

machine shop for his company, and utilized prison labor for twenty-five cents a day. Working in Hubbard's plant was an alert young gunsmith, Nicanor Kendall. "Sparking" Hubbard's daughter, "Cain" nearly blew the head off his intended when he drew a rifle from under a carriage robe to shoot a squirrel and accidently caught the exposed hammer. Shocked by the narrow escape, he devised an "under-hammer" rifle with — for the first time— interchangeable parts. The first big order for the new gunshop came from the Republic of Texas, which deeded 2,000 acres of land to the company in payment.

The third of these founders of the Windsor machine tool industry was Richard Smith Lawrence, who went to work for Kendall in 1838 and became a partner five years later. A crackerjack salesman, he got a government contract to supply rifles at $10.90 each. Outgunned, perhaps, by his partner, Kendall withdrew from the firm and followed his father-in-law to Iowa. The successor firm of Robbins and Lawrence found a ready market for the new rifles, and soon had more business than it could handle.

What is now the American Precision Museum in Windsor, opened to the public in 1966, is the last of the old Robbins & Lawrence plants, erected in 1846 as an armory. In 1851, interchangeable rifles sent to London for exhibition brought an order for machine tools and, in 1855, for 25,000 guns. Even with a work force of one hundred and fifty skilled mechanics, R & L was unable to meet the contract deadline; the order was rescinded, and by a decree of foreclosure, the armory was transferred to Her Majesty's Artillery in 1857. The Vermont Arms Company took over, completed the unfinished Enfields, and began manufacturing sewing machines as well. The rifle business boomed, naturally, during the Civil War, but after it the plant was transformed into a cotton mill.

Meanwhile, the dismayed artisans banded together to establish the Windsor Machine Company, which was nearly wrecked by the depression of 1893-96. Eventually, both Cone-Blanchard and Goodyear Tire & Rubber became the major industries in town, but both shut down in the mid-1980s.

Windsor's most famous nineteenth-century public figure was William Maxwell Evarts, whose wife, Helen Wardner, was a native. Evarts' career was unusually varied. When he entered Yale in 1833 he was one of the founders of the *Yale Literary*

Magazine. After Harvard Law School and marriage in 1843, a union that produced seven sons and five daughters, Evarts became a celebrated constitutional lawyer in New York. As acting Attorney General, he successfully defended President Andrew Johnson in his impeachment trial; served as President Hayes' Secretary of State (1887-1881) and as Senator from New York (1885-1891). His extensive properties in Windsor were called "Runnemede"; the capacious 1796 house at the heart of the family compound, to which he rather imperiously retired, was known as "The White House." Evarts' great-grandson, Archibald Cox, was fired in 1973 as Watergate special prosecutor by the embattled President Nixon, a few months before the president's impeachment hearings began.

One of the Senator's daughters produced the legendary book publisher, Maxwell Evarts Perkins, who nursed several of the best American writers of the twentieth century for Charles Scribner's Sons during his thirty-six-year tenure as editor after 1910. He discovered and nurtured the talents of F. Scott Fitzgerald, Ernest Hemingway, and Thomas Wolfe, and also edited Erskine Caldwell, Taylor Caldwell, Marcia Davenport, Majorie Kinnan Rawlings, and, finally, James Jones' *From Here to Eternity*, just before his death in 1947. For Max Perkins, his biographer A. Scott Berg wrote, Windsor was "the most glorious place on earth. Some seventy years earlier, just beyond the shadow of Mt. Ascutney, his maternal grandfather had built a compound of houses in which to assemble his family around him. 'Windsor was the personal heaven of my grandfather's grandchildren,' Max's sister Fanny Cox wrote...'In the winter we lived in different settings...but in the summer we gathered together in the big place behind the picket fence where six houses faced the village street and the grounds stretched back across green lawns with clipped hemlock hedges and round begonia-filled flower beds to slope down the hill to the pond.' Rising behind the pond was a particularly lovely part of the acreage, where streams raced down hills and footpaths wove through stands of pine and birch. The family called these special woods 'Paradise.' "

The extended family enjoyed climbing Mt. Ascutney, the lonely monadnock in West Windsor (Brownsville), from which granite was quarried as early as 1808, and where a summit house once topped the upward trail. For generations, Ascutney guarded its serenity: a state park and a discreet ski area were eventually developed on its slopes, and broadcasting transmitters were planted on its peak. In the mid-1980s, however, the glossy Ascutney Mountain Resort colonized the base lodge area with a large hotel and conference center, condos and sports center.

Although the resort has nearly devoured its hamlet host, Brownsville clings to a fifty-four-year tradition of summer baked bean suppers that link generations of the town's families. Since they became an institution during the depression in 1935, Brownsville's baked bean suppers have paid for a new roof for the Methodist-Episcopal church, a town history, and produced continuing support for the Grange, the PTA, and the West Windsor Historical Society. In the beginning, the suppers drew two to three hundred diners every Saturday night, at 25 cents a head. Now, the number is limited to two hundred and twenty five, and the price has gone up to $4.50. But the aromatic baked beans, salads and desserts remain unaltered. Each volunteer baker prepares six pounds of yellow eye, pea, or red kidney beans, accompanied by green salad, potato salad, quick-breads, sour pickles and pies.

The Windsor-Cornish covered bridge is the longest such span in (or partly in) Vermont. Constructed in 1866, it was recently closed to automobile traffic to permit the state of New Hampshire to reinforce it.

A few miles north on Route 12A in Cornish, New Hampshire, lies the Augustus Saint-Gaudens National Historic Site, a charming property developed by the famous sculptor between 1885 and his death in 1907. His summer home, studio, sculpture court, Blow-Me-Down nature trails, and formal gardens were taken over by the National Park Service in 1964, and provide a delightful interlude, especially on summer Sundays when there are chamber concerts on the grounds.

The songs of the artistic Loreleis along this bank of the river were also reflected in the works of other Cornish summer colonists — the poets Percy MacKaye, Witter Bynner, and William Vaughan Moody; and the American novelist, Winston Churchill, whose estate was used by Woodrow Wilson as the Summer White House in 1914 and 1915. Maxfield Parrish also had a home and studio there, as did Charles Dana Gibson, Finley Peter Dunne, and Ethel Barrymore. Contemporary American literature is personfied by the reclusive J.D.Salinger.

White River Junction

The town of Hartford was settled in 1761 by a few families from Lebanon, Connecticut. One of the earliest was Joseph Marsh, from whose farm in Quechee he became Vermont's first lieutenant governor. The celebrated Marsh family is remembered for several notable accomplishments; but who recalls that Horace Wells, discoverer of laughing gas for dentists, was born here? White River Junction has been the largest community in the town of Hartford because of its location at the confluence of the White River and the Connecticut, and because it became the principal railroad hub in the state.

Northfield, Rutland, St. Albans, and Island Pond stand out in the history of Vermont railways, but White River Junction epitomized the Age of the Iron Horse when it steamed in and radically transformed the state for forty years after 1845 with a cat's cradle of trunk and short lines linking nearly all population centers with Boston, Montreal, New York, and "points West." Vermont's native railroad magnates never matched their Robber Baron contemporaries on the national stage in corruption and conspicuous consumption, but they flexed their political muscles.

Three systems (Vermont Central, Rutland, and Connecticut and Passumpsic) were chartered in 1835, but no rails were laid for ten years, when ground was broken in Windsor for the Vermont Central, chartered by Governor Charles Paine, owner of a large woolen mill and extensive property in Northfield. Paine pushed the road toward Northfield, and on June 26, 1848, the line was completed to Bethel and the first train to run in the state left White River Junction. Paine's fellow railroad pioneers were Timothy Follett, a prominent Burlington merchant already involved in Lake Champlain steamer transportation, who chartered the Rutland and Burlington; and John Smith of St. Albans, who organized the Vermont and Canada to build north from the Winooski River to Rouse's Point at the head of Lake Champlain; and later, Erastus Fairbanks, whose Connecticut and Passumpsic eventually reached Newport and the Canadian border.

Topography ruled the routes. The Vermont Central used the White-Winooski River valleys, while Rutland selected the Black River-Otter Creek pathway. Counting on connections to

Boston via the New Hampshire lines being built, Paine and Follett began a race from the Connecticut River to Burlington. Though Paine won with the first train, the Rutland group tracked to Burlington first, and on December 18, 1849, fresh water from Lake Champlain was spiked with salt water from Boston harbor. On New Year's Eve, the Vermont Central chuffed in, pursued by angry investors from Montpelier and Barre, which Paine had bypassed.

The economic power of the new railroads was reflected in political leadership, as the railroad tycoons passed the governorship back and forth like cigars. Fairbanks served twice as governor (1852-53, 1860-61). In 1863, John Smith's son, J. Gregory, became governor, and later president of the Vermont Central. Smith and Frederick Billings of Woodstock were deeply involved in the spectacular Northern Pacific Railroad— both serving as presidents— which they hoped to join to their Vermont lines as parts of a vast transcontinental network. Edward C. Smith, J. Gregory's son, extended the Smith dynastic influence, as governor in 1898-1900, and as president of the Central Vermont up to 1928.

John B. Page, of the Rutland Railroad group, became both governor and president of the railroad in 1867. Percival Clement of Rutland also served both as president and governor in 1919-21.

Well into the twentieth century, White River Junction had a raunchy reputation. Dartmouth College boys congregated in search of booze and dames. There was brawling in the taverns and streets and non-stop gambling. When the Vermont-New Hampshire boundary case was finally settled in the early thirties, Daniel L. Cady, responded in verse:

> I hope that when this law suit ends,
>
> That's run so many rounds,
>
> White River Junction will be found
>
> Within New Hampshire's bounds.
>
> And then White River shacks and pens
>
> Where travelers have to wait,
>
> I hope they'll all turn up outside
>
> Our rather tidy state.

Then, when the poor-mouth railroads raise
The station that we want,
We'll sue to have the place set back
Inside appeased Vermont.

Today, White River Junction is a shadow of its railroading heyday — a few freights and AMTRAK's "Ambassador/Montrealer", whose service was recently restored after two years of suspension. The fifty-mile section of track between Brattleboro and Windsor had deteriorated, forcing the Montrealer to creep along at ten miles an hour. The absentee owners of the trackage refused to make repairs; the Interstate Commerce Commission finally stepped in, expropriated the tracks, and turned them over to the Central Vermont. Congress supplied $5 million for the restoration.

Brand-name motels and shopping plazas cluster where Interstates 89 and 91 converge with Routes 4 and 5; and visitors are refreshed by a visit to the recently opened Catamount Brewery, which introduced a zesty English-type ale.

Norwich

Lots of Dartmouth College faculty members live in this exceptionally attractive town across the river from Hanover, New Hampshire, with which it shares the Dresden School District, one of the few such bi-state jurisdictions. Settled in 1761 by people from Marshfield, Connecticut, Norwich was originally the site of of the American Literary, Scientific and Military Academy founded in 1819 and renamed Norwich University in 1834; after the Civil War it was moved to Northfield.

Architecturally, Norwich is a living museum of Colonial, Georgian, Post-Colonial, and Greek Revival houses built between 1770 and 1830, succinctly summed up as "Simplified Georgian." The earliest dwelling is the Hatch-Peisch House, built by Captain Joseph Hatch in 1773 and the first frame house in the village and perhaps the township.

The latest addition to Norwich is the Montshire Museum on a 100-acre tract near the Exit 13 interchange off I-91. Its natural history collections are being moved across the river from Hanover.

Senator Justin Smith Morrill fathered the Land Grant college system, among other notable accomplishments during his 44 years in Washington. —Vermont Historical Society

Strafford

Nicely insulated from mainstream traffic on Route 132, fifteen or so miles north of Norwich, Strafford basks in the afterglow of its foremost citizen, Justin Smith Morrill, who served as Representative and Senator in Washington from 1855 until 1898, and whose seventeen-room Gothic-Revival home is a fascinating historic landmark. Morrill never got to spend as much time here as he would have liked because he kept getting reelected. Born in 1810, Morrill was a country storekeeper before embarking on a midlife political career on an antislavery platform and a campaign promise that "money should be substituted for [alcoholic] rations in the Navy and groggeries annihilated in and around the capitol in Washington." In Congress, he was the author of the first Morrill Tariff

Morrill's fine Gothic house in Strafford is open to the public.
—Vermont Travel Division

of 1861; instrumental in the design and construction of the Washington Monument, the State, War and Navy Departments building, the Library of Congress, and improvements to the Capitol itself, for which he enlisted the talents of Frederick Law Olmsted. Primarily, of course, he was responsible for the creation of a nation-wide and federally subsidized system of higher education in the Land Grant College Act.

Both houses of Congress adjourned as a mark of respect when Morrill died on January 4, 1899. In his memorial address, Senator Vest of Missouri said: "His great desire was to see Washington city the most beautiful capital in the world, and this Capitol building in which we are assembled worthy of the greatest republic upon the earth." Morrill's colleague Senator Proctor said: "The people of Vermont never considered his retirement. If his noble life had been spared to the end of his term, and he himself had not forbade it he would have been elected to his seventh term just as heartily. Long ago, by tacit consent, the people of my state resolved to make him a life Senator, and they never wavered in that purpose...Though he grew mightily in wisdom, and his wonderful talents and traits of character were greatly refined by many years of public service, Vermonters love to think that, however great may have been the measure of his character, in kind at least, even unto the end he was a typical Vermonter."

"There was no wire running to his seat from any center of patronage," Senator George Hoar of Massachusetts, declared. "He did not come out of his door and cry cuckoo when any clock struck elsewhere."

Fairlee/ Orford, N.H.

Summer camps and resorts on nearby Lakes Fairlee and Morey sustain the livelihood of Fairlee. Chauvinism aside, one should cross the river to New Hampshire and Route 10 to admire Orford's "Bulfinch Row," a tier of seven elegant houses built between 1773 and 1839 by merchants and professional men. The Bulfinch-style Wheeler house at the southernmost end of the low ridge was probably designed by Asher Benjamin, one of Charles Bulfinch's associates.

Fairlee and Orford share a common heritage in the extraordinary person of Samuel Morey, who resided in Orford and lumbered in Fairlee. Morey was the inventor of the first steamboat: in 1793, fourteen years before Robert Fulton launched his *Clermont*, Morey was puffing up and down the Connecticut River in a primitive craft barely big enough to hold him and his firewood. Morey exhibited his model to Fulton, who reportedly also came to Fairlee. The remains of this little steamer are believed to lie at the bottom of Lake Morey, scuttled by its creator when the $100,000 in stock allegedly offered him by Fulton turned out to be worthless. After some four thousand experiments, Morey patented an internal combustion engine in 1825, anticipating the automobile age.

Ely, south of Fairlee on Route 5, is the turning off point for Lake Fairlee, and once the railway depot for the Ely Copper Mines at Vershire, ten miles northwest on Route 113. These fabled copper mines supported a population of two thousand or more after the great "copper rush" of the 1820s. Two decades of small-scale mining preceded the arrival of Thomas Pollard, a Cornishman, who formed the Vermont Copper Mining Company in 1853. By 1860, three million pounds of copper, then worth more than twenty cents a pound, were shipped in one year; and at the peak of its production, the company bought by a New Yorker, Smith Ely, supplied three-fifths of America's total copper output. Greed overtook president Ely: he and his family had gradually acquired a ninety-percent control of the company; he had the name of the town changed to his own, raised his salary to $50,000, discontinued dividends, and had all the surplus converted into improvements to the plant, most of them unnecessary. Then, "management mysteriously changed hands," W. Storrs Lee wrote in *The Green Mountains of Vermont*, and there was a "long, expensive, disastrous litigation. Capital was short and production slow for the first time in two decades. In 1883 the managers became more and more desultory in meeting the wages of loyal miners and in July remittances stopped altogether. For a while the workers charged their grocery bills and lived on credit, but shortly they sensed that something was drastically wrong with the company finances. When back pay reached an astronomical total of $25,000 and demands went unanswered, all work ceased."

Then followed the most dramatic revolt of labor in Green Mountain annals. The miners seized rifles and ammunition, flooded the works, tore down buildings, threatened to dynamite the mines and burn the company's tenements in Ely and West Fairlee.

Overnight, management skipped town; but news of the insurrection reached Montpelier, and Governor John L. Barstow despatched five companies of the National Guard to Ely by special train. At dawn, the striking ringleaders awoke to face fixed bayonets. But the guardsmen sided with the strikers, who pried open the cash boxes and distributed some four thousand dollars— the only remaining assets. "It was a total disaster. Families of workers, many in abject poverty, moved on. On April Fool's Day in 1884 a few of the remaining miners got their revenge when clouds of smoke billowed up from the plant. It should have been the big Vermont disaster story of the year, but state sentiment was so strong against mine management that the *Burlington Free Press* reported the event in three short sentences: 'The engine and boiler house of the Ely mine was burned this morning. The engine and machinery cost over $100,000 two years ago. The fire was probably of incendiary origin.' That was all."

Other entrepreneurs made periodic attempts to reopen the mines, and a new Vermont Copper Company was formed in the 1940s; but the veins have been pretty much played out.

The Vermont Journal, *May 16, 1798*

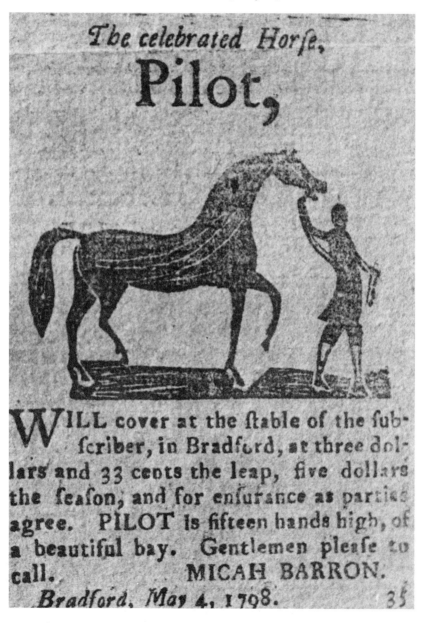

The celebrated Horſe,

Pilot,

WILL cover at the ſtable of the ſubſcriber, in Bradford, at three dollars and 33 cents the leap, five dollars the ſeaſon, and for enſurance as parties agree. PILOT is fifteen hands high, of a beautiful bay. Gentlemen pleaſe to call.   MICAH BARRON.
Bradford, May 4, 1798.   35

Bradford

Here, the Waits River flows into the Connecticut over a waterfall that used to power a mill. Bradford was unique in Vermont in that it was settled in the 1760s without any deed, grant or charter, thus setting an early lesson in contrariness.

Among its more notable offspring were James Wilson, an ingenious farmer who made America's first geographical globes in the early 1800s; and Captain Charles Clark, the naval officer who commanded the battleship *Oregon* on its strategic 15,000-mile dash around Cape Horn from the Pacific to help defeat the Spanish fleet at Santiago Bay in 1898.

Bradford nearly doubles its population of 1,700 on the Saturday before Thanksgiving when hungry visitors pour into the Congregational Church for the town's annual Wild Game Supper. Some 2,800 pounds of buffalo, venison, moose, pheasant, coon, rabbit, wild boar and bear, cooked up by parishioners as roasts, steaks, burgers, stews and sausages, are devoured.

Newbury and the Bayley-Hazen Military Road

People once called it the "road from nowhere to nowhere." Aimed from the upper reaches of the Connecticut River northwesterly toward the Canadian border, the corduroy path through the wilderness begun by General Jacob Bayley in May 1776, two months before the Declaration of Independence, is a ghost of the grand strategic purpose intended for it by General George Washington. But the observable remains of the Bayley-Hazen Road, like all historical artifacts, reveal an overshadowed chapter of Vermont's emergence as an independent republic.

The Green Mountain state shares the distinction of being one of four American states (with Hawaii, California and Texas) that were independent nations. Vermont's sovereignty between 1777 and its admission to statehood in 1791 was never intended to be permanent, although its leaders behaved as if it were when they annexed lands from the neighboring states of New Hampshire and New York and conducted diplomatic negotiations with Great Britain.

Jacob Bayley moved with characteristic dispatch that summer of 1776. The road was finished and open to wagons for 14

The terminus of the Bayley-Hazen military road is marked at Hazen's Notch. —Vermont Travel Division

miles from Newbury to Peacham, then the last outpost of settlement in the area. The 50-year-old Bayley, a veteran of the French and Indian War, and one of the major landholders of Coos County which straddled the Connecticut River, pushed the road through with 110 men working 45 days for the equivalent of $10 a month, food, and a half pint of rum daily. The project cost him the princely sum of 732 pounds, which he was never able to collect from a distracted Continental Congress. Washington and his advisers wanted the road as a short-cut bypass or alternative route to the historic Lake Champlain trough, which, for more than a century, had been the militarily strategic link between New York and Canada. The new road would have to be blazed through virgin forest for 90 miles to St. Johns in what is now the province of Quebec, thus outflanking the British on Lake Champlain and serving as a potential invasion route.

The realization that it could equally help the British march into New England halted the road in its tracks when Benedict Arnold failed to take Montreal. In the early spring of 1779, however, with Burgoyne's army defeated and France the colonies' ally, schemes for another Canadian incursion were revived, and work on the road resumed. A labor force of armed militia was commanded by Colonel (later General) Moses Hazen, the brother of Jacob Bayley's close friend and associate, John Hazen. Under Hazen, trees were felled and covered with earth and the road was pushed another 40 miles, with camps and blockhouses constructed along the way, with a final camp on the site of the present village at Lowell. From here on August 24, 1779, beset by reports of imminent attack by the British, Moses Hazen wrote Colonel Bedel:

> We are determined to put an end to our work here by next Saturday night and therefore have ordered out all the provisions that will be wanted up to that time, viz: 2600 lbs of Flower and about 3000 wt. of fresh Beef (no more ox teams or Stinking beef.) We shall not find much difficulty in getting up to the notch of the mountains....I have directed Major Reid, three Captains, two Subalterns and eighty-five men, including those at the Block House, as an escort for provisions; who come on and return with the pack horses, and I shall pay very particular attention to secure the woods on my left from our van to Onion River, so that I hope I may not be surpised. If I shall find that a party is coming to attack me I shall endeavor to draw them further into the woods by filing off to the right toward the upper "Coos" and gain a little time for your militia to assemble and get in their rear when I think we can manage any party they can send.

Construction was suspended, however, in what is still called Hazen's Notch, which rears up 2000 feet in Westfield in sight of Canada, presumably because Hazen decided he was too vulnerable to attack. While never fulfilling its primary purpose, the road accelerated the settlement of Orleans and Caledonia counties (a vision which probably impelled Bayley and the Hazens to such strenuous exertions as much as their patriotic duty).

Jacob Bayley not only gave his name to an historic road, but soon, as one of the maverick leaders of the Dresden Party, very nearly split the infant commonwealth of Vermont in half. While the names of the Allen brothers, Ethan and Ira, reverberate, deservedly, through the pages of the early histories of the state, Bayley has never been as rightfully or widely recognized as the Jefferson Davis of his day.

Born in Newbury, Massachsetts in 1726, Bayley was surrounded by a family and community of intellectual and religious interests. At 19 he married, moved to Hampstead, New Hampshire, and then enlisted in the army. After the surrender of Montreal in 1760, Lieutenants Bayley, Jacob Kent and Timothy Bedel and Captain John Hazen trekked south to the Connecticut River valley, where they decided that the Lower Coos lands which had been partly cleared by the Indians would make ideal sites for settlements. Back home in Massachusetts, the quartet's influential friends helped secure Governor Benning Wentworth's charters, in 1763, to Newbury on the west side of the river and to Haverill on the east bank. By 1770, Bayley was able to write: "The whole country is rapidly filling up with a very desirable class of settlers, and what was ten years since, a howling wilderness is now fast becoming fruitful farms."

Bayley soon found himself embroiled in a political tug-of-war. Vermont, then a patchwork of overlapping land grants issued by New Hampshire and New York, had declared its independence of everyone in January 1776 and adopted a constitution in July 1777. In June the following year, 16 New Hampshire towns dissatisified with their underrepresentation in that state's legislature petitioned for annexation to Vermont. Governor Chittenden and his council, trying to manage the fledgeling republic from their homes in Arlington, opposed this union but realized the trouble rejection would cause. Eastside Vermont towns, resenting the Arlington clique dominated by the Allen brothers, might secede from Vermont. Bayley himself disagreed with Ethan Allen politically and was morally outraged by his free-thinking irreverence. Accordingly, the rebellious New Hampshire towns were admitted to Vermont. Discovering that this action worked against Vermont's recognition by Congress, the Arlington junta, never happy with the union because it gave the eastern towns and their New Hampshire allies a political majority in the legislature, reversed itself and expelled the towns east of the Connecticut River early in 1779, prompting Bayley's next move. He and other landowning leaders of "The Dresden Party" were plotting to join politically with Massachusetts, New York or New

Hampshire, or even to organize New Connecticut, a separate state incorporating towns on both sides of the river, whose capital would be Dresden, the section of Hanover occupied by Dartmouth College. The controversy simmered for two years until the second East Side Union briefly pried loose some of the eastern Vermont towns.

In February 1781, however, Ira Allen negotiated with 43 discontented New Hampshire towns which were pressing New Hampshire to lay claim to all of Vermont and shrewdly switched the signals by having Vermont claim most of western New Hampshire, and promised them that they could seek union with Vermont; 34 did, and were accepted by the Assembly when it met in Windsor. The creation of the second East Union threatened the westside, which responded quickly to the petition of a group of eastern New York towns to join Vermont. In June 1781 the Vermont Assembly, in another flare of imperialism that must have given sardonic pleasure to George III, voted 53-24 to seat the representatives of 15 New York towns and to extend the state's jurisdiction west to the Hudson and thence north through the Champlain valley to Canada. New Hampshire and New York retaliated, threatening to send troops. In Philadelphia the Congress, upset by the chaos in the region, offered admission to Vermont if it would give up claims to land in the other two states. In February 1782 Isaac Tichenor, an opponent of the Chittenden group, dissolved "Greater Vermont," but Congress balked again, and would continue to do so until New York claims were settled nine years later.

Meanwhile, the Allen brothers had been dickering since the summer of 1780 with the British governor of Quebec, Sir Frederick Haldimand, discussing Vermont's return to the empire. While historians have differed about the motivations of these backwoods Talleyrands, most agree that their courtship of Haldimand was a crafty way to neutralize a British military threat to Vermont's unprotected frontier and at the same time to pressure the Congress for recognition and admission to statehood. Jacob Bayley regarded the Allens' gambit as nothing short of treason. Haldimand, hoping to silence Bayley, despatched secret service agents to kidnap him.

Bayley was plowing his field one day when a British Lieutenant Pritchard and his Tory followers sneaked up on him. Forewarned, Bayley escaped the trap and fled across the river

140

to Haverill, but Pritchard took four prisoners from the Bayley home, including one of Jacob's sons, who was shortly released.

General Bayley lived until March 1, 1815, when he died in the house of his son Isaac. At the 150th anniversary of the settlement of Newbury in August 1912, a monument on the village common was dedicated to his memory.

Today's travelers can retrace parts of the Bayley-Hazen Road, through remarkably beautiful upland country in the state's unexploited Northeast Kingdom. Of its original 56 miles, some 14 have achieved numbered blacktop status; about 33 miles are dirt or gravel in various states of repair; and nine miles have been abandoned — some jeepable, others walkable, and one section near Joe's Pond in Danville so overgrown with spruce and fir thickets as to be barely crawlable, as a *Vermont Life* writer reported some years ago. The route, roughly, takes one from Wells River to Ryegate, Peacham, East Cabot, Walden Station, Hardwick Street, Greensboro, East Craftsbury, Albany and Lowell to Hazen's Notch. Here it meets the Long Trail on Route 58, a scenic road, dappled with sunlight through thick foliage in summer, with a fine picnic site near the historic marker. That stretch of Route 58, however, is closed in the winter, when deep snow temporarily erases all evidence of Hazen's persistence.

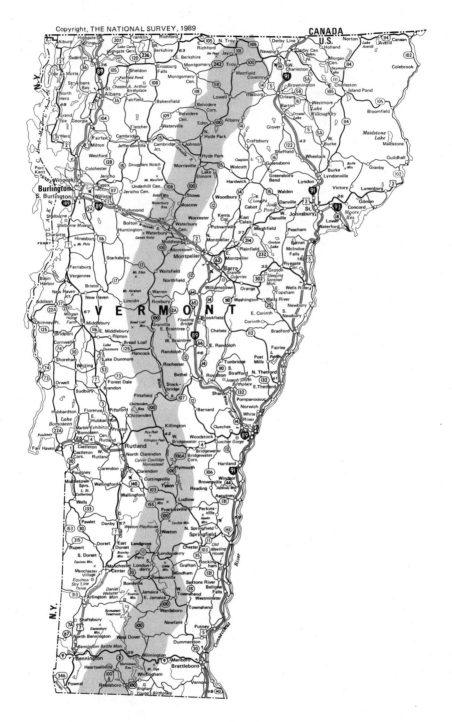

Route 100: Spinal Tap

Chapter Three

Route 100 — Spinal Tap

"If the spirit of liberty should vanish in other parts of the Union and support of our institution should languish, it could all be replenished from the generous store held by the people of this brave little state of Vermont."

— President Calvin Coolidge,
Bennington, September, 1928

In the early 1800s able-bodied men could work out their taxes by maintaining the roads — here, between Williamsville and Newfane.
—Vermont Historical Society

Vermont's south-north Route 100 could be called the Snow Bunny Trail because it links most of the state's major ski resorts, from Mount Snow to Mount Mansfield and Jay Peak, touching Stratton, Bromley, Okemo, Killington, and Sugar Bush along the way. The narrow artery is a study in contrasts, revealing vintage villages like Weston; Plymouth and the spartan shrine to Calvin Coolidge; deceptively rustic Rochester; the enchanted Granville Gulf; and the gentrified resort towns of Waitsfield and Stowe. Sugar houses, body shops, woodworking plants, used car dealers, and other tangible, often gritty manifestations of rural society alternate with world-class hotels for affluent vacationers.

Just north of the Massachusetts border, this highway shows signs of internal indecision, as it proceeds first north, as an extension of Route 8 from North Adams, veers south at Heartwellville, east at Readsboro to Jacksonville, then north again to Wilmington and beyond.

Whitingham

First settled in 1770 when it was granted by New York to Colonel Nathan Whiting, this village lies between Sadawga

Pond and the elongated Harriman Reservoir. There's a floating island on Sadawga Pond, and nearby is the "Green Mountain Giant," a 3,400-ton freestanding boulder. Whitingham was once the site of a mineral spring spa said to cure cutaneous eruptions, humors, dropsey, gravel, chronic ulcers, liver complaints, tic doloreaux, nervousness, general delibility, constipation and various other disorders.

Brigham Young, the Mormon prophet, was born here in 1801. After the murder of Joseph Smith, the founder, who was born in Sharon, Vermont, and led the Latter-Day Saints from

Monument to Brigham Young, the man of "wonderful equipment." —Vermont Travel Division

Palmyra, New York, to Carthage, Illinois, Young rallied the faithful to push onward across the prairies to found a new city of Zion on the barren wastes beside the Great Salt Lake. In the village of his birth, Brigham Young is commemorated by a stubby granite shaft inscribed, "A man of much endurance and superb equipment," attributes surely needed by the husband of seventy wives and the sire of fifty-six children.

Wilmington/Dover

Route 100 intersects Route 9, the Molly Stark Trail, at Wilmington, and winds about seven miles north through West Dover, the actual center of the township, to Mount Snow. This popular ski destination made its debut in 1954, when Reuben Snow's farm was invaded by ski lifts and trails, lodges, skating rink, and a vigorous geyser. Ski lodges and second homes burgeoned rapidly, and the resulting impact on rural village services helped precipitate the state's first environmental protection law. By the early 1970s, bust followed boom: Mount Snow went through a revolving door of owners until it was finally acquired and expanded by S.K.I. Ltd., which also owns Killington.

This "sledge-coach" linked Williamsville and East Dover.
—Vermont Historical Society

Stratton

Stratton Mountain's legions of winter skiers and Volvo International Tennis fans in the summer are not unprecedented.

Hikers around the mountain are surprised to encounter a boulder commemorating Daniel Webster's presence here on July 8, 1840. To hear the famous orator and presidential candidate argue that only the Whigs could save the Union, more than ten thousand hardy souls gathered on foot, on horseback, and in buggies. Hard cider for the multitude was served from a five-hundred-square-foot log cabin thrown up for the occasion. Why Webster chose to deliver an address in such a remote spot has mystified most historians. One explanation is that, invited while in Boston to make speeches at three places in New England, and unable to accept, Webster drew a triangulation of the three locations that landed him at Stratton Mountain. Actually, the "Tippecanoe and Tyler too" campaign of 1840 was the most spectacular ever staged in Vermont. More people voted (56,117) than in any previous election or in any subsequent ones until 1868.

The Stratton Mountain ski resort, located atop a five-mile access road from Route 30 in Bondville, is an especially well-groomed area. With a vertical drop of 2,003 feet, eighty-six trails and slopes, it includes Stratton Village, a complex of thirty shops, several restaurants, condo-hotel, indoor parking garage, a sports center and scores of condominia. Arts and crafts festivals are annual features, along with the Volvo International Tennis tournament.

Weston

This tiny hill village on the West River, with its oval green, is perhaps Vermont's most picturesque hamlet, the home of a respected summer playhouse, the Kinhaven Music School, and the Weston Priory, a Benedictine monastery noted for its contemporary spiritual ballads and as a sanctuary for Central American refugees. The meticulously-maintained Farrar-Mansur House, built as a tavern in 1797, is open to the public.

What has been attracting the most visitors for nearly fifty years, however, is the famous Vermont Country Store, an old-fashioned, nostalgia-steeped emporium created by the late

Vrest Orton, whose tartly conservative political views punctuated the enormously successful mail order catalogue, *The Voice of the Mountains*. Born in Hardwick, Vermont, in 1897, Vrest K. Teachout Orton spent his boyhood in Calais and other northern Vermont towns, and was educated in Massachusetts, attending Harvard. He served in the American Expeditionary Force in World War I and wound up in New York City in 1925 with *The American Mercury*, Alfred A. Knopf, book publisher, and *The Saturday Review of Literature* until helping to start *The Colophon*, a book collector's quarterly, in 1930. Moving back to Vermont, he founded the Stephen Daye Press, a Brattleboro book publisher, and in the mid-thirties, the Countryman Press in Weston. Before its acquisition by John Lowell Pratt and the A.S. Barnes publishing company, the Countryman imprint appeared on several illustrated, signed, limited editions that Orton designed and printed, including *Rudyard Kipling's Vermont Feud* by Frederic Van de Water, *The Golden Fleece of California* by Edgar Lee Masters, and two books by Stephen Vincent Benet, *The Devil and Daniel Webster* and *Johnny Pye and the Fool Killer*. (After twenty post-war years of dormancy, the imprint was revived by this writer for a new trade book publishing company in Woodstock in 1973.)

Orton, a poet as well as the author of several nonfiction books, promoted such oldtime products as the Vermont Common Cracker. He died in 1986, but the Vermont General Store flourishes under the management of his son, Lyman.

Ludlow

Ludlow, in the Black River Valley, one produced "shoddy," reworked wool introduced after the Civil War during a cloth shortage. Today, the recreation industry is its mainspring, with skiers crowding Okemo Mountain. The Black River Academy, now an intriguing museum, is the high school attended by Calvin Coolidge. Here the future president and one of his chums, John Garibaldi Sargent, perpetrated a youthful prank by heaving and hauling a donkey up the stairs to a classroom. Sargent was later rewarded with Coolhand Cal's appointment as Attorney General. Ludlow was also the home of Abby Maria Hemenway (1835-90), who compiled town histories for the entire state, adding up to a prodigious five volume *Gazeteer* of 6,000 pages.

Whether the small town of Cavendish has been infiltrated by the KGB can only be conjectured, but it in fact harbors one of the most celebrated Soviet emigres, Alexander Solzhenitsyn. The controversial author of *The Gulag Archipelago* and other anti-Soviet works first came to the state to lecture at the Russian Studies Center at Norwich University in 1975. The atmosphere, climate (not unlike Russia's, especially in winter) and countryside suiting his mood, Solzhenitsyn decided that here he could be physically isolated yet within reach of influential political and educational centers, and in 1976 he purchased a fifty-acre property up a dirt road four miles from Cavendish. The property, including a spacious house and outbuildings, was soon surrounded by an eight-foot chain-link fence surmounted by barbed wire and accessible only through an electronically controlled gate. Townspeople were understandably, at first, upset by this alien presence, but after the Cassandralike author, resembling an Old Testament prophet of doom, made a dramatic appearance at a Town Meeting, neighbors closed ranks protectively around his privacy, as so often happens in Vermont where eccentricity is usually prized, and his personal think-tank and international publishing center function undisturbed. A son has attended the local public schools and has been making a name for himself as a pianist.

Plymouth

An austere stone appropriately marks the grave of Calvin Coolidge, America's thirtieth President, a few hundred yards from the Plymouth Notch house in which he was born on July 4, 1872. Many historians have tended to deride the Coolidge administration for its passive, pro-big-business policies, but the man himself has in recent years been transformed into a nostalgic national icon, personifying Yankee simplicity, plain speaking, economy, and probity in an age of excess. One has only to witness the the bus tour pilgrims who flock to his isolated native hamlet in the summer to realize how deeply these virtues have been ingrained in the minds of uneasy older Americans who deplore their absence in today's hypocritical political arena.

Chartered as Saltash and first settled in 1771, the town's name was changed to Plymouth in 1797. A minor gold rush animated the area in the 1850s, and during the years when nearby Tyson Furnace prospered with iron foundries and the manufacture of stoves, Plymouth boasted a dance hall whose floor rested on rubber balls. Coolidge was a man of two worlds — rural upcountry Vermont, and the complex seats of government in Boston and Washington. He learned the art of democratic government in Plymouth's annual town meetings, by watching his father as the local Justice of the Peace and member of the state legislature, and carried with him to the White House the lessons of self-restraint and self-discipline. As Massachusetts legislator, governor, and President, Coolidge always returned to Plymouth to renew the values that sustained him as a farm boy: hard work, frugality, neighborliness and a genuine respect for the land.

A presidential boomlet for Calvin Coolidge was touched off in Woodstock in December 1919 when the Windsor County Republican Committee exhorted Vermonters everywhere to get to

Calvin Coolidge was born in this cradled hamlet of Plymouth. —Vermont Historical Society

work for his nomination. At the Republican National Convention in 1920, the high command picked Warren G. Harding, Senator from Ohio, as the nominee and were about to select one of his cronies for Vice President when the delegates rebelled and nominated Coolidge. The Governor of Massachusetts had recently won national acclaim for having declared in the course of a strike by Boston police that there was "no right to strike against the public safety by anyone, anywhere, anytime." The Governor and his wife, Grace Goodhue from Burlington, were warmly welcomed in Plymouth that July by three thousand people. Coolidge addressed the throng with the words: "I am here by right of birth...it is a great heritage to be reared here among these hills, given to thrift and industry and all that is noblest and best."

After the election of Harding and Coolidge, friends of John Coolidge, Calvin's father, kidded him about going to Washington. John Coolidge only smiled and allowed as to how Plymouth had been good enough for him for the past seventy-two years, and he guessed it would be good enough for the rest of his life.

On August 3, 1923, John Coolidge, as Justice of the Peace, administered the presidential oath of office to his son. Calvin was in Plymouth, helping his father with the haying, as President Harding lay mortally ill in San Francisco. "The optimistic tone of the bulletins from the bedside of President Harding," the *Vermont Standard* reported August 2, "have greatly relieved the tension under which the vice president has been laboring and he has decided to remain in Plymouth with his family for the next few days....During the day he was besieged by newspaper men from the metropolitan papers....It is a matter of satisfaction that he remains untarnished by the artificialities of politics and social stress."

Since there was no telephone in the Coolidge homestead, news of Harding's death was personally carried to Plymouth by William A. Perkins of the Bridgewater telephone office after midnight on August 3. John Coolidge answered the knock on the door, read the message, and carried it upstairs to his son. Calvin thereupon telegraphed his office in Washington for the text of the oath, to which he was duly sworn by his father at 2:47 A.M. by the light of a kerosense lamp. Once asked why he thought he had a right to administer the oath, the elder Coolidge replied, "I didn't know I couldn't."

A premature campaign banner for Coolidge flies in 1988 over current U.S. District Judge Franklin S. Billings, Jr., former Chief Justice of the Vermont Supreme Court.
—Vermont Historical Society

Calvin Coolidge expressed his most memorable tribute to Vermont at the end of a two-day train trip in September 1928. The President made a loop by rail through the state to survey the amazing recovery that had been made from the devastating flood of 1927. In Cavendish, the presidential party viewed the most spectacular aftermath of the flood, a chasm nearly four hundred feet deep carved by the Black River, into which had toppled seven houses, ten barns, four garages and most of the main street. In Bennington, five thousand people crowded around his train and cried "Speech, speech!" Until then, the President had avoided oratory, but now, in what reporters said was an unusual display of emotion, he spoke of "the splendid recovery from the great catastophe which overtook the state a year ago," and then delivered his extemporaneous, often-quoted tribute:

"Vermont is a state I love. I could not look upon the peaks of Ascutney or Mansfield without being moved in a way that no other scene would move me. It was here I first saw the light of day; here I received my bride; here my dead lie pillowed upon the everlasting hills.

"I love Vermont because of her hills and valleys, her scenery and invigorating climate, but most of all because of her indominatable people. They are a race of pioneers who almost beggared themselves for others. If the spirit of liberty should vanish in other parts of the Union and support of our institutions should languish, it could all be replaced from the generous store held by the people of this brave little state of Vermont."

His fellow Vermonters were sorely disappointed when Coolidge declared "I do not choose to run" in 1928. An editorial in the *New York Sun* crystallized popular sentiments at the time, and, increasingly, the presumptions of Reaganomics sixty years later:

> This New Englander was born and bred in an atmosphere of thrift....The hardness of Vermont farming is not nothing. Save, pay, don't squander. And these very old-fashioned policies, sneered at in some quarters as the narrow conclusions of the rustic mind, resulted in the greatest economic revival, the most abundant and widely spread prosperity, that the world has known. He and the head of the Treasury proved that the scientific reduction of taxes stimulates industry and buying power and yet increases the Government's revenue. In the last four years America has enjoyed the phenomenon, hitherto unknown, of rising wages together with falling commodity prices. Small wonder that President Coolidge had but to say "Yes" to be chosen for another term!

Perhaps the canny Coolidge foresaw the economic twister that destroyed his successor, President Hoover.

Several of the myths surrounding Coolidge were dispelled by Vermont historian Charles Morrissey in the winter 1979 issue of *Vermont Life*: "Silent Cal? The myth persists. Yet as President he delivered more speeches than any of his 29 predecessors. During the 67 months he was in the White House he made radio addresses about once each month. He held 520 press conferences, an average of 7.8 per month. Franklin D. Roosevelt, who is famous for his Fireside Chats, averaged 6.9 press conferences per month during his presidency....A man of little humor? It may be hard for us to imagine, but as a youth in Plymouth Notch, Coolidge was an end-man in the village minstrel show. As a senior at Amherst College he delivered the humorous oration at graduation time — and did it well. Will Rogers has commented that 'Mr.Coolidge has more subtle humor than almost any public man I ever met. I have often said I would like to have been hidden in his desk somewhere and just heard the little sly digs that he pulled on various people that never got 'em at all. I bet he wasted more humor on folks than almost anybody.' "

The Coolidge tradition and presence are tangibly evident in Plymouth Notch today, in the homestead, in an overly modest museum, and in the small cheese factory where John Coolidge, the president's surviving son, may sometimes be found. The Calvin Coolidge Memorial Foundation has been growing in membership and activity in recent years.

While Plymouth Notch now seems preserved in amber for eternity, the surrounding area of forests and lakes is being colonized by Hawk Mountain's second homes and condo-hotel.

Sherburne

The lordly Killington ski resort, at the junction of Routes 100 and 4, is described in Chapter Four.

Rochester

With its serene patina, Rochester is deceptive. On the surface, this vintage village appears archetypical, a small rural center where nothing much happens. Located on the White River where Route 73 climbs through the Brandon Gap westward to Route 7, the town harbors a sizable group of sophisticated urban refugees. Tom Wicker, the *New York Times* columnist, has a vacation home here, and a New Age book publishing company has set up shop on the green.

Seven miles north, past the lumbering villages of Hancock and Granville and the intersection of Route 125, which ascends to Bread Loaf and the Middlebury Gap, the highway snakes through the lovely Granville Gulf State Park. The first six hundred acres along both sides of the road were given to the state by Governor Redfield Proctor in 1927. Moss Glen Falls is an especially appealing place to pause and savor the natural beauty of the narrow, wooded valley.

Warren

Named for General Joseph Warren, the physician who died in action at Bunker Hill, the mountainous town was settled in 1797. Warren's Gore, comprising nearly six thousand adjoining acres, is one of several unincorporated and uninhabited areas in the state, wedge-shaped pieces of land such as Warner's Grant, also in Essex County, and Avery's Gore in Chittenden County. Avery's Gore in Franklin County was divided by legislative action in 1961 and made part of the towns of Bakersfield and Montgomery.

One of the most challenging side roads in the state winds precipitously through the Lincoln-Warren Gap between Mount Grant and Mount Abraham to Bristol. It is closed in the winter months, and not recommended for recreational vehicles of the QE 2 variety or trailers.

As in other parts of the state, the names of these peaks have stories of their own. In *The Green Mountains of Vermont*, W. Storrs Lee wrote that Mount Abraham was originally called Potato Hill or Lincoln Mountain: "The older generation in the village of Lincoln nestling at its feet still prefers the vegetable allusion because it represents their conception of an outsized, well-banked potato hill, but they have long since lost out to the map publishers who succeeded in removing the vegetable aspect, if not the confusion. Lincoln, the town, was established long before Abe was splitting rails, and was probably named for General Benjamin Lincoln, who distinguished himself in the Revolution and later in Shay's Rebellion. But when the connoisseur of mountains, Joseph Battell, bought the mountain and with it the right to call his property what he wanted, he brushed General Benjamin aside. Colonel Battell reverenced the author of the Emancipation Proclamation more than Revolutionary gold braid and converted Potato Hill into Mount Abraham, and the contiguous elevation into Lincoln Peak. To assure the President of good company, he assigned an adjacent rise to the President's mother, Nancy Hanks, and another mountain to General Grant. The Green Mountain Club, with conciliatory intent, calls the whole section of the range from Mount Abraham to Mount Ellen, 'the main peaks of Lincoln Mountain,' but Lincolnites still remember General Benjamin and Potato Hill."

The Mad River Valley adjacent to Warren has become a sophisticated ski resort, including Sugarbush, Mount Ellen, and Mad River Glen. In the early 1960s, Sugarbush developed the first bottom-of-the-lift village, which attracted the mink-lined, sun-tan set, who built their own chalets, landing strip, and formed summer polo teams and fox hunts.

Waitsfield

General Benjamin Wait settled this resort town in 1789 when he was over eighty years old, a veteran of the French and Indian Wars and of the capture of Fort Ticonderoga. Eleven of the thirteen earliest settlers here were Minutemen at Lexington and Concord, memorialized by a monument dedicated in 1906.

Round Barn Farm on East Warren Road, a bed and breakfast inn, is a landmark because of its remarkable round barn, built in 1810, and one of the few remaining.

Waterbury

This crossroads town on the Winooski River was settled in 1784 and is known principally as the location of the Vermont State Hospital for the mentally ill, founded in the late nineteenth century, and for a satellite complex of state government offices.

Routes 100 and 2 intersect here with Interstate 89; skiers bound for Sugarbush and Stowe sleepily disembark from AMTRAK's Montrealer soon after dawn — whenever it's on time.

Ben and Jerry's ice cream is almost as well known nationally as Vermont maple sugar. The youthful entrepreneurs who started their business in a Burlington storefront built a new plant between Waterbury and Stowe in 1986; visitors are welcome to watch their favorite flavors being made and to sample them afterward.

Mount Mansfield overlooks the Waterbury Dam in early spring.
—Vermont Travel Division

Stowe

Mount Mansfield, the highest in the state at 4,393 feet, is often snowcapped in June. About five miles long, its crest rsembles an upturned face, with forehead, nose, lips, chin, and an adam's apple. Just beneath the Chin is the Lake of the Winds, more of a marsh than a body of water. The Rock of Terror and the Cave of the Winds, Wall Street, and Needle's Eye are hikers' milestones, and there's an automobile road to the summit.

There was a carriage road almost to the crest as early as 1858, leading to a modest hotel between the Nose and the Chin, both engineered by a small hotel owner in Stowe, who thus set the stage for the town's dramatic transformation over the next hundred years. With big money from southern New England investors, the Mount Mansfield Hotel Company was brokered in 1859, intent on competing with the White Mountain summer trade. The first step, according to W. Storrs Lee, "was the construction of a plush hotel with all the dressings from pillared portico to ice water. It took five years to complete the great edifice, but on June 24, 1864, the doors of the Mount Mansfield Hotel were ceremoniously swung open to the first guests. They had a choice of two hundred guest rooms and a choice of almost as many items on the menu. There were lavishly furnished parlors and a ballroom brilliantly illuminated with kerosene chandeliers. Even the hotel stables were luxurious, with stalls for a hundred horses and space for half that number of carriages." The place was an overnight success. An annex of another hundred rooms was added, with a bowling alley in the basement, and a pond improvised for bathing and boating.

"This village has quite the appearance of a watering place, Abby Hemenway observed in her 1867 *Gazeteer*. "For three or four months of the summer, from three to five hundred strangers are thrown into it, with all the means of show and parade they bring with them, of fine apparel, fine carriages, and fine horses."

Hemenway, a shrewd chronicler of the times, went on to express an opinion shared by many contemporary Vermonters:

> Let us do all we can to keep up the notion among our city cousins that to live "away up in Vermont" is the American equivalent for being exiled to Siberia. Let us tell them that we like to have them *visit* us during the few fleeting days in midsummer when we can safely walk about with them in our fields without our buffalo coats and bear-skin gowns, but that *they* belong to altogether too delicate a race to think of *living through* our severe winters with any comfort.
>
> Not that we do not think very highly of our city cousins, especially *when we see them in the city*. But when they come with their long baggage-train of trunks and band-boxes, and take possession of a country village, bringing their livery and their minister with them, occupying all the finest building sites, ordering all their groceries and toggery from the city, and importing into industrious communities the seductive fashion of doing nothing and doing it elegantly, they turn the heads of the young, demoralizing the whole tone of society, convert respectable villages into the likeness of suburban Connecticut and New Jersey, and for all these losses do not compensate by adding any appreciable amount to the circulating capital or to public improvement.

The owners of the big hotel soon completed the circuitous carriage road to the summit house, which they acquired and expanded. Finishing the road was a challenge, for there were long stretches of nearly forty-five-degree inclines hugging the sheer slopes, sections where cliffs had to be rounded on narrow shelves of ledge, and one frightening passage of a hundred yards built entirely of corduroy logs overhanging a chasm. At the rate of $12 a week, the summit house was a bargain for the many public figures of the era who registered there, including Ralph Waldo Emerson, who evidently relished his sojourns in several of the state's hostelries. The famous transcendentalist noted the spectacular view from the Chin: "Lake Champlain lay below us, but was a perpetual illusion, as it would appear a piece of yellow sky, until careful examination of the islands in it and the Adirondac summits beyond brought it to earth for a moment...This summer, bears and a panther have been seen on the mountain, and we peeped into some rocky caves which might house them. We came on the way, to the edge of a crag, which we approached carefully, and lying on our bellies...The next morning a man went through the house ringing a large bell, and shouting Sunrise, and everybody dressed in haste, and went down to the piazza. Mount Washington and the Franconia Mountains were clearly visible, and Ellen and I climbed now the Nose, to which the ascent is made easy by means of a stout rope firmly attached near the top, and reaching down to the bottom of the hill, near the House. Twenty people were using it at once at different heights. After many sharp looks at the heavens and the earth, we descended to breakfast. I found in this company...many agreeable people."

The magnificent hotel in Stowe burned to the ground on October 4, 1889, but the more modest hotel on the summit survived. In 1923 it was rebuilt and enlarged, and when the Stowe area became Vermont's ski capital, a new Mount Mansfield Company took over the Summit House and Toll Road and built the luxurious Smugglers Notch Lodge, which, in turn, was turned into condominia in the early 1980s.

A few hardy Stowe residents were skiing on barrel staves around the turn of the century, but as a popular sport, Alpine skiing did not catch on until the early 1930s, when one of the first modern ski trails in America was cleared on Mansfield by Albert Gottlieb and the Civilian Conservation Corps. The Nose

Dive Trail got national attention when it was skied by the American Women's Ski Team, brought there by Roland Palmedo, president of the Amateur Ski Club of New York. In 1936, Frank Griffin, a businessman from Burlington, built the Toll House ski lodge and hired Sepp Ruschp, the professional Austrian skier, to organize a ski school.

Palmedo helped finance the first chairlift in the East on Mansfield in 1940, and then developed Mad River Glen in 1949. On a blustery day in March 1938, on the Nose Dive Trail, Minot "Minnie" Dole, with Palmedo's backing, introduced the first organized first aid and rescue squad for skiers, credited as the birth of the National Ski Patrol.

Ruschp, as president of the Mt. Mansfield Corporation by the mid-1960s, was responsible for its post-war expansion. By 1988, the area included three base lodges, forty-four trails, a gondola to the Cliff House just below the Chin, double, triple, and quad chairlifts. The village of Stowe has become almost like Pompeii, nearly buried in an avalanche of inns, lodges, motels, and restaurants.

Among Stowe's year-round, four-star inns, the Trapp Family Lodge is one of the most popular. The late Baroness Maria von Trapp settled here because the terrain resembled her native Austria, and guests are attracted by echoes of "The Sound of Music" as well as spectacular views from the lodge and chalets.

Smugglers' Notch

This 2,162-foot pass north of Stowe on Route 108 is traversed by Vermont's most dramatic road, which is closed to traffic in the winter months because of the impenetrable snow. Some of the drama has been provided every fifty years or so when a huge boulder came crashing down from the towering cliffs, and the road simply curved around it. During the War of 1812, cattle and other supplies destined to be smuggled into Canada to feed the British army were hidden in this mountain fastness. A path through the high pass has existed since Indian times, but not until 1910 was the road built, which, with its eighteen percent grade is as steep as many ski trails. Motorists can pause to savor the wild and wonderful scenery at a Forest and Parks turnoff by Big Spring, from which gushes the finest water in the state. Nearby landmark rock formations for hikers include

Elephant Head, King Rock, the Hunter and His Dog, Singing Bird, the Smugglers' Cave, and Smuggler's Face.

In 1963, a group of investors headed by IBM board chairman Thomas Watson developed the Smugglers' Village ski area around Madonna Mountain, a self-contained Aspen-style resort, accessible in the winter from Jeffersonville.

Jay

From Stowe, Route 100 meanders north through Morrisville, Eden and Eden Mills, where the asbestos industry flourished, Lowell, to Westfield, thence northeasterly to Newport, which figures in Chapter Six. At Westfield, a side road leads five miles to Jay, the northernmost ski resort.

Granted in 1780 under the name of Carthage, the village reverted to the state from 1809 until 1814, because the only residents were the twenty children of the first settler, and was regranted to the statesman John Jay, who never visited. His son sold it to Azarias Williams, who in turn deeded it to the University of Vermont. Jay Peak, which rises 3,861 feet, is the last major summit on the Long Trail. On a clear day, one can see Montreal distinctly, Champlain and the Adirondacks, and the Presidential Range of the White Mountains.

About 30,000 acres on and around Jay Peak were owned by the Weyerhaeuser lumber and paper company, which acquired the ski area in the early 1960s and installed a Swiss-built aerial tramway to the summit, plus a Tyrolean complex. Ownership then passed to the Canadian-based owners of St. Sauveur, a major ski area in the Laurentians, which further developed it into a destination resort for Montrealers.

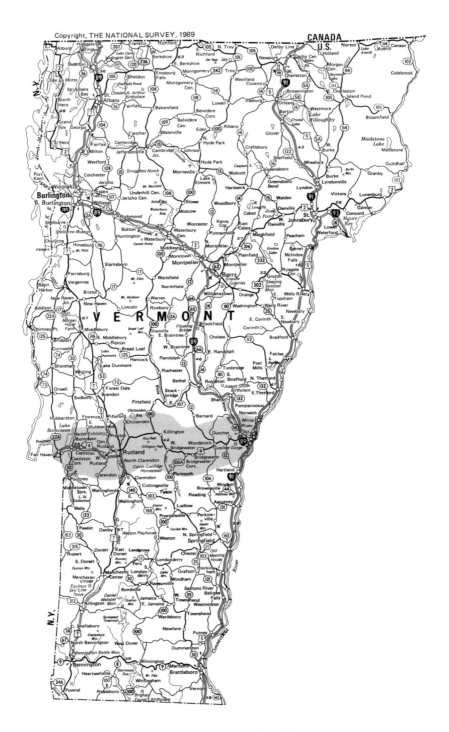

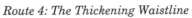

Route 4: The Thickening Waistline

Chapter Four

Route 4—
The Thickening Waistline

"The [railroad] Extension Bill will have to pass on its merits or not at all. I do not propose to buy my way through Congress . . . You may understand that every thing that can properly be done for the passage of the Bill, will be done; but as to buying its way through Congress, that is not possible while I am head of the enterprise."

—Frederick Billings, Woodstock, president of
the Northern Pacific Railroad, 1879

Vermont cannot seem to make up its mind what to do about Route 4, the principal East-West highway that suffers from arteriosclerosis and galloping "striposis" (or "roadside rash"). Stretching from White River Junction westward to Fair Haven, the mostly narrow road is overloaded with foliage tour busses, skiers' cars, and 18-wheelers that are undermining the foundations of the stately Federal houses that line Woodstock's famous Green.

Significant, limited-access improvements have been made between Fair Haven and the Killington-Pico ski areas east of Rutland, but topography defeats by-pass schemes proposed for the twenty or so miles through the winding Ottauquechee River valley (Killington's leach field), where creeping strip development grows like kudsu vines. A new East-West connector with I-91 is overdue, but there's no Robert Moses — New York City's onetime parkway czar — on the horizon with enough zeal and leverage to bull it through.

Quechee Gorge was spanned for the Woodstock Railroad in 1875.
—courtesy Vermont Historical Society

Few vestiges remain of White River Junction's sooty, sometimes boistrous history as a significant New England railroad hub, but the pleasantly gritty town still harbors freight trains and a depot for AMTRAK's *Montrealer*, which shuttles passengers between Montreal and Washington, D.C. The kinetic convergence of I-89, I-91, Routes 5 and 4 has spawned a cluster of household-name motels, and the venerable downtown Hotel Coolidge recalls the era of steam and drummers. (See also pages 128-9.)

White River Junction and its adjacent neighbor, Lebanon, across the Connecticut River in New Hampshire, form the burgeoning urban core of a rapidly growing commercial-industrial metropolitan area, enhanced by Dartmouth College's educational and medical centers in nearby Hanover.

For nearly sixty years, 1875-1933, the notable short-line Woodstock Railroad between White River and the town of Woodstock fueled the latter's fame as a year-round resort, carrying fashionable vacationers from Boston and New York to the old Inn. Today's Route 4 follows or parallels the railroad's right of way, crossing Quechee Gorge on the steel railway bridge reconstructed in 1911. Conceived by prosperous Woodstock leaders and chartered in 1863, the railroad was completed in 1875 when the first, wooden span was thrown across the Gorge. J.J. Porter, the longtime superintendent of the road, once took a lot of ribbing at a banquet of railway executives: bridling when the head of a major line sneered at the "fourteen-mile stem...don't remember it," Porter replied, "Yes, it's little and short, but it's just as wide as yours." Plagued by diminishing freight traffic and rising deficits during the 1920s, the Woodstock Railroad was almost literally washed out by the 1927 flood. It struggled on until the proposed concrete highway became a reality; service was abandoned in April 1933. Older local residents still chuckle over its widely-heralded last run, when the"special" spun its wheels on pranksters' grease smeared on the tracks over Shallies Hill.

Quechee

If White River Junction reflects the reality of the past, the village of Quechee (in the town of Hartford) is the wave of a future most Vermonters deplore. Here, the invasion of the

The 1798 Hutchinson House (with contemporary landscaping) marked the southern terminus of the Woodstock and Royalton Turnpike.
—Gordon Sweet, Woodstock Historical Society

condos has been consolidated in an upper middle-class, suburban second-home colony superimposed on 6,000 pastoral acres, absorbing a once-prosperous community that grew up around Albert Gallatin Dewey's woolen mills during the sheep-craze decades. In 1841 Dewey installed a patented rag-picking machine constructed by Reuben Daniels of Woodstock to turn out the first American "shoddy," the material made from reworked wool rags, tailors' cuttings and new threads. By 1870, 1,300 yards a day were rolling out, and when A.G. died in 1886, the firm was taken over by his sons — the inventive, mechanically ingenious John J. and shrewd, financially-minded William S. The mills lasted into the fourth and fifth generations of the family well into the second half of the twentieth century.

The only remnant of indigenous industry in Quechee today is the Simon Pearce Glass works, for which the noted Irish designer has harnessed the Quechee waterfall to provide hydropower.

Quechee Gorge, under Route 4, is one of Vermont's natural wonders, arresting hordes of sightseers, including more than a few of the morbidly curious drawn by the chasm's fatal attractions — accidents, homicides, suicides. In 1972, for instance, a

166

despondent motorist smashed his car through a guardrail and plunged into the gorge; in 1988, a love-bugged New Hampshireman tossed his estranged girlfriend over the cliff and then made his own swan-dive. As impressive as the 167-foot drop is the engineering feat achieved in 1875 when it was spanned by a wooden bridge for the Woodstock Railroad.

Woodstock

This Shire Town, the Windsor county seat, is, arguably, the most cosmopolitan small (3,500 persons) town in Vermont. Visitors have long admired the graceful coincidence of natural and man-made beauty that distinguishes the moated village and its surroundings, cradled between the plump promontories of Mt. Tom and Mt. Peg, on the banks of the Ottauquechee River. As lawyers, doctors, teachers, and merchants were drawn to the Shire Town and its court house late in the eighteenth century, Woodstock grew in wealth and sophistication, and its Green became today's internationally famous architectural showcase.

Woodstock's elliptical Green remains the heart of this vintage village.
—Woodstock Historical Society

The legendary elliptical Green— sometimes reputed to have been laid out in the length and shape either of the fabled paddle-wheeled transatlantic liner *Great Eastern* or Commodore Dewey's flagship *Olympia* — was acutally enlarged to its present dimensions in 1793. Folklorists claim that when the body of "the Corwin boy," thought to be a vampire, was disinterred in 1830, the heart was boiled in an iron cauldron and the remains buried fifteen feet deep in the common under a granite slab. The Green was indeed the site of a macabre spectacle in February 1818 when ten thousand people from all around eastern Vermont massed to witness the hanging of Samuel Godfrey, convicted of the murder of the Keeper of the State Prison in Windsor.

A pleasanter image rises from the final stanza of "A Vermont Pasture," a poem by the local poet Daniel Cady (1861-1934):

> My! such a peaceful, fambly day,
> It makes you Congos Quakers;
> You can't have no such day as that
> On top of tillage acres;
> It beats a day on Woodstock Green,
> Or 'mongst the Highgate sedges;
> There ain't no day that's like a day
> Upon your pasture ledges.

Early dwellers in the handsome brick and frame Federal houses achieved wide-ranging fame. One of the more commanding figures in the late eighteenth century was the Rev. Aaron Hutchinson, who could quote the New Testament in Greek, preached evangelically in barns in the winter and meadows in summer, and read the Boston newspapers aloud to his friends and neighbors. His son Titus, a lawyer and five-term representative to the General Assembly, was appointed district attorney for Vermont by President Madison and later became chief justice of the state supreme court.

Charles Marsh, who settled in Woodstock in 1788, practiced law here for sixty years. President Washington appointed him attorney general in 1797, and he later served a term in the House of Representatives. A roadbuilder and Dartmouth trustee, Marsh was a man of great cultivation: his gracious house on the slope of Mt. Tom was the social center of the town, where visiting worthies were stylishly entertained.

George Perkins Marsh, shown with his son in Italy, was America's first environmentalist.
—Frederick Billings Archive

George Perkins Marsh, his son, achieved distinction as a linguist, conservationist, Congressman and diplomat. Marsh spent seventeen years (1825-1842) in Burlington as a lawyer after graduating from Dartmouth College. He married Caroline Crane after his first wife died, raised sheep and cattle on his farm in Shelburne, helped bring woolen mills to Winooski, and lost money as an investor in the Central Vermont Railroad. Elected to Congress in 1842, he opposed the annexation of Texas and the war with Mexico, and championed the formation of the Smithsonian Institution. In 1849 he was appointed minister to Turkey, which gave him a chance to broaden his scholarly interests in geography and linguistics. Five years later Marsh came home, wrote and lectured. In 1861 Lincoln appointed him minister to the new Kingdom of Italy, where he served for twenty-one years, an unprecedented term in the foreign service, following the government from Turin to Florence to Rome.

Here he completed his most notable and influential work, *Man and Nature*, published in 1864, the first book to dramatize man's destructive impact on his natural habitat, anticipating by a century public concern and remedial efforts to contain further ecological damage. Marsh died in July 1882 and is buried in Rome near the graves of Keats and Shelley.

Marsh's notable library was purchased by Frederick Billings of Woodstock, who gave it to the University of Vermont with a $250,000 robust, romanesque building designed by H.H. Richardson. Billings, born in Royalton in 1803, could have been the model for a true Horatio Alger tale. When his father, Oel, ran aground financially in 1834, he had to move his large family to Woodstock to be within reach of the sheriff, at a time when debtors were often jailed. Young Frederick, driving a pig down the dusty Woodstock-Royalty Turnpike and past the Charles Marsh mansion on the slope of Mount Tom, promised himself never to be poor again. The family, which could barely pay the toll of thirty-one cents for wagon and cow, got a fresh start in Woodstock. Frederick attended local private schools and Kimball Union Academy before graduating from the University of Vermont in 1844. He was admitted to the bar and also served as Secretary of Civil and Military Affairs in the state capital.

In 1849 Frederick joined his sister and her sea-captain husband in the difficult trek to California. In gold-rush San Francisco, Frederick hung up his shingle as the first lawyer on the Barbary Coast. He prospered, making a fortune in law and real estate; Charles C. Frémont (the "Pathfinder") and his famous Mariposa Ranch were among his clients, and Billings had a lot to do with the founding of the University of California at Berkeley. He remained in California until the Civil War and married a New York belle in 1862. Seven years later, they returned to Woodstock and bought the 270-acre Charles Marsh farm. Billings reforested the hillsides, remodeled the house extensively in the fashionable "stick style" of the day, and began importing and breeding blue-ribbon Jersey cows.

Frederick Billings, a prominent Forty- niner in San Francisco, rescued the Northern Pacific Railroad from financial disaster.
—Matthew Brady, courtesy Frederick Billings archive

At the same time, he bought a one-twelfth interest in the ailing Northern Pacific Railroad, which was being refinanced by Jay Cooke, the Philadelphia banker. After Cooke's failure, Billings rescued the line from insolvency, and as president supervised its transcontinental construction. In an age of rampant corruption and financial chicanery among railroad tycoons, his biographers believe that Billings was evidently the only honest entrepreneur of his generation. Billings, Montana, was named for him in 1882, but by the time the final spike was driven a year later, Henry Villard had wrested control of the railroad away from Frederick and his associates. Billings turned then to another major remodeling of his Woodstock house, building the library in Burlington, and to making substantial philanthropic gifts to schools and churches. He died in 1890, at sixty-seven. One of his old friends said he died at such a relatively young age because he had "led three lives already."

The remarkable Marsh-Billings-Rockefeller coincidence of interest in environmental concerns, land conservation and historic preservation, has been perpetuated because Laurance S. Rockfeller married Frederick Billings' granddaughter, Mary French, in 1934. Together, they have been responsible for much of Woodstock's economic health, as owners of the luxurious contemporary Woodstock Inn and Resort (golf club, indoor sports center, and Suicide Six ski area) and creators of the Billings Farm & Museum, where farming methods of the 1890s have been dramatically enshrined.

Woodstock bred other distinguished nineteenth-century lawyers political leaders, artists and educators, more than any other single town of its size in Vermont. Among them were Jacob Collamer (1791-1865), a state supreme court justice, Congressman, Postmaster General in President Zachary Taylor's administration, and who was elected by the newly-created Republican Party in 1854 to the United States Senate, where he strenuously opposed the admission of Kansas as a slave state. He was re-elected in 1860 but died shortly before the expiration of his second term.

In his eulogy, Charles Sumner referred to Collamer as "the Green Mountain Socrates." Jefferson Davis reportedly declared that before the outbreak of the Civil War he would have been willing to submit the differences between the North and the South to Senator Collamer for decision, so great was his confidence in the Vermonter's honesty and sagacity. And, according to historian Walter Hill Crockett, on a stormy Sunday morning during that war, after the Northern army had suffered serious reverses, a man called at Senator Collamer's home while the latter was at church, and left a card on which was written: "If not at church please call on me at once, and if at church please call as soon as convenient" — signed "A. Lincoln."

Collamer made the memorable remark, "The good people of Woodstock have less incentive than others to yearn for heaven."

Julius Converse (1798-1885) was elected governor of Vermont in 1872, following the death of his friend and neighbor, Governor Peter T. Washburn. In 1924, Franklin S. Billings — Frederick's nephew — was elected governor after serving four terms in the legislature. His son, Franklin, Jr., was Speaker of the House, Superior Court Judge, Chief Justice of the State Supreme Court, and was appointed Federal District Court judge by President Reagan.

Between 1830 and 1850, Woodstock was the site for an important medical college. The Norman Williams Public Library, built in 1884, was the gift of Dr. Edward H. Williams, a physician and engineer, who was general manager of the Pennsylvania Railroad and later chief executive of Baldwin Locomotives. John Cotton Dana, scion of another early Woodstock settler, was the noted librarian and museum director who did more than anyone else to make books and art more accessible to the general public. He and his equally distinguished brothers are memorialized in the Dana House museum of the Woodstock Historical Society, which has an oustanding collection of antiques, porcelains, portraits, coin silver, costumes, and early toys.

Among the town's artists and writers were Benjamin Franklin Mason, the popular portrait painter; and Hiram Powers, expatriate sculptor of the "Greek Slave," which shocked the prudish when it was exhibited in the 1840s. More than seventy of John Taylor Arms' meticulously detailed etchings are displayed in the Dana House, given by Ward and Mariam Canaday of Pomfret, where Arms had a studio. Canaday, a patron of the arts in his home city of Toledo, Ohio, developed and built the famous World War II Jeep.

The Woodstock area has also been home base for other artists, notably the late painter Ivan Albright, and including the sculptor Judith Brown; glassblower Peter Bramhall; the late Byron Thomas, who painted many wartime scenes for *Life* magazine; printmaker Sabra Johnson Field; and George Tooker, who contributed a magnificently-conceived religious tryptich to the Roman Catholic Church in Windsor. For more than twenty-five years, the work of Vermont artists has been featured in Ellison Lieberman's famous Gallery Two.

Nobel-prize novelist Sinclair Lewis and his wife Dorothy Thompson, the foreign correspondent, were familiar figures in

Woodstock when they lived in nearby Barnard in the 1930s —
playing host to titled and otherwise notable central European
refugees from Nazidom. In September 1929, Lewis gave a
prophetic talk to the Rutland Rotarians:

> Right now I can visualize a great New York syndicate
> holding a meeting. Someone will mention Vermont. Probably
> members of the syndicate will say, "Yes, Vermont, let's go
> up there and be benefactors—build a 3000-room hotel on
> Mt. Ascutney—never mind the road, just get the hotel up."
> I can visualize the development in Rutland when the
> syndicate buys up all available property and builds
> magnificent Spanish gardens in barren orange groves and
> Czechoslovakian beerless beer gardens to clutter up the
> landscape....Florida was ruined by that mania. It must not
> happen in Vermont. You have priceless heritages—old
> houses that must not be torn down, beauty that must not
> be cluttered with billboards and hot dog stands. You are to
> be guardians of this priceless heritage and you are fortunate
> to have the honor of that task instead of being horn-
> blowers.

*The legendary Woodstock Inn dominated the village from 1892 until its
replacement in 1969.* —Woodstock Historical Society

Lewis's *It Can't Happen Here*, a novel about a small-town newspaper editor resisting American fascism, was set in Vermont.

Otis Skinner, the celebrated actor, had a home on the Green for several years after 1929.

The Vermont Symphony Orchestra, unique in the United States because of its eclectic, semi-professional membership, was born here in 1935, an outgrowth of Alan Carter's Pomfret chamber orchestra. Carter, who later headed the Middlebury College music department, conducted the Vermont Symphony's inaugural concert in the Town Hall in December 1937.

The renowned "old" Woodstock Inn (1892-1969) was a popular resort for winter sports enthusiasts from Boston and Montreal, and in the mid-thirties, Woodstock became the Eastern ski mecca when the first rope-tow in the United States was rigged up on Gilbert's pasture in 1934.

The Green Mountain Horse Association, which sponsors the popular 100-mile trail ride and other events, attracts serious equestrians to South Woodstock, where there are several stables and horse farms.

Woodstock has never been shy about its own virtues. In October 1913, the gifted Dana brothers published the first issue of *The Elm Tree Monthly*, declaring:

175

Frank "Old Age" Dana directed the newfangled automobile traffic in Woodstock for many years. —Woodstock Historical Society

Woodstock village is the best village in Vermont. Few doubt this and none can prove it isn't true. Woodstock has more good people in more comfortable homes than any village of its size in the world. It is on a beautiful, winding stream, with a fine brook attached, and the water in both is clean enough to drink. We eat it when it's ice and do not drink it because good water comes to us in pipes under pressure from the hills. Electricity is abundant and cheap. Telephones are everywhere. The sidewalks are concrete and never muddy. Highways are good, are improved every year, and are oiled besides.

The schools are approved and grow better steadily. The churches are overabundant; but we wish for all kinds, to pay the cost. The Inn is known and praised wherever travelers meet. The library is better than we need, but not above our tastes. The natives are of good old Yankee stock, with enough Canadians, Italians, and negroes to give a little zest. Fortunes are wanting; but a tidy stream of money trickles into two banks. Newspapers are old and worthy, and now that The Age has changed to this form and title, Woodstock has the handsomest journal in the state.

The summer resident is of the Woodstock kind, not much in the public print, but greatly on the job of getting rest and recreation.

Nearby are fishing and hunting clubs, which are precisely what they are called. On sunny slopes and sightly knolls are summer houses of city folk, which fit the landscape as neatly as their residents fit the local economy....

Bridgewater

Zadock Thompson, the naturalist and historian, was born here in 1796, the grandson of pioneers from Middleborough, Massachusetts, who settled on a hill farm in North Bridgewater at the close of the Revolution. Short, sedate and studious, Thompson was fascinated by the natural world, and translated his curiosity into an almanac of flora and fauna, which he sold door-to-door for enough money to pay his tuition at the University of Vermont, which he entered in 1819. While peddling his almanacs in the summers, he visited on foot or horseback nearly every town in the state, and decided to glean information from town reports and from the recollections of elderly residents for a history and gazeteer of the state. Working as an editor and publisher in Burlington, Thompson produced school texts, geographies, a *Guide to Lake Champlain, Lake George, Montreal and Quebec*, and his first state gazeteer in 1824. Thompson was ordained an Episcopal minister in 1835, and from 1841 until his death in 1856, he served as the state's geologist, naturalist, as well as curator of the State Cabinet (forerunner of the Vermont Historical Society). In 1853, the final, 700-page edition of his *Civil, Natural History, Gazeteer, Botany and Geology of Vermont* was issued. In it, he wrote, plaintively: "During the last ten years I have spent a large part of my spare time in collecting and preserving facts in relation to the civil and natural history of the State...If life and health should be spared for a few years longer, it would afford me much satisfaction to re-write the whole work and by incorporating into it the additional material make it more worthy of the approval and patronage of my fellow citizens. But as the great expense would preclude me from the possibility of being able to publish a new edition, that satisfaction is not likely to be realized."

Sherburne/Killington

At 4,241 feet, Killington Peak is the second highest in the state. From its summit in 1763, the Rev. Samuel Peters, a clergyman from Connecticut, is said to have surveyed the glorious views around him and christened the state "Verdmont," pronouncing it "worthy of the Athenians and ancient Spartans, in token that her mountains and hills shall be ever green and shall never die." Perkins later complained that the "Vermont" variation that was officially adopted meant "Mountain of Maggots." Given to fabrications, Rev.Perkins was nevertheless elected the first Bishop of Vermont at a convention of Episcopal clergymen in Rutland in 1794, although the Archbishop of Canterbury refused to consecrate him.

In June 1946, three thousand-plus acres of forest land in Sherburne were purchased as a state forest for less than $7 per acre, and it was surveyed as a possible ski area. In 1954, Preston Smith, a twenty-three-year-old from Connecticut with snow crystals in his eyes, approached the Forest and Parks Commissioner to see if he could lease Killington for a ski area. The legislature obliged with funds to build an access road and a warming hut in 1957, and Smith opened up his resort in December 1958 with three Poma lifts serving Snowden Peak. Since then, Killington has become the largest ski area in the East, embracing six mountains, the longest ski run and season in the Northeast, and the most extensive snowmaking in the world. In 1988 it boasted 107 trails and slopes, six double chair lifts, four triple chair lifts, five quads, and a three-and-one-half-mile gondola. In that year, its twenty-ninth of consecutive, profitable operations, Smith's S.K.I.,Inc., which also owns Mount Snow, reported revenues of $76 million.

Surrounded by concentrations of several thousand condominia, hotels and lodges, what some call "imperious Killington, the ski state within a state, with an insatiable hunger for Lebensraum" appears to be planning for a self-contained resort community with a population approaching ten thousand.

Mendon

In a lordly gesture, Fletcher Proctor gave Pico Peak to his son, Mortimer, as a twenty-first birthday present in 1910. In 1937, Bradford and Janet Mead leased the area from Lt. Gov. Proctor and the Vermont Marble Company, and opened a ski area with an 1100-foot Fra-Mar rope tow. The resort grew gradually. The Mead's daughter, Andrea, distinguished herself as an Olympic skiier, winning two gold medals in slalom races in the 1952 Olympics. Bradford Mead drowned in a boating accident on Chittenden Pond in the summer of 1942; and Mrs. Mead sold the area to Karl Acker, who had directed its Pico Swiss Ski School.

Rutland

Vermont's second city is described in Chapter One, with other Route 7 communities. "The ride over the range from Woodstock is one of the joys of motoring, and is one of the urgent reasons for seeing Rutland," the Dana brothers reported in their August 1917 issue of *The Elm Tree Monthly*. "It is not a joltless road up the beautiful Ottauquechee Valley to Sherburne; there are rough and sandy spots, and sections of it are deeply rutted at certain seasons by the heavy wheels of freight teams owned by the insatiable lumber and pulpwood people, who are skinning the hills of Bridgewater, Sherburne and Plymouth, and even the slopes of Killington, Vermont's next-to-the-highest mountain peak. There is some compensation, perhaps not much, in the fact that over these jumpy places a devouring motor can't shoot along at thirty miles an hour, which it generally does if the track permits — making a blur of the roadside scenery and densely wooded slopes, whose green trees, and the streams, flowers, and ferns, and pure air, are meant for rational enjoyment.

"The mountain road — the 'Green Mountain Highway,' as the motoring maps now call it, is a good one for a high-built thorofare, and does very well in dry times, while we are waiting for a 'cross-state boulevard [in 1988 we're still waiting]....The road is too narrow in places for a model highway; the wind has a free sweep as it descends the west side of the range, and one wonders how George Bradley ever got through, on a winter's day, with mail and passengers, behind one or two or four horses....

"The Deer's Leap tea house, half hidden in the spruces near the top of the mountain, is not open this season — at least there are no signs of occupancy now, so there is no welcoming place to rest between the Sherburne general store and the Rutland hostelries. At the height of land is Rooney's mill, and here the traveler gets a glimpse of the famous Long Trail, crossing the highway there, which is slowly becoming a real trail. The distance from this point to Killington Peak is five and one-half miles, while Pico is two miles nearer....

"The car zips through Mendon and into the edge of Greater Rutland. Here it must be allowed the road is not interesting, even on a very good road. There are fertile farms and fields and green trees, but as a whole the highway's surroundings are not altogether satisfying. Then comes the City itself.

" One doesn't see all of the Marble City in an hour, and we don't wish to be unfair to the Capital of the Otter Creek Valley. To the transient tourist, however, it appears that Art has not laid a-hold of Rutland with an uplifting and embellishing grasp, and architecturally it is discouraging and behind the times. The motoring entrance to the town from the east perhaps doesn't reveal its better side, and this handicap might be remedied for the sake of silencing the more critical travelers, if they are wanted!....

"The motorist's return trip to Woodstock is in some cases, largely a test of his car's ability to make Mendon 'on high' and some of them can do it. This spurt is short, however, and detracts little from the pleasure of the ride over the range."

Today, Route 4 partially bypasses Rutland; west of the city, Route 4A links West Rutland, Castleton, and Fair Haven, intersecting Routes 30 and 22A, with digressions to Clarendon Springs, Proctor, and Poultney.

Clarendon Springs

Almost literally hidden on a side road off Route 133 south of Rutland Center and tricky to find, this hamlet was once one of the most active summer resorts in the state. Clarendon Springs was a spa, "a resort for valetudarians," two years before it was an organized town. In 1776, Asa Smith, a mystic, divined the location of a miraculous spring in a dream. His vision included not only the site, but the "chalybeate water impregnated with carbonate of lime," W. Storrs Lee wrote in *The Green Mountains of Vermont.* "A victim of 'a scrofulous humor,' Smith was in no condition to go on an exploration tour; nevertheless with tacit faith in the veracity of the dream and in his waning strength, he set out on foot and was not at all surprised after a treacherous day's tramp to come upon the scene exactly as it had been depicted the night before. Smith drank freely of the water, bound his swollen limbs in a compress of clay and algae, and walked away a permanently cured man."

People accepted his story of the miracle as readily as they recognized the curative power of the impregnated water. Smith, more interested in mysticism than money, sold out his discov-

180

ery to George Round, who built a log cabin bath for boarders, and by the time the Revolution was over, he had a thriving business, and he built a hotel that could accommodate more than a hundred guests. Clarendon Springs was launched as one of the country's great spas. Patients suffering from salt rheum, scrofula, and cancer found relief in drinking the water, baths, and mud applications. For seventy-five years, Virginians and Carolinians came in large numbers to compete with each other in the number of glasses of bubbly water they could consume in a day, to rock on the wide verandah, play croquet, and absorb the restorative scenery. "Locally the Springs were credited with having a remarkable effect on human fertility," according to Lee, "when a census revealed that eight families living there had produced a total of one hundred and thirteen children...Further investigation also confirmed that not one of the eight husbands possessed more than one wife and that there was only one pair of twins..."

The ghost of the graceful old brick hotel looms mysteriously over the nearly forsaken village; partial restoration has begun, but it yearns for the kind of multi-million-dollar adaptive preservation that saved the Equinox House in Manchester.

Proctor

Eight miles north of Center Rutland on Route 3, the Vermont Marble Company in Proctor embodies both a political dynasty and one of the state's historic, principal industries.

The first marble quarry in North America did not open here, but in Dorset, where Isaac Underhill exploited the great underground deposits of this age-old stone in 1785. Marble was later found along the whole range of the Taconics bordering Lake Champlain, as far south as Bennington and with isolated deposits as far north as Swanton and Isle LaMotte. The Champlain marbles belong to an older period than the white veins to the south, embodying shades from red, brown, green, to black. Quarrying with primitive methods slowed the use of this great natural resource, but quarries were opened in Pittsford in 1795, and in Rutland in 1807. Extracting blocks of the stone was only half the problem; they had to be cut and transported, a daunting task before the advent of gang saws, channelers, and the coming of the railroads. In 1837, blocks for the U.S. Bank Building in Erie, Pennsylvania, were quarried and laboriously

"Mud season" stranded this car in 1913 on the road between East Proctor and Rutland. —Vermont Historical Society

dragged behind oxen from Dorset to Whitehall. From here they were shipped down the new Champlain Canal and across the Erie Canal. The mills in Middlebury transported their product on barges down the Otter Creek into Lake Champlain, and from there along the St. Lawrence River to the Atlantic Ocean to eastern seaboard cities.

When the railroad progressed up to Rutland and Pittsford in 1849, the industry was revolutionized. Several new quarrying and finishing firms were built up in the Rutland area, notably the Rutland Marble Company, under the absentee ownership of New York City financiers, who skimmed off all the profits. But Redfield Proctor, who invested every cent he could raise in the bankrupt Sutherland Falls Marble Company in 1870, plowed back every dollar he made to expand and strengthen the company. The New Yorkers asked him to take over the Rutland firm; in 1880 he merged the two into the Vermont Marble Company, which became the largest single marble company in the world.

Behind this impressive growth lay the organizing genius of Proctor and his sons. Born in 1831 in Cavendish, where his grandfather, who was a lieutenant at the Battle of Lexington, created Proctorsville, Proctor graduated from Dartmouth College and went West to seek his fortune in Minnesota. Having spent his patrimony, he came back to Vermont, served in the Civil War as an officer in the Vermont regiments, and practiced law in Rutland. Like other industrialists of the era, Proctor sought and achieved political power as well. From local politics he rose to the governorship in 1878. Ten years later, his influence in the Republican Party at the national level was recognized by his appointment as Secretary of War in President Benjamin Harison's administration. Following the death of Senator George F. Edmunds in 1891, Proctor was appointed to his unexpired term and served continuously in the Senate for sixteen years until he died in 1908.

Senator Redfield Proctor was the catalyst for what John Hay called "that bully little war with Spain" in the summer of 1898. Late the previous year, Proctor had enlisted the help of Theodore Roosevelt, assistant secretary of the Navy, to promote Commodore George Dewey to command the Asiatic Squadron over the heads of seven senior officers. President McKinley was not overly eager to declare war, but miscalculated the momentum created when the *U.S.S. Maine* was blown up in Havana harbor and a popular clamor arose to free Cuba from Spain's despotic grip. With American and Cuban refugees crowding the docks of Key West, Senator Proctor returned from a factfinding trip, and on March 17 made a fateful speech that galvanized official and public opion.

"The plain, explicit and unvarnished statement made by Senator Proctor on the floor of the senate last week, of the horrors he witnessed in Cuba," the *Vermont Standard* commented, "will probably accomplish more for the relief of the starving and plague-stricken people than could have been brought about in any other way. For months and months the people of this country have heard almost incredible stories of the destitution and misery resulting from Spanish barbarity; but the majority of people did not know how much was true and how much exaggeration, and they failed to grasp the awful reality of it all. Senator Proctor's testimony is worthy of perfect confidence....It makes the matter real and tangible. It arouses

Redfield Proctor, the marble baron, served as governor and U.S. Senator. —Special Collections, Univeristy of Vermont Library

the people to the necessities of the case and is followed by action throughout the land."

Proctor's powerful plea for armed intervention encouraged the Senate war party, but Maine Congressman Reed, Speaker of the House, aimed a caustic barb at "the marble king" — "a war will make a large market for gravestones." There were grounds for his sarcasm: in 1894, Proctor's company won the contract for supplying marble head and footstones for Civil War battleground cemeteries, whose wooden headboards were rotting. Woodrow Wilson later called Proctor's speech "one of those rare utterances which have really shaped public policy."

War with Spain was declared April 19 and Dewey was cabled to take Manila. He smashed the Spanish fleet with no American casualties. "Every Vermonter is proud of Commodore Dewey, the latest 'favorite son' of the Green Mountain state," the *Standard* rejoiced. "It was characteristically a Yankee contest, fought by Americans, in American vessels, with American guns and equipment, planned with Yankee audacity, begun with Yankee fervor and accomplished by Yankee backbone and Yankee efficiency."

A four-stanza ballad called "A Regular Yankee Trick" circulated widely:

> Well, here! Hurrah for Dewey, fer he sunk the hull concern!
> An' what he didn't perferate he managed fer ter burn!
> All the time the flag was flyin' an' a-floatin' like a star;
> Say, what's the use o' talkin' 'bout a-lickin' us in war?
> When he quit, the other vessels that were lyin' in the bay
> Jes' yelled like howlin' coyotes fer the flag that won the day,
> Durn me, but I'm tickeld, Sal—they didn't git a lick;
> Fer Dewey's a Vermonter, an' he
> Knows a Yankee Trick!

Commodore George Dewey drove the Spanish fleet out of Manila Bay.
—Vermont Historical Society

Paralleling Dewey's stunning victory was the 14,800-nautical mile race of the battleship *Oregon* under the command of Captain Charles Clark from San Francisco to Cuba. A *Rutland Herald* editorial commented wryly: "Commodore Dewey, who is a Vermonter, has with him a commander who is a Vermonter. The commander of the *Oregon* is a Vermonter, and the first man to give the United States senate and through it the country a clear statement of Spanish barbarities is a Vermonter. It is difficult to say just how long the war between Spain and Vermont will continue."

In partnership with leading architects and engineers, the Vermont Marble Company pioneered improved methods of utilizing blocks of marble for load-bearing walls, a form of construction no longer in wide use. But many of the nation's classic buildings, such as the U.S. Supreme Court, and the Jefferson Memorial, were constructed this way. A more contemporary example of the use of Vermont marble is the Beinecke Rare Book and Manuscript Library at Yale University, where Vermont Montclair Danby marble was employed as translucent window wall material in panels eight inches square and one and three-quarters inches thick, cut, finished, and installed to regulate the intensity of exterior light.

Redfield Proctor died in March 1908, and ten thousand admirers attended the funeral. The industrial and political dynasty he founded and bequeathed effectively controlled the state for nearly fifty years. His son Fletcher was governor in 1906-08; Redfield Proctor, Jr., occupied the governor's office in 1923-24; Fletcher's son Mortimer was elected governor for the 1945-47 term; and F. Ray Keyser, also a president of the company, served as chief executive in 1961-63.

The family company's feudal structure was severely shaken when the marble workers struck in 1935. The bitter strike polarized the Rutland area, and drew an unusual degree of national attention, partly because labor strife contrasted starkly with Vermont's pastoral image, and because several prominent leftwing activists made it a cause. The workers, many of them immigrants from Europe, especially Italy, had lived in company houses or tenements, bought their groceries in company stores, and were generally beholden to the paternalism of the Proctors. What began as a "holiday" walk-out in early November during wage negotiations quickly escalated into violent confrontations. On the second day of the work stoppage, a truck driver from Albany attempted to drive a load through the company gates with a helper on the running board carrying a sub-machine gun. He did not open fire, however, even under a shower of rocks thrown by the three hundred men milling outside the gates. Later, the cars of two of the non-union polishers who had stayed on the job were damaged, and one of them injured by broken windshield glass.

The press release on the strike was brief: business was down to one-fourth of normal; Vermont Marble's $80,000 weekly payroll was the largest single factor preventing unemployment and relief in Rutland County; the company's minimum wage rate was already 25 percent higher than its Southern competitors, but if the demands of 37 1/2 cents per hour and a forty-hour work week were granted, the company would have to price marble — a luxury product — out of what small market remained. The company vowed to continue negotiations and permit peaceful picketing.

The sheriff recruited fifteen deputies to protect the non-striking workers, mostly Swedish, as they entered and left the mills; more than five hundred members of the Quarry Workers International soon voted to end the "holiday" and call a strike, but about six hundred workers stayed on. Company management thereupon called up eighty-one special deputies from around the state, paid them five dollars a day, and tried to force workers to house them! The small army of deputies failed to prevent damage. Several ten-ton blocks of marble were sabotaged, ruined by waste oil; some heads and windows were broken, and in the middle of December a section of railroad track was dynamited after members of a striker's family were beaten up by deputies. Incredibly, the deputies, who were costing the company $2,800 a week, were transferred to the state payroll. Governor Charles M. Smith defended this decision as preferable to calling out the National Guard.

Students at Dartmouth and other New England colleges began collecting food and clothing for the strikers. Sinclair Lewis arrived from New York to find out what was going on, told the press he had "soured" on the strike, but soon joined Archibald MacLeish and other writers at a rally in New York City. One speaker described workers who were dying of silicosis for less than $12 a week, before the company started making deductions for rent, light, coal, wood, water, insurance and groceries: "I saw one weekly pay slip for two cents."

The Department of Labor despatched the Commissioner of Conciliation and waved the Wagner Act in the face of besieged management. In January, four strikers were arrested for blowing up a railroad bridge and a power line transformer. The company retaliated with eviction notices to the strikers living in company houses, and ordered white-collar employees on town relief boards to withhold help. Eventually, the violence abated; the strike was submitted to arbitration; and in the spring of 1936, the strike ended.

The Vermont Marble Company was bought by a Swiss conglomerate in 1976. Its visitors' center exhibit in Proctor, open between May and October, is a popular attraction. Among its features are a geological display, and a sculpture gallery.

Wilson's Castle, off Route 3 between West Rutland and Proctor, is a thirty-two room chateau built by a Proctor physician and his rich English wife in 1874. More than a million dollars were spent, and European craftsmen and materials imported to construct what reminds one of a central Europen "folly" worthy of a bush-league Bavarian King Ludwig. Crammed with elaborate, florid European and Oriental furnishings, stained glass and an incredible array of wood paneling, it is a memorable monument to extravagent bad taste. No wonder the builder's wife wouldn't live there, and decamped with what remained of her fortune. The town eventually seized the place for taxes; it's open to the public in the summer.

Castleton

An architectural showcase on Route 4A, Castleton was granted its charter in 1761, but settlement did not really begin until 1770, when three families arrived from Salisbury, Connecticut. The first dwelling was built in 1769, and Fort Warren in 1779. In those early years, Puritanism reigned: a pastor named Matthias was dismissed by his irate parishioners because he "holds that no infants are guilty of actual transgression before they are born into the world." By 1775 there were thirty families when Ethan Allen blew into town in May leading a large pack of Green Mountain Boys. Refreshing themselves at Remington's Tavern, Ethan plotted the capture of Fort Ticonderoga, Skenesborough (now Whitehall) and Crown Point.

The news of the fighting at Lexington and Concord had triggered Allen's determination to strike a blow for the colonies. Why the Grants should have undertaken the first concerted military action against the Crown, which had been more of an ally than enemy, is puzzling; Ethan probably realized that he could no longer rely on the British to protect his own real estate in the territory, and his friends and followers went along. Fort Ticonderoga was thought to be undermanned and in poor condition; the desire to obtain its cannon for use against the British in Boston led men from Massachusetts and Connecticut to consider their own assault on the fortress. As the attackers gathered in Castleton on May 8, Captain Benedict Arnold, captain of the Connecticut Foot Guards, rode into town

The Ransom-Rehlin House in Castleton was built in 1846 from plans smuggled out of England. —Vermont Historical Society

with a commission from the Massachusetts Committee of Safety to lead the expedition against Ticonderoga.

Ethan and his force rejected Arnold's credentials, but granted permission for the temperamental captain to march alongside him at the head of the rag-tag force. With a great deal of luck, eighty-three men rowed across the narrow channel of the lake in the early hours of May 10, sneaked through a hole in the fort walls, and overcame two sentries on the parade ground.

The ensuing face-off between Allen and the British officers in charge have been described many times in many places. Richard G. Carlson, who has taught history at the University of Vermont and Yale, portrayed it this way: "Climbing the stairs to the officers' quarters, Ethan confronted a trouserless officer whom he took to be Captain William Delaplace, commander of the fort. Actually, it was Jocelyn Feltham, a lieutenant. In a tableau familiar to generations, Ethan demanded the surrender of the fort. Some witnesses lated recalled that he cried, 'Come out of there, you dmaned old rat,' or 'Come out of there you sons of British whores, or I'll smoke you out.' Ethan recalled the scene differently. When asked by the surprised officer by whose authority he demanded Ticonderoga's surrender, Ethan replied, 'In the name of the great Jehovah, and the Continental Congress.' " One sidelight of the successful raid was the fabled feat of Vermont's own Paul Revere, the blacksmith Samuel Beach, who is said to have run some sixty miles in twenty-four hours from Castleton to recruit more men for the attack on Ticonderoga.

Ethan's victory drove him to folly. He had confidently expected to be placed in command of the growing army, but at a meeting in Dorset to elect officers for the Green Mountain regiment-to-be, his exploits were completely ignored. Twenty-three officers were elected, including his brothers Hemen and Ira, with Seth Warner as commander. For Ethan there was not even a lieutenancy. More stunned than angry, his ego bruised, Ethan decided on a reckless plan to invade Canada, occupy St. John's, and try to take Montreal. As the poorly organized expeditionary force straggled to the lower narrows of Lake Champlain, the war in the region started by Ethan at Ticonderoga four months earlier claimed its first victim. On a scouting forray not far from St. John's, his cousin and close friend, Remember Baker, was beheaded by Caughnawaga Indians.

Proud of their trophy, the Indians paraded Baker's head through St. John's on a pole until British officers bribed them to part with it.

Ethan thereupon exceeded his orders, and with a modest force of just over a hundred men set out to attack Montreal, whose population of nine thousand made it one of the largest cities on the continent. It was thinly defended, however, and there was panic in the streets when word spread of Ethan's approach. Instead of attacking at once, Ethan waited for reinforcements, giving Governor Carleton time to rally volunteers to support the regulars — over three hundred British, Canadians, and Indians poured out of the city. "When I saw the number of the enemy as they sallied out of the town," Ethan later wrote, "I perceived it would be a day of trouble, if not rebuke....I thought to have enrolled my name in the list of illustrious American heroes, but was nipped in the bud."

Ethan's men put up a stiff, two-hour fight, but were forced to surrender. General Richard Prescott, commander of the British garrison, told Ethan he would be sent to England to be hanged for treason: "You shall grace a halter at Tyburn, God damn you." Ethan was shipped to England in chains and jailed for nearly three years before being brought back to New York and exchanged for a British officer. In 1779, he published a book with the record-setting title: *A Narrative of Colonel Ethan Allen's Captivity, from the time of his being taken by the British, near Montreal on the 25th Day of September, in the year 1775, to the time of his exchange on the 6th Day of May 1778; Containing his Voyages and Travels, with the most remarkable Occurences respecting himself and many other Continental Prisoners of different Ranks and Characters which fell under his Observation, in the Course of the same; particularly the Destruction of the Prisoners at New York, by General Sir William Howe, in the Years 1776 and 1777. Interspersed with some Political Observations, written by himself and now published for the Information of the Curious in all Nations.*

The only Revolutionary War engagement actually fought in Vermont occured in nearby Hubbardton on July 7, 1777. Westsiders were frightened because more than eight thousand British regulars, Hessians, Indians and Tories, led by General Burgoyne, were advancing down the Champlain valley to join General Howe. General St.Clair abandoned the American position at Fort Ticonderoga and retreated toward Rutland. Bringing up the rear were Seth Warner's Green Mountain Boys. While St.Clair encamped in Castleton, Seth Warner and about a thousand men held their ground on a knoll in Hubbardton, where they were attacked at dawn by British troops. Warner held firm until Baron Riedesel's Hessians came to General Fraser's aid. Then the American lines broke, Warner shouting "Scatter and meet me in Manchester." The battle, called as bloody as Waterloo in proportion to the troops involved, nevertheless prevented the British from attacking St.Clair's main force, which fought again at Bennington and Saratoga. A monument marks the site of the battle, and a small museum displays a relief map detailing the action.

After the Revolution, Castleton grew rapidly, and by 1850 there were more than three thousand inhabitants. The village's "Pillar Town" nickname arose from the distinguished architectural record left by the gifted Thomas Royal Dake, a builder who arrived in town around 1807. The first house he built was his own, on South Street, in 1809. A fine spiral staircase believed to have been made by Dake may be seen in the Ransom-Rehlen house, a Greek Revival mansion with seventeen Ionic columns, built in 1846 from plans smuggled out of England. Dake's masterpiece, the Federated Church, was designed in similar style will a colonnade of six Doric columns, and an austere interior except for the beautiful pulpit, which Dake completed by hand when the budget was exhausted.

Underlying the town's nineteenth century prosperity was the slate industry. Slate was first quarried just north of Fair Haven in 1839. Water rights on nearby Lake Bomoseen became vital to the growth of Castleton, Hydeville, and other towns in the area because some of the best slate was hauled from Cedar Mountain on the lake by barge. Between 1850 and 1870, the West Castleton Railroad and Slate Company was the largest producer of marbleized slate in the country. During these years, many Welsh settled in the vicinity. This principal industry along Vermont's western border suffered a severe setback in 1907 when a strike halted production for several months, causing customers to turn to suppliers in Pennsylvania.

A notable son of Castleton was Edwin L. Drake (1819-1880), called the "founder of the oil industry" because he drilled the first modern oil well in the world on August 27, 1859, at

The Langdon-Smart House is another prize of Castleton's architectural showcase. —Vermont Historical Society

Titusville, Pennsylvania. Drake, unfortunately, died impoverished.

Castleton College is the linear descendant of the Rutland County Grammar School, chartered in 1787, and of Vermont's first medical school (1818). The institution was formerly known as the Castleton Normal School and Castleton State Teachers College. It is now part of the state college system.

The town has been immortalized in a children's book classic, *The Blue Cat of Castle Town* by Catherine Cate Coblentz, still in print nearly forty years after it was written. Castleton is the home of the New England humorist, Keith W. Jennison, whose droll photo and text books —like *Vermont is Where You Find It, Green Mountains and Rock Ribs, "Yup...Nope" & Other Vermont Dialogues* — have delighted visitors since 1941.

The site of the Battle of Hubbardton is not far from the small island where the Battle of the Wits was fought. Neshobe, in the middle of Lake Bomoseen, was in the 1930s the summer retreat of the celebrated Alexander Woollcott, the caustic drama critic and radio star, whose wicked wit sparked the Algonquin Round Table of New York's glitterati in the late 1920s. The original, basic housekeeping arrangements on the island were tended by a Man Friday known as "Bathless Bill" and a cook with whom he lived in sin and contentiousness. Some of the luminaries who formed the Neshobe Island Club preferred these primitive conditions, but another, larger faction sought a more luxurious setting. What developed was "the Revolt of the Classes against the Masses," led by Woollcott, who demanded — and won— running water, electric lights, and a refrigerator. Dues were raised, Bathless and his consort were pensioned, and Woollcott gradually took over the establishment as his private playpen. Aleck's guests called him *der Fuhrer*, and he was cast for that part in an elaborate home movie written by Howard Dietz and Charles Lederer, with photography by Tanis Dietz, and played by Alice Duer Miller, Neysa McMein, Beatrice Kaufman, Harold Guinzburg, and Harpo Marx. The climax came with the burning at the stake of Fuhrer Woollcott after he had kicked his croquet partner for failure to go through a wicket. Dorothy Parker, Noel Coward, Ethel Barrymore, Cornelia Otis Skinner, S.N.Behrman, Moss Hart, Thornton Wilder were also frequent guests. To its Lake Bomoseen natives, Neshobe was a mixture of Valhalla and a madhouse. The islanders frequently figured in the press, which was good for local trade.

Samuel Hopkins Adams, in his 1945 biography of Woollcott, relates the story of a party of picnickers, who innocently landed at the far end of the island, supposing it uninhabited. "They came back to the mainland with a dire tale of having heard voices in murderous altercation (the usual croquet game) and being pursued by a naked man, painted blue, who chased them to their boat with hideous roars. (Harpo, returning from a swim, had spied the intruders, endowed himself with some effective stripes from a blue crayon, and put on a one-man show.)

Bomoseen is the site of another kind of battle — the grim invasion of Eurasian milfoil, a weed that threatens to clog this and other lakes permanently.

Poultney

Six miles south of Castleton on Route 30 is the town of Poultney, where two eminent nineteenth-century newspaper editors and publishers learned their vocations: Horace Greeley, founder of the New York *Tribune*, boarded at the venerable Eagle Tavern while he was learning to set type for the East Poultney *National Spectator* in the 1820s; working with him was George Jones, who was Henry Raymond's partner and successor as proprietor of *The New York Times*.

Poultney was settled in 1771 by Thomas Ashley and Ebenezer Allen, who later moved to Grand Isle. Green Mountain College, at the western end of Main Street, began life in 1836 as the Troy Conference Academy of the Methodist Episcopal Church, became the Ripley Female College for a spell, and assumed its present name in 1931 as a junior college for women. It is now a four-year institution.

The Eagle Tavern in East Poultney, a stagecoach stop built in 1790, was the scene of much post-Revolutionary revelry. On one such occasion, a Captain William Watson raised his glass in a classic toast: "The enemies of our country! May they have cobweb breeches, a porcupine saddle, a hard-trotting horse, and an eternal journey." Once again open to travelers, The Eagle is surrounded by an unusually pristine cluster of beautiful colonial structures.

"Go West" Greeley was the son of indigent New Hampshire farmers who moved to Vermont and then to western New York. His first editorial assistant on the *Tribune* was Henry Jarvis Raymond, a black-bearded graduate of the University of Vermont, "no bigger than a snuff-box." Raymond worked for Greeley three years, and launched the *New York Daily Times* in 1851. Greeley's spirited competition with his New York rival, James Gordon Bennett, the misanthropic Scot who published the *New York Herald*, is legendary in the history of American journalism. Greeley's outspoken thirty-year editorship of the New York *Tribune* landed him the nomination for the presidency in 1872 as the candidate of the third-party Liberal Republicans who had turned against the "corrupt and debauched" adminstration of General Ulysses S. Grant. Endorsed by the Democrats as well, Greeley made a strong speaking campaign, "but the regular Republicans had the

Horace Greeley began his newspaper career as a printer's devil in Poultney.—Special Collections, University of Vermont Library

money and the organization," according to Samuel Eliot Morison, "and the average citizen, having to choose between an old soldier whose very name stood for patriotism, and a journalist who had been as often wrong as right, voted for Grant." The President carried all but six states with a popular vote of 3.6 million as against 2.8 million for his opponent. Greeley, exhausted, broken-hearted, and at the age of sixty-one turned out of his editorial chair by the *Tribune*'s owner, Whitelaw Reid, went out of his mind and died before the end of November.

Fair Haven

"Fair Haven joins on Skeenesborough [Whitehall, New York], and is the most flourishing manufacturing town in the State," John A. Graham wrote to his British patron in 1797. "It owes its consequence to its founder, Colonel Lyon, whose enterprise and perseverance in promotion and carrying on manufactories has been of infinite utility to the Public, to the gratitude of which he has the strongest claims. He has erected a furnace for casting all kinds of hollow iron ware, and two forges; a flitting mill for the making of nail rods, a paper mill, a printing press, and corn and saw-mills. It is a curious fact that Colonel Lyon has executed a good deal of printing at his Office, on paper manufactured by himself of the bark of the basswood tree, and which is found to answer every purpose for common printing. He has held some of the first offices of the State, and no man in it can be more qualified to do so, as his knowledge of the finances and situation of the country is scarcely to be equalled; nor does his integrity ever suffer him to lose sight of the real good of the people...

"Benson and Orwell adjoin on Lake Champlain...these towns on the lake abound with iron ore, and they have a number of iron founderies and forges among them. The great road from Fair Haven to the Northern part of the State, and to Canada, leads through the above places; and in winter, the travelling in sledges, drawn by horses, is both convenient and expeditious."

Graham's laudatory sketch of Matthew Lyon coincided with the versatile, fire-eating, red-headed colonel's election to Congress. Arriving in the colonies as an indentured Irish lad, Lyon landed in New Haven, Connecticut, in 1755 and was sold for a pair of oxen to pay the captain for his passage. (Lyon's favorite oath thereafter was, "By the bulls that bought me.") Moving to Litchfield, he attached himself to the Allen brothers, and at twenty-one moved north to the Grants with Thomas Chittenden just in time to join the Green Mountain Boys in 1770. Lyon took part in the capture of Ticonderoga; most of the conventions leading to independence and statehood; married Governor Chittenden's daughter, Buelah, after the death of his first wife, an Allen cousin; and founded Fair Haven, where the Allens owned property.

In Congress, Lyon— a Jeffersonian— got his first taste of national notoriety by getting into a floor brawl with Roger Griswold of Connecticut, an ardent Federalist. When Griswold accused him of an act of cowardice during the war, Lyon spit in his face. Colleagues separated the two. Later, Griswold hit Lyon over the head several times with his cane; Lyon roared in with fireplace tongs, but Griswold emerged on top. Federalists in Congress, according to William Doyle's *Vermont Political Tradition*, referred to Lyon as a "nasty, brutish, spitting animal." One Massachusetts Representative demanded that "this kennel of filth" be expelled, but the House failed to achieve the necessary two-thirds vote.

Samuel Williams, editor of the *Rutland Herald*, was Lyon's Federalist opponent for election in 1798. The *Herald* constantly referred to Lyon as a "Vermont beast," and when it refused to print any of Lyon's rebuttals, Lyon started publishing his own newspaper, *The Scourge of the Aristocracy*. The first editorial expressed its position graphically: "When every aristocratic hireling from the English Porcupine [a Federalist editor]...down to the dirty hedgehogs and groveling animals of his race...are vomiting forth columns of lies, malignant abuse and deception, the *Scourge* will be devoted to politics."

Two days later, a grand jury in Rutland indicted him as "a dangerous domestic enemy of the government" under the new Alien and Sedition Act, passed when the Adams administra-

Matthew Lyon won re-election to Congress while jailed under the Alien and Sedition Law. —Special Collections, University of Vermont Library

tion believed it would have to go to war with France. Unable to obtain legal counsel, Lyon conducted his own defense, and was found guilty of stirring up sedition and bringing "the President and Government of the United States into contempt." A fine of $1,000 and a four-month prison term were imposed. The Federalist press rejoiced. The Hartford *Courant* declared that "the beast was now caged and on exhibit in Vergennes [where he was jailed]...the same creature that had been seen in Philadelphia cavorting like a monkey...where he was taken for an Ass for his braying, for a Cur by his barking, and for a Lyon, by nothing but being the greatest of beasts."

In Vergennes, where the General Assembly was meeting, Lyon was paraded through town and thrown into a cell that had a glassless window, no heat, and "a stench about equal to the Philadelphia docks in the month of August." Some of his followers proposed to free him, but Lyon wrote that he preferred to "suffer any kind of death here, rather than to be taken out by violence." Lyon remained a candidate for one of the two seats in the House of Representatives. [Between 1813 and 1821, Vermont had six Congressional districts; they gradually shrank back to two from 1883 to 1933, and stayed at one seat since.] While in jail, Lyon won a runoff election. Jeffersonians rallied to his cause, and collected the gold to pay his fine. When he was released from jail in February 1799, he was greeted by a throng of supporters and driven to Middlebury in a sled drawn by four horses in a procession twelve miles long.

Federalists in Congress did not cheer his return, branding him a "notorious and seditious person, and of a depraved mind, and wicked and diabolic disposition." Another attempt to expel him failed. In 1800 he was in the limelight again. Neither Jefferson, Burr, nor Adams won a majority of presidential electors, and the election was thrown into the House. On the thirty-sixth ballot, Lyon cast the decisive vote for Jefferson.

Although his arrest and conviction galvanized opposition to the Alien and Sedition Act and helped cost Adams the election, Lyon pulled up his Vermont stakes and moved to Kentucky in 1801. He was again elected to Congress, and started voting with his former arch-enemies, the Federalists. At one point he said of Jefferson, "I made him and can unmake him." He moved again, to Arkansas, and was once more elected to Congress, but died, in 1822, before he could serve.

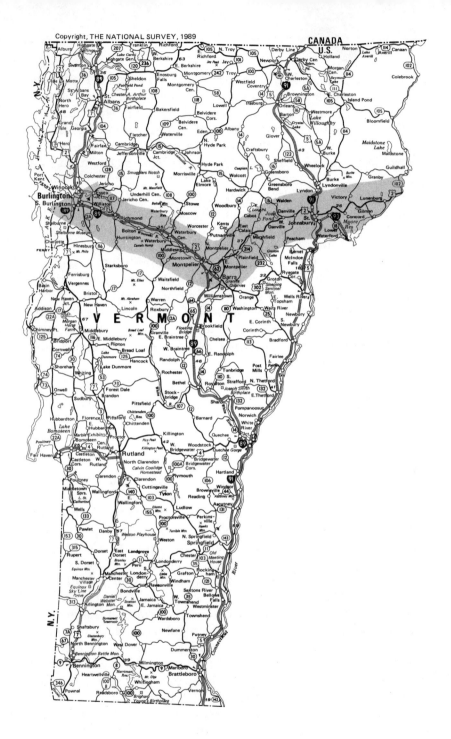

Route 2: The Beltway

200

Chapter Five

Route 2 — The Beltway

*"The element of disunion which, in a portion of the
United States, for many years vented itself in threats and
menaces has culminated in open rebellion, and an unnatural
and causeless civil war has been precipitated against the
General Government. . . . All partisan differences are ignored
and lost in the higher principle of patriotism. In this
patriotic enthusiasm, Vermont eminently participates. Her
citizens, always loyal to the Union, will in this hour of peril,
nobly rally for the protection of the Government and the
Constitution."*

— Gov. Erastus Fairbanks,
April 23, 1861

Extending eastward from the pastoral Champlain islands, crossing Chittenden, Washington and Caledonia counties, Route 2 connects Burlington, the state's only modern metropolis, and St. Johnsbury, a principal nineteenth-century center of industrial power. The financial and educational capital in Burlington is also linked today with the Capitol in Montpelier by Interstate 89, permitting a convenient forty-minute commute for Vermont's economic and political elite.

For most of its distance, the road follows the Winooski River Valley, which bore the deadliest brunt of a natural disaster in November 1927 that still scars the consciousness of the state's older residents. Double the normal rainfall was recorded that October; on November 1, two rainstorms locked over Vermont's saturated ground, and by nightfall the next day the main streets of almost every town in the state were impassable. Telephone circuits and electricity failed; roads, bridges, and railroad tracks were washed out. Mills, houses, stores, barns and livestock swirled away in the darkness. In Barre, Lieutenant Governor Hollister Jackson stepped out of his car to his death in the swift black water of Potash Brook.

By morning, Friday, November 5, most of the nearly ten inches of rain in thirty-nine hours had fallen. Tales of individual heroism circulated, but the flood had drowned fifty-five people in the Winnoski corridor alone and caused damage estimated at $30 million, statewide. The Central Vermont Railroad lost 253 miles of track and fifty-four bridges, but was back in operation within three months.

Governor John E. Weeks found it hard to admit that he would have to ask for help outside the state's borders. As soon as a telephone trunk line could be used, he called his friend in the White House, where Calvin Coolidge was wondering what had happened to his native state. Weeks asked Coolidge if he would send up "your man Hoover." After touring the devastation, Secretary of Commerce Herbert Hoover reported, "I have seen Vermont at its worst — but I have also seen Vermonters at their best."

Hoover was right. Speaking at the Burlington Chamber of Commerce, Weeks was optimistic: "Calamities, like the Vermont flood, are invariably followed by a period of renewed energy on the part of the people affected. Vermont is facing a new era of progress and development. I have absolute confidence in the ability of the people of Vermont to overcome every obstacle in the pathway of progress and to measure up to the highest standard." Outside aid came from unexpected sources: the banking house of J.P. Morgan, for example, which marketed $5 million of the state's flood bonds, refused to accept a commission. The *Boston Transcript* pointed out that proportionately the state's $100 per capita loss would add up to $400,000,000 in Massachusetts. Vermont's reconstruction was praised by the nation's press. "It is a tribute to the pluck of the little Green Mountain state that it managed to carry on somehow and eventually get back on its feet," *The New York Times* observed. "Miracles of energy," declared the *Providence Journal*. "What Vermont has done is remarkable," said The *Philadelphia Bulletin*. "In a few months it has accomplished reconstruction which experts thought would take more than a year. It has raised money, and done the work. Its example of self-reliance is inspiring. The resolute sturdiness of the old New England hills is still a part of its people. The rest of the country is proud of Vermont."

And L.C. Rogers, an Underhill native, composed an ode that began:

> Vermont is ready f'r bus-ness,
> Yes sir — Yes siree!
> An' tain't no time f'r dizz-ness,
> No sir — No, siree.
> Fer th' Gov'ner haz said so,
> An' I guess he'd orter know,
> An' all he sez is spread so,
> Fr'm here t'—Mexerco
> By all th' leadin' papers,
> We jes got t' help 'im go.

And ended:

> But t'day th' trains er goin'
> And the roads er opened up,
> An' nor-mal-see's a-showin'
> In th' bitter uv th' cup,
> Whar th' milk o' human kindness
> An' th' sugar uv its deeds,

Hez neu-trol-ized th' bitter
To a tonic thet she needs—
An' ol' Vermont's a-sprucin' up,
Fr'm Senerter t' yaller pup.

By 1935, more than two thousand Civilian Conservation Corps were working on flood control projects, including the largest earth-filled dam east of the Mississippi on the Waterbury River, a project inspected by President Franklin D. Roosevelt when he visited the state in July 1936. At the immense dam's dedication in 1939, Governor George D. Aiken, at odds with Washington's flood control policies, was given huge key signifying the transfer of the dam to the state. "From the size of this key," Aiken said, "I would say that it would open the Panama Canal."

The sixteen-sided Old Round Church in Richmond was built as a community center in 1812-13.
—Vermont Travel Division

In the flood's aftermath, governance gradually began to shift from nearly complete local autonomy to a more centralized concept and form. In 1931 the legislature adopted the first income tax, and established a state highway system, since many of the washed out railroad spurs and inter-urban trolley lines were never replaced.

Richmond

This village at the intersection of Routes 2, 124, and I-89, is chiefly known for the Old Round Church. Completed in 1813, this unique sixteen-sided meeting house was built cooperatively by five sects — Congregationalists, Universalists, Baptists, Christians, and Methodists. All these denominations held services here for many years, but they gradually separated into their own places of worship, and the structure reverted to the town. Henry Ford once offered to buy it for removal to Dearborn, but Richmond residents refused to part with it.

George F. Edmunds, the man who might have been President, was born here in 1828, destined to become one of the nineteenth century's finest leaders of the United States Senate. "In intellect no New England senator except Daniel Webster ever surpassed him," the *New York Times* declared on the centenary of his birth. Compelled by poor health to abandon his college career, Edmunds read law and was admitted to practice in Burlington, where he married Susan Lyman, a niece of George Perkins Marsh, the ecologist, Congressman and diplomat. From 1855 to 1862 he served in the legislature, as Speaker of the House and President Pro Tem of the Senate. Following the death of U.S.Senator Solomon Foot, Governor Paul Dillingham appointed Edmunds to fill the vacancy. He quickly established himself as a learned and effective member, and from 1872 until his retirement in 1891 he was chairman of the Judiciary Committee except for two years when the Democrats were in control.

With Ohio's Democratic Senator Thurman, his close friend, Edmunds framed the bill requiring transcontinental railroads to repay the government bonds lent for construction, and later wrote the basic provisions of the Sherman Anti-Trust bill. In the wake of the contested election of 1876, Edmunds drafted

the Electoral Count bill, and served on the commission that certified the election of Rutherford B. Hayes.

President Grant offered him the post of Minister to Great Britain, and both Presidents Hayes and Arthur wanted to appoint him to the United States Supreme Court, but he declined.

The principal candidates for the Republican presidential nominee in 1880 were ex-President Grant and James G. Blaine. The leaders of the Vermont delegation to the convention, Frederick Billings of Woodstock, and former governors Smith and Stewart, nominated Edmunds. "Gentlemen," Billings thundered, at the height of his renowned oratorical flair, "we bring you this breeze from the Green Mountains. How quickly it will swell into a gale and how surely it will sweep the land."

Edmunds name remained on thirty-five ballots. On the thirty-sixth and final roll call, his name disappeared, and the Vermont delegation joined other states in selecting James A. Garfield. The Grant delegates had planned to shift to Edmunds as a last resort, and he would have won on the thirty-fifth ballot, but they waited too long. Vermont-born Chester A. Arthur was nominated as vice president.

The Vermont delegation tried again at the 1884 convention. This time, most of the Massachusetts delegates were also for Edmunds, and owing to a deadlock in the New York delegation between the followers of Arthur and Blaine, the friends of the president threw their support to Edmunds. They included the young Theodore Roosevelt. *Harper's Weekly* commented: "Mr. Edmunds' strength is undeniable. He unites eminent public ability and service with the greatest availability — a very unusual combination in a Presidential candidate." Governor Long of Massachusetts made the late-night nominating speech: Edmunds' name "will carry over all the land a grateful feeling of serenity and security, like the benignant promise of a perfect day in June. It will be as wholesome and refreshing as the Green Mountains of the native state of him who bears it.

> Their summits tower not higher than his worth; their foundations are not firmer than his convictions and truth; the green and prolific slopes that grow great harvests at their feet are not richer than the fruitage of his long and lofty labors in the service of his country...

Only four ballots were needed to nominate Blaine, who was defeated in the election by the Democrats' Governor Grover Cleveland of New York. Edmunds' Vermont supporters were sure that he would have drawn more independent votes than Blaine.

When Edmunds resigned his seat and retired in the spring of 1891, *Harper's Weekly* said: "the retirement of a Senator of such integrity, grasp, experience, and simplicity of taste and character impoverishes public life." Because of his bronchial problems, Edmunds moved to Philadelphia and then Pasadena, California, to escape Vermont winters. For several years, he represented clients before the United States Supreme Court, winning in one case a verdict that declared unconstitutional the income tax act of 1894. He died in 1899.

Five miles, more or less, north of Richmond off Route 117 is Jericho Center and the Old Red Mill, a National Historic site, where a new rolling process for flour was introduced in 1885. The village of Jericho was the home of Wilson A. "Snowflake" Bentley, the first person in the world to photograph individual snow crystals through a microscope, and who also discovered a way to measure raindrops. By nature musical and artistic, he grew up something of a loner on a remote farm. Bentley was obsessed by the unique characteristics of the snowflakes that fell in such profusion, and won his nackname by the time he was twenty. When he died in 1931, he had pursued his unusual talent for forty-five years, amassing a collection of more than five thousand glass plates, some of which were sold to Tiffany for jewelery designs.

Montpelier

In 1805, the legislature anointed Montpelier as the capital, after meeting forty-six times for twenty-eight years in fourteen different towns. Randolph, in the geographical center of the state, had vigorously sought the honor, even building an extra-wide avenue and designating a proper executive mansion — a

Vermont's first state house evoked Shakespeare's Old Globe Theatre.

The state's second, granite Capitol was designed by Ammi Young and built in 1836. —Vermont Historical Society

perq no Vermont governor has enjoyed. Montpelier had to agree to two conditions: to donate the land for the capitol building, and see to it that the State House was built by September 1808. Thomas Davis, son of the town's first permanent settler, Col. Jacob Davis, donated the land. The first State House, a three-story, ten-sided wooden structure that bore a close resemblance to Shakespeare's Globe Theater, was then built on a site adjacent to the present capitol at a cost of $9,000.

It was replaced in 1838 by a Greek Revival granite building designed by Ammi B. Young, a Burlington architect, inspired by the temple of Theseus, at a cost of $132,000. The granite was drawn ten miles by horse and ox-cart from the quarries in Barre.On a subzero night in January 1857, the box stove that heated Representatives' Hall exploded, and the resulting conflagration burned up everything but the shell. The Doric portico was incorporated in the third and present State House, designed by Thomas Silloway — Young's thirty-year-old apprentice — and dedicated in 1859.

The fire revived a hot-tempered argument over where the capital should be, with Burlington in the vanguard of contenders. In a special session of the legislature convened by Governor Ryland Fletcher, Montpelier prevailed, again; the assemblymen appropriated $40,000 to rebuild the State House, and Montpelier was to match that sum. Stanford White called the new capitol the finest example of Greek Revival he had ever seen.

The dome, made of wood, sheathed in copper, and gilded with 23.75 carat gold leaf, is surmounted by a statue of Ceres, goddess of agriculture, carved originally by Larkin G. Mead of Brattleboro. In 1938, workmen found the wooden figure to be permeated with dry rot; Dwight Dwinell, the octogenarian Sergeant-At-Arms, carved the pine replica. Charles Morrissey, one-time editor of *Vermont Life* and director of the Vermont Historical Society, has written that, back in the 1930s, "Ceres

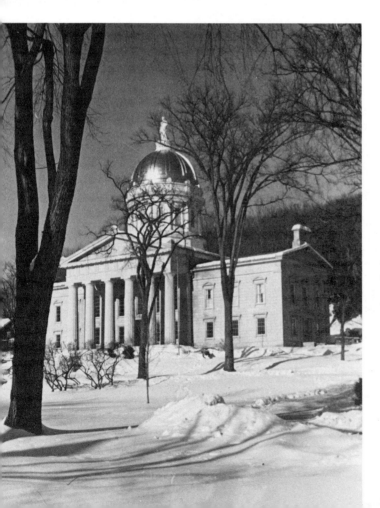

The present State House with its gilded dome has lasted since 1857.
—Vermont Historical Society

was said to be Dorothy Thompson, the newspaper columnist who lived with her (then) husband, Sinclair Lewis, in Barnard, on her way to deliver a copy of the *New York Herald Tribune* to the Republican loyalists down below." Ceres is also the goddess of brewing, Morrissey added, "and some think that is appropriate for Vermont because in its early days, and recent days also, Vermonters have kept themselves warm and have jollified occasions by drinking prodigious amounts of intoxicants."

Mead also carved an Italian marble statue of Ethan Allen in 1861, but it deteriorated and was replaced in 1939 by Aristide Piccini's of Rutland from Danby marble. Opposite the Allen statue on the portico is a cannon captured from the German Hessians at the Battle of Bennington. On the lawn are two Spanish naval cannons retrieved from a cruiser sunk by Commodore Dewey in Manila Bay in 1898— trophies of the "Vermont-Spanish War."

There are two portraits of Admiral Dewey in the State House; one of Vermont's icons, he was born in 1837 in a house that once stood across the street when his father was a founder of the National Life Insurance Company, whose home office remains in Montpelier. Dewey's stature as a national hero was somewhat eroded in later years: he was, like General Douglas MacArthur, a poseur who enjoyed the limelight. In 1910, urged again to run for President, Dewey told the press, "If the American people want me for this high office, I shall be only too willing to serve them....Since studying this subject I am convinced that the office of the President is not such a very difficult one to fill." Before his death in 1917, he said that longevity was the result of "buttermilk, lots of fresh air and a simple life."

Inside, the State House exudes the solidity of marble and mahogany and simplified Victorian grandeur. Vermont's one hundred and fifty Representatives sit in an ample D-shaped chamber under a huge bronze chandelier. The thirty-seat Senate Chamber has a domed ceiling in the shape of an ellipse with twenty lobes joining in the center.

The Governor's Reception Room is dominated by Julian Scott's massive 20'x10' painting of the 1864 Battle of Cedar Creek, Virginia, where more Vermont units came under fire than in any other engagement of the Civil War. Scott had enlisted in the Vermont Brigade from his home in Johnson at the age of fifteen. Being undersized as well as underage, he

An unknown Civil War volunteer reflects on the battlefield carnage he survived. —Vermont Historical Society

joined as a drummer boy, later becoming the first Vermonter to receive the Congressional Medal of Honor. Scott was commissioned by the legislature to do the painting, which he worked on almost constantly from 1871 to 1875, recreating the battle as he remembered it, and including faces from life-sketches. (Many Vermonters gaze at the painting and exclaim, "Why, there's my great-grandfather!")

For a fundamentally pastoral society, Vermonters have tended, over the generations, to be remarkably belligerent. It was the first state to respond to Lincoln's call for troops in 1861, and pledged $1,000,000 to the defense of the Union. Vermont lost more of its sons to the cause, proportionately, than any other Northern state. During the course of the war, sixteen Vermont regiments and nearly 35,000 volunteers were involved. The Second Vermont suffered particularly severe casualties, losing forty percent of its men killed and wounded—eight times that of the Union Army as a whole. In a single afternoon at the Battle of the Wilderness, the Vermont regiments sustained more than a thousand casualties. As the Union forces marched to Gettysburg, General Sedgewick issued a famous command: "Put the Vermonters up front and keep the column well closed up."

From Groton came Private William Scott, the lad President Lincoln saved from the firing squad in one of his controversial acts of compassion. Scott, twenty-two, was the eldest of Thomas Scott's five sons who volunteered for duty. Scott was assigned to Company K, Third Regiment of Vermont Volunteers commanded by Brigadier General "Baldy" Smith. On August 31, 1861, two months after he enlisted, Scott was found asleep at his sentry post near the Chain Bridge outside Washington, D.C. He had been on duty several nights and was taking the place of a comrade who was sick. Nevertheless, he was promptly court-martialed and sentenced to death by firing squad. A petition for presidential clemency was signed by 191 officers and men, including General Smith, and a delegation met with E.L. Chittenden, a Vermonter, who served on Lincoln's staff. The President ordered General George McClellan to pardon Scott, but when he received no confimration that his stay of execution had arrived, Lincoln went to the army post on September 9 to deliver the order in person. McClellan had secretly rescinded the death sentence, as Lee Goodman wrote in *Vermont Saints & Sinners*, "but only after he had ordered a full-dress brigade muster to impress upon the troops the imperative for obedience to orders and the price to be paid for violating them. The regiments were assembled on the parade ground, 'to form a hollow square' presumably to witness Private Scott's execution. The firing squad faced the prisoner. The death sentence was read. The drummers beat the traditional tatoo. Then instead of the order to fire, the president's pardon was read. It ended with the declaration that Pvt. William Scott was 'to be released from confinement and returned to duty.' The troops were reported to have cheered wildly." Seven months later, Scott was killed at Lee's Mill in the Vermont Volunteers' attack on Confederate emplacements along the Warwick River, during the Peninsula Campaign aimed at Richmond.

Only two of the five Scott brothers survived the war.

Such zealous courage had been bred in the bone, because Vermont had been the most articulate anti-slavery state. The first bill to abolish slavery nationally was introduced in Congress by Vermont's Representative William Slade in 1837. For more than fifty years, the state had an active "underground railroad" for fugitive slaves fleeing to Canada. And Supreme Court Justice Theophilus Harrington, challenged by a slave owner, demanded, "What proof do you have?" The owner produced a bill of sale and the judge asked, "Is that all?" When the plaintiff responded, "What more proof do I need," Harrington thundered: "A bill of sale from Almighty God."

Vermont's anti-slavery attitudes drew broad public attention, and generated both support and antagonism. They were so resented in the South that the Georgia legislature, for instance, protested to President Pierce that "able-bodied Irishmen be hired to dig a ditch all around Vermont, till the thing could be detached from the rest of the union and towed out to the middle of the Atlantic Ocean."

Once again in the vanguard, the First Vermont Infantry reached the U.S.-Mexican border ahead of any other National Guard unit in July 1916, when President Wilson mobilized them in response to Pancho Villa's raid on Columbus, New Mexico. Governor Carroll S.Page called a special session of the legislature, which voted to pay each guardsman an additional $10 a month to supplement his War Department pittance.

Vermont's bellicosity was then aimed at the Germans in March 1917, when Governor Horace F. Graham exhorted a joint session of the legislature to appropriate $1,000,000 for "war purposes," specifically for equipment and supplies for the National Guard, and also called for legislation to permit the arrest without warrant of persons suspected of aiding the enemy in case of war. The million-dollar appropriation was promptly passed, causing the national press to applaud Vermont for having declared war on the Central Powers before the United States did. "Vermont was always a patriotic state, perhaps the most patriotic in the whole Union," the *New York Sun* commented, "but in this glorious achievement she has surpassed itself. A million dollars! And her chief industry is dairying. We salute the Green Mountain State with admiration and respect. If the Vermonters are not proud, they ought to be."

Admiral Henry T.Mayo of Burlington was Commander in Chief of the Atlantic Fleet.

On the brink of World War II, Vermont's Senators Ernest Gibson and Warren Austin were among the first to call for the repeal of the 1937 Neutrality Act; and in September 1941, the legislature decided once again to move faster than Washington by declaring, three months before Pearl Harbor, "a state of belligerency with Germany." Major General Leonard F. Wing assumed command of New England's 43rd Division in the field, the only National Guard officer to receive such a post. His 172nd Infantry regiment was composed largely of Vermonters, but, as in the First World War, the state's fifty thousand fighting men and women were scattered.

Vermont's nineteenth-century passion for the causes of abolition and temperance was gradually channeled into women's suffrage, although not as vigorously. Lucy Stone, Julia Ward Howe, and William Lloyd Garrison stumped the state in 1870 to dramatize the issue, which was being adopted by leaders of the Women's Christian Temperance Union. Suffragettes and their allies concentrated on the legislature: six times between 1888 and 1917, a bill granting taxpaying women the right to vote in town meetings was passed by one house only to be rejected in the other. Around 1900, Laura Moore saw her Vermont Women's Suffrage Association dwindle in membership and activity, but the momentum gathered force in 1910 when a "No Vote, No Tax" strategy was promoted by Mrs. Annette Parmalee of Enosburg Falls and Miss L.C.J. Daniels, a wealthy Grafton landowner who refused to pay her property taxes.

Deborah Clifford, who has taught Vermont history at Middlebury College, described the penultimate victory in the summer 1979 issue of *Vermont History*:

"In the 1916-17 session of the Vermont Legislature no fewer than six separate measures relating to woman suffrage came before the House and Senate. For a time it looked as though municipal suffrage was doomed for failure. On February 27 a House committee reported unfavorably 'an act allowing women to vote in town meetings.' The anti-suffragists had sent a large delegation to Montpelier to fight the measure, and discussion was heated if inconclusive. The bill was reintroduced on March 8. This time various efforts were made to amend it. The opponents of the measure made their final plea that if woman suffrage bills must be passed, they should be submitted to a referendum, either to the women of the state or to all the voters. Not yet sure of their following, the suffragists opposed putting the matter before the people. Fortunately, however, all attempts to amend the measure failed, and it finally passed by a bare majority of six. Municipal suffrage had an easier time in the Senate, though one Senator, the Reverend Mr. Leach of Montpelier, could not resist one final stab at reform. Women, he said, should not be burdened with the ballot. Furthermore, he claimed his wife would vote against him on some issues and thus cancel his vote. Despite Leach's sophistry and similar objections, the bill passed the Senate on March 21; on March 30 the governor signed it into law."

Thus Vermont became the first state in New England to do more than allow women to vote in school elections.

In the spring of 1918 an amusing antidote to the grim news from the European war front surfaced in the press. Don Tobin, editor of the *Swanton Courier*, wrote an editorial poking fun at the women who voted in town meeting for the first time. The barb stung Ann Batchelder, a poet from South Woodstock and later food editor of *The Ladies Home Journal*, who wrote a letter to the editor of *The Burlington Free Press*, that Mr. Tobin should know that in Woodstock, "which is quite as much of a town as Swanton, the women went to town meeting in good round numbers, they voted and even nominated a selectman, got him elected, and the men, far from seeming to be injured, enjoyed having the women share the privilege of the franchise, and they didn't feel they were being cheated out of their time-honored prerogatives, either. But then, here in old-fashioned Woodstock, we don't have sawdust on the floor, we don't sit in a ring at town meeting, and we don't have tobacco-spitting, swearing, women-hating men, either. We have instead men who think women are good for something besides making them comfortable, men who are progressive enough to keep up with the procession and not belong in the Age of George the Third, men who are willing to accord women the rights and privileges that are theirs by reason and justice, and who do not expect an emasculated politics from the accession of women to the list of voters, either."

Tobin fired back: "Swanton, as perhaps Ann does not know, is peopled by men 'strong for the rage of battle — men who are grit to the core.' A rugged border town, far up in the frozen heartless north country, where men have no time but to do things, where the product of one short hour's labor of the horny hands of her men, and women [in the Remington Arms plant] would be sufficient to blow fair Woodstock off the map. Is it to be wondered that her men are a bit leonine?

"With Woodstock it is different, naturally. Her hills are bathed in the sunny warmth of a more southern clime, the favored haunt of the idle rich and the gilded Gotham youth, she has a different environment. There are no dudes or spoiled debutante children to loll about our shady nooks, or pelt the tennis ball or tramp the dewy links, spreading culture and propriety in graceful promenading. Men do not wear wrist watches in Swanton."

After tartly reminding Tobin that Woodstock's fighting men "wear wrist watches," Miss Batchelder counter-attacked in verse:

> Come down to Woodstock, men of iron,
> Ye horny-handed crew;
> We need such sons, friend Tobin says,
> To make more virile our childish ways,
> And say — for many years
> Bring down your horny-handed women, too.
> Come down to Woodstock, Swanton's best,
> We'll spread the sawdust on the floor.
> There you shall sit and spit and spit
> As you never spat before;
> And think you of the nice long rest
> For your horny hands and sore.
> For work is all unknown and green
> The waiting golf links lie,
> In Woodstock, town of great renown
> Beneath the flawless sky;
> Come down, ye Swanton men, come down
> Ye horny-handed crew,
> And take a rest from all your toil—

And say—
Those horny-handed girls—
Give them a good rest, too.

But, "If Vermont enjoyed a brief reign of glory as a pro-suffrage state, her reputation was soon tarnished," Professor Clifford concluded. "In 1919 a presidential suffrage bill passed both houses of the Legislature, but Governor Percival Clement refused to sign it on the grounds that it was unconstitutional. In early 1920 when the nineteenth amendment to the United States Constitution was making the rounds of the states for ratification, Vermont came under considerable pressure to become the thirty-sixth and final state to ratify. Again Governor Clement refused to cooperate and resisted efforts to make him call a special session of the Legislature. Vermont women waited for the supreme law of the land to grant them the vote."

Voters were quick to respond. In 1921, Edna Beard, a housewife from Orange, was the first woman elected to the legislature. Born in Illinois in 1877, Mrs. Beard moved to Orange with her family in 1883, and before her election, she served as Orange's school superintendent from 1906-08, later as district school director and town treasurer. In 1923, Mrs. Beard broke another political barrier for women with her election to the state senate. Her portrait by Ruth Mould (1894-1979) hangs in the State House — most recently in the ceremonial office of Governor Madeleine Kunin.

The nature of politics changed radically in the post-war years, as the monolithic Republican establishment began to crack. In 1946, Ernest W. Gibson, Jr., an "Aiken Republican," veteran of the South Pacific, and son of the senator, challenged and defeated Governor Mortimer Proctor. Gibson scalded the administration as a "study in still life" and Proctor as "burning with all the intensity of a five-watt bulb." Gibson resigned the governorship to accept President Truman's appointment as Vermont Federal District Court judge. His successor was Governor Lee Emerson, an ardent anti-communist who forced the University of Vermont to fire its ablest scientist for taking the Fifth Amendment; the legislature balked, however, and rejected his efforts to censor school books and ban the communist party from the ballot. Emerson was narrowly re-elected in 1952.

A Vermont "first" was scored in 1953 when the legislature elected Consuelo Northrop Bailey as Speaker; a year later,she became the first woman in the nation to be elected lieutentant governor. In 1958 the Democrats began to emerge from the woodwork, with William Meyer capturing Vermont's lone seat in the House of Representatives, coming within 700 votes of the governorship, and electing more state assemblymen than ever before.

The Democrats finally won the governorship, for the first time, in 1962 with Philip Hoff of Burlington, with the slim margin of fifteen hundred votes. Hoff introduced several significant federally-funded programs to the state, and in his third term turned to national issues. He opposed the Vietnam war and was the first Democratic governor to break with President Lyndon Johnson. Hoff had, indeed, moved Vermont toward a two-party state, but not far enough to win a U.S. Senate seat in 1972.

One of the most admired and effective governors was Deane C. Davis, who served two terms after 1968. Admitted to the Vermont bar in 1922 when he was twenty-two, Davis practiced law for eighteen years, earning a reputation as one of the state's outstanding trial lawyers. At thirty-one, he was appointed a Superior Court judge. In 1940, Judge Davis began a new career with the National Life Insurance Company in Montpelier, which had been founded in 1850 by the father of Admiral George Dewey and was the state's largest financial institution. Davis served as general counsel, then president and chief executive officer, and chairman until 1968. He had been influential in Republican circles, and was finally persuaded to run for governor.

His two terms were remarkable. The need for a sales tax had been discussed for several years, but Davis was the first governor with the courage to sponsor and get it through the General Assembly. He also reorganized state government by instituting the cabinet form of administration at the executive level. His most enduring legacy is Act 250, enacted in 1972 to put the brakes on rampant, uncontrolled development.

In the 1960s, Vermont's dormant population began to increase rapidly, growing more than seven times as fast as it had in previous decades. Expanding ski areas and second-home colonies were profoundly changing the nature of small towns and rural landscapes, especially in the southern villages of Wilmington and Dover around Mount Snow, the most accessible of the state's ski resorts. There, municipal facilities and services were being strained beyond comprehension. During the Hoff administration, some preliminary, public and private, defensive measures materialized: the Scenery Preservation Council, the Vermont Planning Council, legislation banning billboards, Regional Planning Commissions, and a statement of future planning goals entitled *Vision and Choice: Vermont's Future*.

Davis realized that Vermont was in for trouble "unless we did something about the invasion of the state by people and the type of quick development that was going on to make a fast buck. As I studied the development that was going on in Windham County, I realized that the so-called second homes before long turned out to be first homes and when they are first homes, there are children in the home, schools have to be taken care of, roads have got to be built to them and they are building $200,000 houses on dirt roads up on the mountain where the soil was fragile." In 1969, the governor convened a special conference on natural resources and appointed a Commission on Environmental Control chaired by Arthur Gibb. The commission presented a report to the 1970 legislature that touched on land development, pesticide regulation, water quality and resources, state government reorganization, and open-space protection. The legislature responded with the pioneering State Land Use and Development Bill (Act 250), and other environmental protection measures. Although the land-use plan was never implemented, Act 250 has been utilized by District Commissions to review applications for large-scale residential or commercial developments, using criteria intended to control — but not prevent — growth.

Several years after his retirement, Governor Davis published *Justice in the Mountains* (1980), a collection of "stories and tales by a country lawyer" that became a best seller. Typical of the anecdotes is one called "A Matter of Economy", which deals with one of Vermont's peculiar attributes:

> One of Vermont's unique institutions is the office of assistant judge, colloquially called the "side judge." This institution was originally borrowed from the Pennsylvania constitution. Pennsylvania, and every other state that had

such an office or one similar to it, has long since done away with it. The "side judge" is an elective officer, and two are elected in each county. They are uniformly not lawyers. However, they have equal authority with the Superior Court judge, who is the presiding officer of the three-member court.

In a few instances the two lay judges have overruled the presiding judge, even on questions of law. One interesting case came from Bennington County, where two lay judges overruled the presiding judge, who was a lawyer, on a legal question. The case went to the Supreme Court and the lay judges were sustained!

....The reason for "side judges" in those early days was the fear of authority. In those days the prevailing philosophy was to divide up all kinds of power among judicial, executive, and legislative and then to provide further checks and balances in countless situations so that no person would become possessed of dictatorial authority.

The reason the institution has remained so long in Vermont is that the assistant judges are provided for in the state Constitution, and therefore the office cannot be discontinued without an amendment to the Constitution, with all its attendant delays and difficulties. Periodically, however, an attempt is made in the legislature to remove the office from the constitutional provisions. Some years ago such an attempt was made, with the following colloquy.

The sponsor of the bill, on the third reading, made an impassioned plea to get rid of the the office of assistant judge by providing for a referendum to be submitted to the voters to amend the Constitution. Winding up his eloquent plea, he said, "These assistant judges are perfectly useless. Moreover, they are a great expense. Why, we might just as well carve a couple of 'side judges' out of basswood and set them up there on the bench and save money."

Just about that time a member from a remote section of the state, who had been overimbibing in one of Montpelier's kitchen dives during the noon hour, was taking his seat. Immediately he arose, somewhat unsteadily, and addressed the Speaker: "Mr. Speaker, I resent that statement. I don't think we have to spend money carving our 'side judges' out of basswood. The ones we've got are just as good as that."

After Democratic Governor Thomas Salmon's terms, the Republicans recaptured the executive office in 1976 with Richard Snelling, who, after his nearly unprecedented re-election for a fourth time, became the third governor in the state's history to serve eight years or more. Snelling took a lead in amending Vermont's Constitution to include the Equal Rights Amendment, securing low-cost Canadian electrical power, and, nationally, in promoting federalism and warning the public about the dire consequences of the massive national debt.

Most Vermonters were astonished when Madeleine Kunin of Burlington won the governorship in 1984 — the first woman to reach the executive office, and a Democrat! A Swiss-born journalist and political scientist, Mrs. Kunin had served two terms as lieutentant governor from 1978-82, and was re-elected for a third term as governor in 1988.

Vermont's population growth rate of 30.5 percent since 1967 (from 420,000 to 548,000 people) brought renewed attention to the impact and problems of growth management in 1987. Vermonters had become self-conscious, and a bit vain, over their popularity as tourist attractions, and acutely aware of the inroads caused by second-home colonizers. In one of its periodic spasms of self-analysis, the state convened the Commission on Vermont's Future, appointed by Governor Kunin, which held a widely-attended series of public hearings. Most spokesmen tended to agree with Peter Bramhall, the noted glassblower of Bridgewater, who declared: "We must be willing to say that the beauty and quality of life in Vermont is not for sale. That if you can find a way to enhance the quality of life here, come join us, if you cannot, or care not to, please visit another state." Far less comprehensive demographically than the report of the Country Life Commission in 1931 (see Chapter Seven), the latest commission delivered a provocative summary of its findings. While people spoke of the benefits of a booming economy and were generally optimistic about the state's ability to solve its problems, the Commission was "struck with the depth of concern for the future of agriculture in Vermont as well as for the declining availability of affordable housing. It also heard much about the inability of the existing regulatory process — both at the state and local level — to effectively manage development. Many witnesses spoke eloquently of the deteriorating quality of life in Vermont, about the threats to our environment and of the rapid loss of open space." People from Springfield, where the machine tool industry had dwindled, and the "Northeast Kingdom" above St. Johnsbury, the most spartan area of the state, said that they suffered from too little growth. Others, from growth centers, argued for manufacturing jobs that paid better than those in hotels and other services.

The Commission found that the absence of state land use policies and the lack of strong regional planning had produced a major gap in Vermont's planning system. Important resources such as prime agricultural and forest lands cross town lines and require planning at the regional level, as do commercial or residential developments that have a cumulative impact on more than one town. The Commission's report and recommendations, issued in January 1988, became the basis for a vigorously debated "Growth Bill," which finally emerged from the legislature in its closing hours as Act 200. This new statute mandated greater planning coordination at the local, regional and state level; beefed up the Housing and Conservation Trust Fund with an increase in the property transfer tax; and made other provisions — none really definitive — designed to deal with the thorny question of restraining development.

In her 1988 State of the State address, Governor Kunin summed up her position: "As we try to shape our future, we want to retain our grasp on our shared Vermont values; to adhere to our allegiance to the land, even as our interdependence with it has changed; to retain our sense of community, even as our communities have become more diffuse and varied; and to continue to value one another as individuals, worthy of respect....I believe Vermonters are ready...to enter a new planning era, taking more direct responsibility for decision-making in order to assure greater control over our destiny." During her re-election campaign, when unemployment in Vermont was the lowest in the country, she added:

"In the past, we have always assumed that we had to make a choice between being tough on the environment and jobs. And whenever we had tough environmental laws, a lot of people who were representing the economic side of things said, 'Hey, you can't be that tough on the environment, it's going to hurt our state economy.' Vermont has a reputation for being a tough environmental state and having an environmental ethic. What we've really proven is that you don't have to choose, that you can do both, and that that in the long term is the best investment, that good environmental policy equals good economic policy. I think that is a major turnaround and a major achievement for Vermont."

Flanking the capitol to the east are the State Library and Supreme Court Building and the reincarnated Pavilion. From the time it was built in 1807 as a hotel for legislators until it was razed and replaced by a modern replica in 1971, the Pavilion was the social center of the capital. Most of the Pavilion is occupied by the Governor's Office and state agencies, but the first floor houses the Vermont Historical Society, which was incorporated in Barnet in 1835 and moved to Montpelier in 1851. The society's library and genealogical collections are in constant use, and its distinguished small museum displays absorbing vignettes of Vermont's past in permanent and temporary exhibits.

Eleven miles north of Montpelier, off Route 12 east of Worcester and Maple Corner, can be found the Kent Tavern Museum, which has been restored and maintained by the Vermont Historical Society as a living-history centerpiece demonstrating the relative self-sufficiency of a four-corners community. The museum, open to visitors in the summer months, was built with granite from a local quarry, brick from

The snowy street in front of the Pavilion Hotel (and all roads) used to be rolled, not plowed. —Vermont Historical Society

a family kiln, wood sawed down the road apiece, and iron fixtures forged around the corner.

The work of Thomas Waterman Wood, the notable nineteenth-century painter, is represented in the Wood Gallery of Art on the Montpelier campus of Vermont College. A more contemporary artistic panorama of Vermont life is the huge (50' x 8') mural by Paul Sample which ornaments the lobby of the National Life Insurance Company.

Finally, Montpelier has become the gustatory capital of Vermont as well. Here the New England Culinary Institute trains chefs and sends them out into the world of haute cuisine. Their apprenticeship includes cooking for two Institute-owned local restaurants, Tubbs and the Elm Street Cafe. Both serve outstanding meals at reasonable prices, as does the Horn of the Moon Cafe, a New Age storefront bistro with an enthusiastic following.

Barre

Pronounced "berry," the ethnically cosmopolitan granite center of the world was organized under the charter name of Wildersburgh in 1793. Deciding the name was uncouth, the first settlers held a town meeting to chose another. Tempers flared: two Massachusetts men, Thompson from Holden and Sherman of Barre, got into a fist fight. Sherman won and the settlement was renamed for his home town. Three nondescript villages grew up in the vicinity and eventually merged: Twingville, around Joshua Twing's foundry; Gospel Village, surrounding the 1808 First Congregational church; and Jockey Hollow, used by sporting men to train race horses.

The granite industry was started soon after the War of 1812 by two army veterans, Robert Parker and Thomas Courser, who opened the first quarry on Cobble Hill. Granite was used initially for millstones, doorsteps, fence posts and window lintels. A finer grade was soon found on Millstone Hill, to which quarrying was transferred and where it remains. These early entrepreneurs got their first big order when the Capitol in Montpelier was being built in 1836. Because of its beauty and flawless texture, light and dark Barre granite that takes a high polish continues to be used for monuments. Between 1880 and 1890, Barre's population leaped from 2,060 to 6,812, the sharpest rise ever recorded by a Vermont town in a decade. The increase was directly attributable to the growth of the granite industry and the influx of Italian, Scotch, French, Spanish, and Scandinavian stoneworkers.

This volatile mix of mostly underpaid laborers who were ready to strike for their rights, elected and re-elected a Socialist mayor, and encouraged even more radical political figures in the early years of the twentieth century— Emma Goldman, for instance, who was arrested in Barre and later charged with abetting the murder of a mayor. During the long strike in the middle of the Depression, the Boston Communist Party sent truckloads of food and clothing to the strikers' families; as a result, Earl Browder got more votes in Vermont than in Rhode Island in 1936.

Today's visitors are awed by the the century-old, 350-feet deep quarry, covering twenty acres, that can be seen on the Rock of Ages tour. Proud examples of granite memorial artistry, statuary, and mausoleums can be seen in the beautifully landscaped Mount Hope Cemetery on Route 14 at the city's edge.

Four stalled winter motorists in Montpelier, the cry was, "Get an ox team!"
—Vermont Historical Society

The Barre Fire Department strung garlands over their rig for a parade.
—Vermont Historical Society

Granite is not Barre's only claim to fame. In 1909, William F. Milne, a young Scottish stonecutter, organized the first Boy Scout Troop in America from among Barre Baptist Church Sunday school lads, several months prior to the founding of the Boy Scouts of America in February 1910.

The Barre Opera House, built in 1899 after fire destroyed its predecessor, occupies the second and third floors of City Hall. Acoustically outstanding, the hall has been restored for current musical productions.

Goddard Seminary, founded in Barre in 1863, moved to Plainfield in 1938 and was reorganized as a small private college with a progressive philosophy and special emphasis on the coordination of classroom and work experience.

Cabot

Located about three miles north of Route 2 between Marshfield and Danville, Cabot was settled in 1783 by Daniel Webster's uncle Benjamin Webster. The immortal Daniel and his brother Ezekiel rode horseback from Franklin, New Hampshire, to spend the summer of 1795 here. During the War of

1812, folks around Cabot carried on a lively smuggling trade with Canada, supplying liquor from the town's numerous stills. An early settler wrote, "The citizens of this place being quite content on obeying the divine injunction, 'if thine enemy hunger, feed him; if he thirst, give him drink.'"

Summer camps surround Joe's Pond and the smaller Molly's Pond, named for an Indian couple who were rewarded for their loyalty during the Revolution with an audience with George Washington and a pension from the Vermont legislature. Cabot was also the home of a freaky child prodigy in mathematics, Zera Colburn, born in 1804, who made a widely-heralded personal appearance tour of Europe, being exhibited on stages in London and elsewhere when he was nine years old and handling complex questions like a human computer.

Cheese has replaced whiskey as the town's principal product ever since the Cabot Farmers' Cooperative Creamery commenced operations in 1919. About six million pounds of cheese are made here annually; its fine cheddars are especially popular.

Chapter Six

The Northeast Kingdom

"The record of Vermont as a resolute champion of individual freedom, as a true interpreter of our fundamental law, as a defender of religious faith, as an unselfish but independent and uncompromising commonwealth of liberty-loving patriots, is not only unsurpassed, but unmatched by any other state in the union."

— George Harvey, publisher
Harper's Magazine

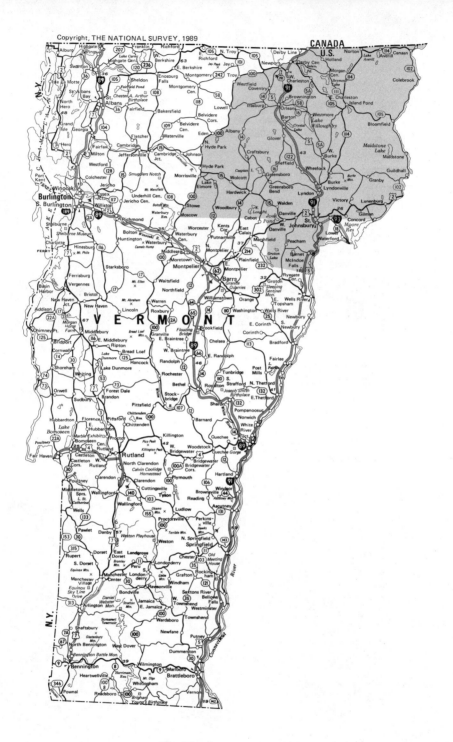

The Northeast Kingdom

The Northeast Kingdom, two thousand square miles of Orleans, Caledonia, and Essex counties, is Vermont's last frontier. The appellation is credited to Senator George Aiken, who remarked to a group in Lyndonville in 1949, "You know, this is such beautiful country up here, it ought to be called the Northeast Kingdom." The most rural, undeveloped part of Vermont, where people hunt, fish, hike and snowmobile across thousands of acres of near-wilderness and open woods, it's also the poorest region, not unlike sections of poverty-striken Appalachia, isolated from the relative prosperity that has benefited most of the state in recent years. The sale of fourteen thousand acres of timberland near Victory by Diamond International to a syndicate of real estate developers may quicken the pulse of the building trades, but it is raising the blood pressure of conservationists, who hope for authorities to intervene with a state or national forest preserve.

In *Vermont Beautiful*, published in 1922, Wallace Nutting, the photographer, delivered a graceful essay on the quality of the roads in Vermont, while most of them were still being tamped down by rollers in the winter and before many had been paved. He even praised the roads in this part of the state, reporting that he had driven from St. Johnsbury to Newport, Eden, Hyde Park and back "at a rate of speed exceeding the possibilities elsewhere in New England." Expanding on his topic, Nutting wrote: "Vermont is unique in the quality of its roads. More solid sense has been directed to their construction than we have observed elsewhere. It is clearly impossible for a state uniquely rural to construct, or even to plan, a general system of cement roads. The usual thing, however, would have been the building of tarred or composite roads, such as break up quickly and are proving so unsatisfactory in other states. We owe a very high tribute to Mr. Stoddard B. Bates of Orleans County for his wisdom in using the materials which he found at hand.... It would be a revelation to some road builders to test these gravel roads, which are not only the best possible at their cost, but strange to say are the fastest roads, excepting only cement....To make these roads so excellent, they must be cunningly compounded of just enough fine matter to permit the packing of gravel firmly. Here and there local attempts at gravel roads have been failures owing to the looseness of the gravel used. This makes a road dangerous to pass over, except very slowly. The beds of the streams which abound through nine parts of the state of Vermont afford admirably screened gravel. There are still some districts in the northwest part of the state where the roads consist of pure clay admirable for smoothness when scraped, but when wet or rough after drying capable of testing the character of a saint. All good men are advised to avoid journeys over such roads, because the duffer at golf is a kind, sweet gentleman to a traveller on clay when it has fallen from grace.

"In most of our states it is dangerous to leave main roads. In Vermont, however, the roads are so good that one may often follow heavy grades over the highest hills, over narrow, winding passes, without a jolt or jar. In fact, a notable feature of Vermont is the generally high character of the minor cross roads and hill roads [Nutting must have stayed home during mud season!]."

During Prohibition, this roof of Vermont leaked bootlegged whiskey and gin. The thinly patrolled border was readily penetrated, mostly by amateurs. One enterprising smuggler cut tree stumps to a uniform height along one stretch, then added two inches to the clearance of his Hudson touring car. In Montreal he would fill the car with cases of real hooch and head south. If and when the border patrol gave chase, he headed for the stumpage and sailed through, hearing the clanking of government cars being disemboweled. Sporadic shoot-outs occured. Nat Worman of Franklin, who used to publish a weekly newspaper, once observed: "Living exposed to both warring parties — the rum-runners and the lawmen — left many border people with bad eyesight."

"Line houses" did a land-office business, serving drinks from bars on the Canadian side of the room to happy customers lined up on the American side. In Montreal, the family that owns Seagram's began to amass one of the world's greatest fortunes.

Vermonters and Canadians are given to cooperative living, forming joint hydroelectric companies and other community enterprises. In some places, only native townspeople know exactly where the border lies. And in Derby Line's Haskell Opera House, actors or musicians on the stage perform in Canada, while the audience sits in the United States.

During the 1840s, poor farming conditions and practices in Quebec propelled the French across the border to mills and railroad gangs. Now, nearly a quarter of the population along the border make a go of farms the Yankees left long ago and speak French at home, but young French-Canadian families tend to play down their origins, and bi-lingual programs in the border schools are rare.

Folks now in their fifties and sixties have nostalgic memories of the St. Johnsbury & Lake Champlain Railroad, often called the "Slow, Jerky, & Late Coming," that meandered leisurely through the small towns under the eaves from St. Johnsbury to Swanton, pausing to pick up a few passengers, freight, milk cans, mail, and gossip.

Vermont's garret is home to several contemporary writers, notably David Mamet, the playwright, poet David Budbill, author of *The Chain Saw Dance* and other poems about Judevine, and Howard Frank Mosher, whose novel *Disappearances* (1977) conveys a realistic portrait of what he calls "Kingdom Come." Not only are his books "rich with authentic observed detail about the realities of Vermont life from mud-season to deer-hunting," Marshall True wrote in *Vermont History*, "they also contain richly embroidered legends which are part of the cultural fabric of Vermont. Tall tales of whiskey-running, black monks, and logging become cultural hymns to Vermont's character and the survival skills of her independent citizens." Mosher reveals a keen sense of place and community; his residents of Kingdom Come are "aware that laws are less important than lives."

Approaching St. Johnsbury from the south on Route 5 or I-91 offers a New Age contrast: one could pause at Barnet Center to find Harvey's Lake, for fishing and swimming, or to visit the Karme-Choling Buddhist Meditation Center, a Tibetan outpost formerly known as "The Tail of the Tiger." From the outside, this appears to be a traditional white farmhouse with red trim and a big barn, but a bright banner fluttering in the breeze identifies its more holistic nature. Inside is a Tibetan-style temple, and housing for guests bent on a week or month of meditation. Large numbers of Buddhists converged there a few years ago for the ceremonial funeral rites of a notable high lama.

St. Johnsbury

Unique in name (the only place in the world) and nearly so as an organically-preserved 19th-century industrial town, St. J. is the portal to the Northeast Kingdom and a monument to the Fairbanks family. Their paternal imprint can be seen on two extraordinary buildings, the Athenaeum and the Fairbanks Museum, two of Vermont's most unusual cultural attributes. Coming upon these two unexpected gems is like finding Hope diamonds in a K-Mart.

Stephen Nash, a Massachusetts resident spying on the Indians in 1775, was the first caucasian New Englander to camp on the town's future site on the Passumpsic River seven miles north of its confluence with the Connecticut River. Eleven years later, Dr. Jonathan Arnold of Providence, Rhode Island, and others petitioned Vermont for a charter and were granted some 21,000 acres. The name of the new settlement was apparently chosen by Ethan Allen, honoring Hector St.John de Crevecoeur, the French explorer, consul, author, and Hudson River gentleman farmer.

Dr. Arnold, an entrepreneur, was gratified by his surroundings. "I must confess," he wrote a friend, "I feel myself happy in having risked so much on the Vermont bottom...here we may retire, a few acres will easily supply all real wants: are we distant from circles of wealth and ambition? We are the same distance from heresy, confusion, chicane and disappointment. Are we remote from friends? We are equally so from flatterers and defrauders." St. Johnsbury's identity was assured by the invention in 1830 of the platform scale by Thaddeus Fairbanks. The inventor had settled here in 1815 with his father; his first patent was granted in 1826 for the exclusive manufacture of cast-iron plows. His device for weighing merchandise changed forever the method in universal use since biblical days, and the E.and T. Fairbanks "shops," as they were familiarly known for generations, built by Thaddeus and his two brothers, Erastus and Joseph, dominated the town. His older brother Erastus, forced to curtail his grand design to make the Connecticut River entirely navigable, devoted his considerable energies to getting a railroad link to Boston; the first train over the Connecticut & Passumpsic Rivers Railroad chuffed into town in November 1850.

Thaddeus Fairbanks. —Special Collections, University of Vermont Library

Erastus was twice governor of Vermont: elected first in 1852, his final official act was signature of the prohibition bill. Elected again in 1860, he presided over Vermont's rush to the Union colors in the Civil War. His sons inherited his public-service genes, Franklin as Speaker of the House in 1872, and Horace as governor in 1876.

Thaddeus accumulated international honors for his scale and its later modifications. He was called "Sir Thaddeus" for receiving the Knightly Cross of the Imperial Order of Francis Joseph from the emperor of Austria; the king of Siam awarded him the Decoration of Puspamala; and the Bey of Tunis conferred upon him the Nishan el Iptaka, Grade of Commander. He died in 1886 at the age of ninety. "In extreme but venerable age," a contemporary wrote, "his puckered eyes, sagacious nose and hair of driven snow commanded the respect which was profoundly intensified by familiar acquaintance, and among the monarchs of industrial art the name of Thaddeus Fairbanks must forever be pre-eminent."

"Sir Thaddeus'" and his brothers first demonstrated their philanthropic largesse by founding the private St. Johnsbury Academy in 1842, whose brick buildings still stand as an imposing group near the southern end of Main Street, serving for many years as the town's high school.

The two other cultural monuments bequeathed by the Fairbanks family overlook the town from the ridge along which the gentry of their era built substantial homes. The Athenaeum, at 30 Main Street, was dedicated in 1871 by Horace Fairbanks as, principally, a public library. Its splendid woodwork and other appointments suitable to a "gentlemen's reading room" resemble those of its Boston namesake. While the library itself is impressive, the adjoining Art Gallery, completed two years later, is what really awes contemporary visitors. The oldest art gallery still in its original form in the United States, its walls and floors of black walnut, leather-bound art books, and collection of 19th-century paintings and statuary are overwhelmed by the huge, dazzling canvas, "The Domes of the Yosemite," by the famous American landscape painter Albert Bierstadt.

Horace Fairbanks' annual New Year's Eve reception in the Athenaeum was the most glittering social event of the year.

St. Johnsbury Athenaeum. —

236

The Fairbanks Museum and Planetarium, given by Franklin Fairbanks "to teach the meaning of nature and religion," was dedicated in 1890. —Vermont Travel Division

Guests of honor at these galas included the explorerers Admiral Peary and Henry M. Stanley.

What could Horace's brother do for an encore? Sharing the edifice complex that characterized the later Rockefellers, Colonel Franklin Fairbanks constructed the Museum of Natural Science at 81-85 Main Street that he presented to the town in 1891. Built of Longmeadow red sandstone in the H.H. Richardson Romanesque style, the museum's lofty exhibit halls are crammed with fascinating collections of Vermont flora, birds, mammals, reptiles, fish and insects, shells, minerals, fossils, foreign ethnological samples, plus domestic and agricultural relics, including objets d'art crafted of polished beetle shells.

"I wish the museum to be the people's school," Franklin declared at the building's dedication; and, in fact, it continues to attract youngsters and older students. A 50-seat planetarium was added, showing the night sky as it appears in this part of Vermont.

St. Johnsbury boasts the third oldest community band in the country; it has been playing weekly concerts in the park since 1830.

In the 1960s, St. Johnsbury's civic pride saved the scale factory from being exported Southward by its new conglomerate owners: townspeople raised the money to subsidize the construction of a new plant. At the old-fashioned Maple Grove factory — the largest in the world — one can watch maple candy made from molds, and view a film on sugaring in the museum.

Peacham

This vintage village, high on a ridge off Route 5 southwest of St. Johnsbury, has changed hardly any since its settlement in 1776, and remains a magnet for sophisticated urban refugees who wish to live simply and anonymously. Far from anonymous was one of the hamlet's most illustrious sons, Colonel George B.M. Harvey, "the President-maker," whose father was a storekeeper. Born in Peacham in 1864, the future newspaper editor and publisher attended the Peacham Academy, married his boyhood sweetheart, and went to work for the St.Johnsbury *Caledonian*. He moved on as a reporter and editor to Springfield, Massachusetts, to the Chicago *Daily News*, and then managing editor of the New York *World*. He made a fortune in suburban electric railways, and in 1900 presided over Harper & Brothers (with the financial backing of J.P. Morgan), the prestigious book and magazine publishers.

Harvey was for several years a political power-broker in New Jersey: he persuaded Woodrow Wilson to give up his academic career as president of Princeton, engineered his election as governor, and articulately supported his presidential aspirations. Harvey might have gone on to become President Wilson's closest political advisor in the White House, but he was shouldered out of play by William Jennings Bryan and the legendary Colonel Edward M. House, who persuaded Wilson that Harvey was too obviously a symbol of Wall Street and J.P. Morgan. Disgruntled, Harvey deserted the Democratic party, to which he had been faithful since he was old enough to vote, and, to the astonishment and chagrin of his friends, transferred his talents and influence to the Republicans. And when the deadlocked delegates to the Republican convention in 1921 turned to Harvey for advice, he told them that Warren G. Harding should and could be nominated and elected. He probably also supported his fellow Vermonter, Calvin Coolidge, as Vice President. Harding's gratitude was tangibly expressed in Harvey's appointment as ambassador to the Court of St. James's.

His potent political skills were subsequently recruited by the backers of Herbert Hoover, who made frequent pilgrimages to Harvey's summer home in Dublin, New Hampshire. Harvey died, however, in August 1928.

Barnet

Henry Stevens, the noted nineteenth-century bibliophile, was born here in 1819. He attended Middlebury College, graduated from Yale in 1843, and studied law at Harvard before going to live in London, where for most of the rest of his life, he was employed by the British Museum as a collector of Americana. He was also purchasing agent for the Library of Congress and the Smithsonian, for the Lenox Library in New York, the John Carter Brown Library in Providence, Rhode Island, and for individual book collectors.

Danville

Branching west from St. Johnsbury on Route 2, the traveler finds Danville, an attractive town on a plateau with a gracious village green where the American Society of Dowsers gathers for its annual meeting in September. Dowsers' Hall, open weekdays and occasionally on weekends, displays the forked sticks, angle rods and pendulums which these prescient folks use— almost infallibly— to locate subterranean water. The small brick Caledonia Bank was the victim of a holdup in 1935, an event so unusual in Vermont as to command national publicity.

Thaddeus Stevens, the grim, resourceful, crusading Abolitionist, was born here in 1792. Despite an impoverished childhood, he earned a good education from Peacham Academy, in the town to which his parents moved so he could attend; the University of Vermont and Dartmouth College. Stevens later settled in Gettysburg, Pennsylvania, where he practiced law. In 1849 and again in 1858 he was elected to Congress, where he served as chairman of the powerful Ways and Means committee during the Lincoln administration and strongly opposed the post-Civil War reconstruction policies, arguing vehemently for sterner measures to punish the former Confederate States. Described by Samuel Eliot Morison as "a sour and angry Congressman who really loved Negroes— at least he lived with one and was buried among them," Stevens wished to disenfranchise former slave owners. As a party leader with a talent for "controlled invective and devastating sarcasm", he failed to accomplish the impeachment of President Johnson and died a few months later. A clause in his will provided funds for planting roses or "other cheerful flowers" at the corners of his mother's grave in Peacham.

A few miles further is Cabot, famed during the War of 1812 for its distilleries and now for its cheese. The Cabot Farmers Co-op Creamery has been in operation since 1919 and is open daily for visitors, who can sample its grades of cheddar and a half dozen other cheeses.

Greensboro

Several routes are espaliered off Route 2 northwest of Danville. Greensboro, off Route 16 at the foot of Caspian Lake, has been a favorite summer retreat for such celebrities as John Gunther, Greta Garbo, and Chief Justice William Rehnquist. The shores of Caspian Lake, covering nearly eight hundred acres, are dotted with summer cottages and camps to which families have been coming for generations.

Craftsbury

The trio of Craftsbury villages off Route 14, especially Craftsbury Common with its tranquil, expansive town green, are among the most picturesque in the state, and were important trading centers in the late eighteenth century. Ebenezer Crafts, the grantee in 1780, was among the first to come and live on the land they owned. A graduate of Yale and an officer in the Revolution, he was forced to sell his tavern in Sturbridge, Massachusetts, to pay off war debts, and moved north over the Bayley-Hazen Road to settle the village in 1788. His son, Samuel, a Harvard graduate, served as town clerk for thirty-seven years, in Congress as representative and senator, and as governor of Vermont for two terms in 1828-31. He founded the private academy that still serves the town as a public high school.

Glover

The internationally-famous Bread and Puppet Theater troupe lives communally in a farmhouse on Route 122 off Route 16. The hauntingly dramatic, oversized puppets representing Good and Evil are created by Polish-born Peter Schumann. A vast meadow is the scene of the annual Domestic Resurrection Circus, a politically-tinged extravaganza in which thousands of spectators share black bread and inspiration during the August weekend happening.

Alexander Twilight built the Old Stone House as the dormitory for a rural academy in 1836. —Vermont Historical Society

Barton

John Paul Jones, the naval hero, was among the original grantees from Rhode Island. Once a railroad town with six passenger trains a day depositing summer visitors to Crystal Lake and Lake Willoughby, Barton stands at the intersection of I-91, Routes 5 and 16 and remains a pivot for exploring the northland. Lake Willoughby, seven miles northeast, is Vermont's most surprising body of water, because, lying between the sheer cliffs of Mt. Hor and Mt. Pisgah on either shore, it resembles a fjord. It was a popular resort area during the grand summer hotel and steamboat era, but is now relatively undeveloped.

Three miles northeast of Orleans, in the village of Browning-ton, is the Orleans County Historical Society's Old Stone House Museum, a four-story granite building dating back to 1835 built as a dormitory for a rural academy by Alexander Twilight. Although he was dark-skinned, there is some doubt as to whether Twilight was, indeed, the first Black graduate of an

Mts. Hor and Pisgah rise abruptly from opposite shores of Lake Willoughby, creating a fjord-like effect. —Agency of Development & Community Affairs

American college in 1823, as Middlebury claims. The museum holds ten rooms of early weapons, tools, paintings, furniture and folk art.

Newport

Occupying the southern shore of Lake Memphremagog, which extends twenty-seven narrow miles north into Quebec, Newport was a significant logging and railroad center. From Newport came the politically-prominent Prouty family: George H. served as governor 1906-08; Winston L. was Vermont's lone voice in Congress from 1950 to 1958, and was then elected to the Senate, where he served until his death in 1970. Tourism in the Newport area has been revived by such annual events as Winterfest, a February week of dog sled races, curling, ice fishing and sailing, and snow golf; and the Memphremagog International Aquafest in July.

Lyndonville

Directly north of St. Johnsbury, this substantial old community at the confluence of Routes 5, 122, 114 and I-91, once a significant railroad hub, serves as a shopping center for smaller villages to the north. Since 1846 it has been the site of the Caledonia County Fair, and plays host to Lyndon State College.

Bag Balm, developed in 1908 as a cure for chapped udders and made here in an old grist mill, has won a national skin-care reputation.

In nearby East Burke, Elmer Darling, who made a fortune with the notable, old Fifth Avenue Hotel in New York, built a dramatic mansion, "Burklyn," from which there's a fine view of Burke Mountain and the 10,000-acre Darling State Forest with its toll road to the summit. The first ski trails on Burke Mountain were cut by the C.C.C. in the 1930s.

In Sutton, three miles west of West Burke, was born in 1823 the famous American book publisher, Henry Houghton. A penniless printer's devil, he nevertheless managed to get through the University of Vermont. By the time the Civil War erupted, he had become one of the finest printers in America with his Riverside Press in Cambridge, Massachusetts. After the war he began publishing the work of notable British and American authors; the Houghton Mifflin imprint, established in Boston in 1880, remains the most significant in New England. For many years, Houghton maintained a rather grand summer home in Burlington.

Island Pond

Eight ponds lie in the township of Brighton; Island Pond, the largest, surrounds a 22-acre island. Crooner Rudy Vallee was born here, but the town's greatest claim to fame was its mid-nineteenth century status as the division headquarters of the Canadian National Railway and its junction with the Grand Trunk, halfway between Portland, Maine, and Montreal, the cities it was designed to link in 1853. Construction began in 1846, the Canadian National building from the west, and from the east the Atlantic & St.Lawrence — which ran out of money when it reached Island Pond. The Canadian National, which had gotten as far as Norton on the border, agreed to complete the last sixteen miles. "The world's first international railway had been completed," Nat Worman has written. "Railroad shops and offices sprang up. Island Pond, like a magnet, had pulled tracks to itself, from east and west."

Today's Island Pond is a shadow of its former prominence, but it offers a jumping off place for hiking, camping, or fishing tours of the northeast wilderness accessible from Routes 111, 114 to Lake Averill, and Route 105 to the New Hampshire border. The town harbors "The Church," a group of several hundred Fundamentalists who migrated here from Tennessee in the 1970s and who were later subjects of widely-publicized charges of child abuse by state officials, accusations which could not be proven.

Chapter Seven

The Little Parkway
That Couldn't

"We mean to knit and lace the state together with the best roadways in the world—roads that feel like velvet, and stand like adamant, and stretch away like a satin ribbon in the shade and sun. And over these shall come seekers of health and beauty, drinking in from many landscapes the enchanted draught that leaves the gazer restless and unsatisfied until he can return. And so we mean to guard with jealous care the nobility and freshness of our scenery. Here is that wealth that can never be exhausted but by our own stupidity."

— "Rural Vermont: A Program
for the Future," 1931.

"If God had wanted a parkway through them mountains, He'd of put one there." This succinct though apochryphal pronouncement by a state senator more than fifty years ago could be the epitaph for "The Little Parkway That Couldn't Make the Grade."

Most motorists today agree that the stretches of Interstates 91 and 89 in Vermont may well be the most scenic in America's super-highway system. They would have a rival if supporters of the Green Mountain Parkway had prevailed in the early 1930s and a companion to the Sky Line Drive in Virginia had indeed been constructed.

But more than panoramic views of Lake Champlain and the Adirondacks were at stake.

Vermont's maverick tradition was dramatized in the early years of the New Deal when the promoters of tourism and conservationists squared off in the first round of a devisive battle that foreshadowed later skirmishes in the 1980s. The Green Mountain Parkway issue symbolized, as well, a deeper philosophical and political struggle between the proud defenders of states' rights and the pragmatists who welcomed federal funding to temper the chill winds of the depression. It was also the first major test of strength between advocates of growth and development and defenders of the environment.

Roadbuilders have always been visionaries, and this was not the first such bold concept. By 1815 some fifty turnpikes with toll houses crisscrossed the state. A circuitous route of less than two hundred miles from Brattleboro to Burlington, via a series of six turnpikes, could cost a family of five close to fifty dollars in tolls alone.

In his eagerness to promote good thoroughfares and reap the profits, Gamaliel Painter, the wealthy town father of Middlebury, petitioned the Assembly for the right to construct the ultimate turnpike, stretching from Pownal to Highgate. But the legislature sensibly recognized the inherent greediness of his scheme, and charitably gave him a chance to withdraw it before a vote.

Conceived by Colonel William J. Wilgus of Ascutney, a prominent civil engineer for whom a state park has been named, and who might have become Vermont's Robert Moses, the 260-mile scenic Green Mountain Parkway was to extend along the western crest of the Green Mountains from North

Adams in Massachusetts to the Canadian border between Jay Peak and Newport, where there would be a 20,0000-acre wilderness park. Wilgus, then sixty-eight, former chief engineer of the New York Central Railroad, had earned considerable acclaim for his bold plan to cover the Central's Park Avenue tracks in New York City, sell air rights to real estate developers, and construct the mighty Grand Central Terminal, completed in 1919.

"The very greatest recommendation which [he] has to his credit," wrote Charles R. Cummings, the editor of *The Vermonter*, "are 'dreams,' which all came true. He reconstructed the New York Central Railroad, for heavier motive power— new rails, new bridges, restored crumbling abutments, with no cessation of tremendous traffic; he directed the change of motive power from steam to electricity, in the New York suburban zones...conceived and created the Grand Central Terminal; gave birth to the new method of tunnel construction first used under the Detroit River...He served as Chairman of the Board of Consulting Engineers of the great Holland Vehicular Tunnel [under the Hudson River]." Colonel Wilgus had also organized the French railroad system for the American Expeditionary Force in 1917-18.

The skyline drive, as contemplated, would have been the grandest east of the Mississippi, stretching from the scattered heights of southern Vermont, through the lower elevations of the Green Mountain National Forest, to the flanks of Salt Ash Mountain in Plymouth. From there, the parkway would be hitched just below the crests of Big and Little Pico and Killington, Carmel, Horrid, and Romance Mountains, thence into valleys from which the traveler would view Vermont's Presidential Range — Camel's Hump and Mt. Mansfield— climbing again to its ultimate destination at Jay Peak.

The genesis of the parkway was nearly buried in the 385-page *Rural Vermont: A Program for the Future*, a remarkable document published in 1931 by the Vermont Commission on Country Life. For three years, nearly three hundred men and women grouped in sixteen committees, chaired by ex-Governor John E. Weeks of Middlebury, studied the state's natural and cultural resources. Its exhaustive report included recommendations on a broad spectrum of topics, from agriculture to tourism.

Native chauvinism motivated the commission's work. "For more than a century, Vermont has been one of the most reliable seedbeds of our national life," the Introduction began. "In the present generation an extraordinary number of her sons and daughters have risen to positions of distinguished service. How may the fertility of this seedbed be maintained and how may the quality of the human stock be conserved are questions which rightfully command the attention of the leaders of today in the Green Mountain State."

The parkway was subsumed among the sixteen recommendations drafted by the promotion-minded Committee on Summer Residents and Tourists, which also had some Polonius-like advice: "In considering the attitude of Vermonters toward summer visitors, two extremes should be avoided. There should be no fawning or servility in the relations toward their guests. On the other hand, a narrow, intolerant, suspicious attitude should be avoided. The traditional dignity and independence of Vermonters should be maintained in a friendly way. A genuine, kindly hospitality should be shown, a willingness to make the stay of guests pleasant, and a cordiality that will induce them to come again...We should consider all our visitors as potential residents"— [provided, one might add, considering the bigotry of the times, that they embodied acceptable racial and religious characteristics]. After concluding that, from an economic standpoint "the tourist seems desirable in every way. He leaves cash, increases the value of property, furnishes employment for local people and both directly and indirectly adds to the volume of business in the local stores," the committee launched its recommendations.

Proposition Ten was the parkway's cradle: "Ultimately, after our main trunk lines are hard surfaced, it may be well to consider the possibility of linking up some of our country roads far up on the hills, on either side of the Green Mountains, into a system of scenic highways which afford vastly better outlooks than the valley roads. A scenic highway, well up on the slopes of the Green Mountains, on either side of this range, constructed in semi-permanent form, would appeal strongly to lovers of beautiful scenery. A similar policy might be followed in connecting the roads nearest to Lake Champlain in a system that would extend from the Canadian border to the southern extremity of the lake, thus affording what might be made one of the most notable scenic highways in the United States."

In June 1933, Wilgus presented the commission's parkway plan to a group of engineers in Vermont. Passage by Congress of a $3.3 billion public works bill stimulated the Vermont Chamber of Commerce to endorse the parkway concept, and in July a special session of the legislature appropriated $500,000 for public works, including flood control and a parkway.

Governor Stanley C. Wilson thereupon wrote President Roosevelt and Col. H.M. Waite, deputy public works administrator, suggesting the Green Mountain Parkway as a worthy project for federal funding. A Wilson-appointed delegation went to see Waite in October. The mission included Wilgus, George Z. Thompson, chairman of the State Board of Public Works, Thomas B. Wright, for the State Chamber of Commerce, and Proctor H. Page, commissioner of finance. Governor Wilson followed up with calls on Waite and the President, who outlined glowing plans for interconnected parkways from Canada to Mexico, and authorized a $50,000 federal survey of the route through Vermont. The Roosevelt administrationn offered $18 million in WPA funds to build the parkway, which was to emulate the Skyline Drive in Virginia, but after three years of argument and several hotly-contested hearings between 1933 and 1936, the proposal was rejected three times by the General Assembly. Eventually, the legislature called for a popular referendum.

The influential Green Mountain Club, which, realistically, saw the project as a fatal threat to the Long Trail, sounded the first alarms. The newspapers of the state took sides, with editorials of the *Burlington Free Press* favoring the project and of the *Rutland Herald* opposing it. "The issue," according to the *Vergennes Enterprise*, "is fundamentally a contest between two opposing schools of thought. The proponents of the Parkway want to carry Vermont into an intense commercialization of its mountain scenery and summer attractions. The opponents represent a school of thought which prefers to have the state's development follow along more traditional lines."

"Keep Vermont Unspoiled," Leon Gay, president of Central Vermont Public Service, wrote in *The Vermonter* in the summer of 1935, arguing against the erosion of small-town values being caused by better and faster cars and roads.

Anti-New Dealers were bitterly opposed to any cooperation whatsoever with the federal government, bargain or not.

Proponents argued that the $500,000 that Vermont would invest to acquire the rights of way would help reduce unemployment in the short run and stimulate the state's economy for decades ahead. "How long are we going to continue to see Vermont [federal tax] money used to help develop and build prosperity in other states and refuse to take advantage of an opportunity to participate in it ourselves?" Dr.Ernest Bancroft asked in an article in *The Vermonter* in January 1936. "How long are we going to listen to that siren song about keeping Vermont unspoiled, and shall we later complain when we see the youth of Vermont follow our money to more progressive states to establish there their homes and live their lives?....Our only opportunity for a greater degree of prosperity and greater opportunities for our youth seems to lie almost entirely in the direction of the development and extension of our tourist, recreational and summer home business, and I believe this Parkway offers an excellent opportunity to promote such a development in a big way." Bancroft organized the Friends of the Green Mountain Parkway.

One of the most articulate critics was Norwich professor and historian Arthur Wallace Peach, who characterized the Parkway as a "tragic mistake, a blunder whose destructive consequences would reach far into the future of Vermont. It would break Vermont into two parts, from border to border, forever."

"If hosts of tourists are to come over the Parkway from the crowded places," Peach declared, "it would mean in the end the destruction of values that Vermonters hold most dear. I cannot see how intelligent Vermonters would wish to run the risk of creating in Vermont conditions similar to those in the Catskills, at certain beaches on the Maine coast and in certain localities in the White Mountains....Vermont can easily become the great summer home state of the east, and do it without cost if the state will follow its traditional lines of growth, not the lure of some spectacular project, golden in promise and not much else....Build the Parkway, lift taxes, flood the state with any kind of people, particularly those attracted by the spectacular, and the tide will turn. We know there are certain types of people who are destructive of values we want to preserve in Vermont: why not be honest about it? Other states have been ballyhooing for these people; let 'em have 'em. If there were no other beautiful places in New England where a certain crowd can bathe their souls in beauty I should say let them come to Vermont. To be a bit more serious New England can afford to have one state where the 'bounce, bang and boom' of resort life and other cheaper phases of our mortal existence do not enter."

The legislature's referendum was scheduled for the March 1936 town meetings.

As the fateful day approached, the press drumbeat—pro and con—reverberated with front-page news items, editorials, and hundreds of letters-to-the-editor. David Howe, publisher of the pro-parkway *Burlington Free Press*, repeated his position: "The day the state of Vermont was recognized by the National Park Service as worthy of a national parkway in the Green Mountains was a great day in Vermont history." Walter Hard, the Manchester poet and newspaper columnist, wrote: "Fundamentally, I cannot for the life of me see what justification there is for the federal government spending anything for things of this sort especially now. The argument that if we don't take it somebody else will is the stock argument used by every grafter since the beginning of that art, probably in Eden." John Spargo, the "voice" of Bennington, denounced the parkway as "a crime against the coming generation."

Ralph Flanders, the Springfield industrialist, and the State Planning Board to which he belonged issued a public declaration supporting the parkway, and were promptly muzzled by Governor Charles Smith for having made an "unauthorized" statement.

About the only prominent person to stand on the sidelines was Lt.Gov. George Aiken, who wrote to one paper, "I simply cannot get nerved up for or against the Parkway."

On Tuesday, March 3, 1936, Vermonters shuffled into the voting booths and checked off a resounding "No"— 42,000 to 30,0000. The issue carried in only four of fourteen counties. Editorial writers across the country applauded. The New York *Sun* summed it up: "Uppermost in the minds of most Vermonters, perhaps, was a strong desire to preserve the ancient beauty of their hills. If a large part of the territory through which the broad parkway was to run is now a wooded wilderness, so much the better....Apparently the old-fashioned idea still survives in Vermont that a man who prefers to fare forth afoot to see the world is entitled to some protection."

A poet born in Nova Scotia has the last words about how Vermonters feel about their state. Ernest F. Johnstone, a dentist who lived for many years in and around Brandon and Bristol, published this in 1915:

No Vermonters in Heaven

I dreamed that I went to the city of Gold,
To Heaven resplendent and fair.
And after I entered that beautiful fold
By one in authority there I was told
That not a Vermonter was there.

"Impossible, sir, for from my own town
Many sought this delectable place,
And each must be there with a harp or a crown,
And a conqueror's palm and a clean linen gown,
Received through a merited grace."

The Angel replied: "All Vermonters come here
When they first depart from the earth,
But after a day, or a month, or a year
They restless and homesick and lonesome appear,
And sigh for the land of their birth.

"They tell of ravines, wild, secluded and deep
And of flower-decked landscapes serene;
Of towering mountains, imposing and steep,
A-down which the torrents exultingly leap,
Through forests perennially green.

"They tell of the many and beautiful hills,
Their forests majestic appear,
They tell of its rivers, its lakes, streams and rills,
Where nature, the purest of waters distills,
And they soon get dissatisfied here.

"We give them the best the Kingdom provides;
They have everything here that they want,
But not a Vermonter in heaven abides;
A very brief period here he resides,
Then hikes his way back to Vermont."

This stretch of Interstate 89 between Montpelier and Burlington follows the Winooski River and the Central Vermont Railroad tracks. —Vermont Historical Society

Recommended Reading

Maps

Official State Map and Touring Guide. The Vermont Travel Division, 134 State Street, Montpelier, Vt. 05602. Free.

Vermont Road Atlas and Guide. Burlington, Vt.: Northern Cartographic, 1985.

Selected Books in Print

Curtis, Jane, Jennison, Peter, and Lieberman, Frank. *Frederick Billings: Vermonter, Pioneer Lawyer, Business Man, Conservationist.* Woodstock, Vt.: The Woodstock Foundation, 1986.

Curtis, Willis and Jane, Lieberman, Frank. *George Perkins Marsh, Versatile Vermonter.* Woodstock, Vt.: The Countryman Press, 1982.

Cheney, Cora. *Vermont: The State with the Storybook Past.* Shelburne, Vt.: New England Press, rev. ed., 1986 (for children).

Doyle, William, *The Vermont Political Tradition.* Montpelier, Vt.: Doyle, 1984.

Freidin, John. *25 Bicycle Tours in Vermont.* Woodstock, Vt.: Backcountry Publications, 1987.

Goodman, Lee Dana. *Vermont Saints and Sinners: An Impressive Assortment of Geniuses, Nincompoops, Curmuddgeons, Scurry Knaves and Characters.* Shelburne, Vt.: New England Press, 1985.

Graffagnino, J. Kevin. *Vermont in the Victorian Age: Continuity and Change in the Green Mountain State, 1850-1900.* Bennington, Vt. and Shelburne, Vt.: Vermont Heritage Press and Shelburne Museum, 1985.

_____*The Shaping of Vermont.* Bennington, Vt.: Vermont Heritage Press, 1983.

Graham, John A. *A Descriptive Sketch of the Present State of Vermont (1797).* Bennington, Vt.: Vermont Heritage Press, 1987.

Hard, Walter. *A Mountain Township*. Middlebury, Vt.: Vermont Books, (1933) 1985.

Hill, Ralph Nading. *Lake Champlain: Key to Liberty*. Woodstock, Vt.: The Countryman Press, 1976.

_____*Yankee Kingdom: Vermont and New Hampshire*. Woodstock, Vt.: The Countryman Press, Reprint edition, 1984.

Jellison, Charles A. *Ethan Allen: Frontier Rebel*. Syracuse, N.Y.: Syracuse University Press, 1969.

Meeks, Harold A. *Time and Change in Vermont: A Human Geography*. Chester, Ct.: The Globe Pequot Press, 1986.

Merrill, Perry H. *Vermont Under Four Flags: A History of the Green Mountain State*. Montpelier, Vt.: Merrill, 1975.

Morrissey, Charles T. *Vermont: A Bicentennial History*. New York, N.Y.: W.W. Norton & Company, 1981.

Mosher, Howard Frank. *Disappearances*. New York: The Viking Press, 1977.

_____*Where the Rivers Flow North*. New York: The Viking Press, 1978.

Muller, H. Nicholas, and Hand, Samuel B., eds. *In A State of Nature: Readings in the History of Vermont*. Montpelier, Vt.: Vermont Historical Society, 1982.

Muller, H. Nicholas, and Jennison, Peter S., eds. *Freedom and Unity: A History of Vermont*. Montpelier, Vt.: Vermont Historical Society, forthcoming (1991).

Nemethy, Andrew. *Travel Vermont: The Best of the Green Mountain State*. Montpelier, Vt.: Vermont Life, 1988.

Sadlier, Heather and Hugh. *Fifty Hikes in Vermont*. Woodstock, Vt.: Backcountry Publications, 1988.

Tree, Christina, and Jennison, Peter S. *Vermont: An Explorer's Guide*. Woodstock, Vt.: The Countryman Press, 1988.

Van Diver, Bradford B. *Roadside Geology of Vermont and New Hampshire*. Missoula, MT: Mountain Press Publishing Company, 1987.

Weber, Susan, ed. *The Vermont Experience*. Montpelier, Vt.: Vermont Life, 1987.

For a complete list of Vermont books in print, write the Vermont Historical Society, State Street, Montpelier, VT 05602

Selected Reference Resources

Bears Ray, ed. *Vermont: A Guide to the Green Mountains State.* Second ed. Boston, MA: Houghton Mifflin, 1966.

Crane, Charles E. *Let Me Show You Vermont.* New York, N.Y.: Alfred A. Knopf, 1937.

Crockett, Walter H., ed. *Vermonters: A Book of Biographies.* Brattleboro, Vt.: Stephen Daye Press, 1932.

_____*Vermont: The Green Mountain State.* New York, N.Y.: The Century Company, 1921 (Five vols.).

Fisher, Dorothy Canfield. *Vermont Tradition: The Biography of an Outlook on Life.* Boston, MA: Little, Brown, 1953.

Lee, W. Storrs. *The Green Mountains of Vermont.* New York, N.Y.: Henry Holt, 1955.

Newton, Earle. *The Vermont Story 1748-1948.* Montpelier, the Vermont Historical Society, 1949.

Van de Water, Frederic F. *The Reluctant Republic: Vermont 1724-1791.* Taftsville, Vt.: The Countryman Press, 1974.

Index

Converse, Julius, 173
Cook, Reginald L., 52
Cook, Warren, 94
Cooke, Jay, 80
Coolidge, Calvin, 143, 144, 148-54,
  202, 239
Coolidge, Grace Goodhue, 151
Coolidge, John, Sr., 151
Coolidge, John, 154
Coolidge Memorial Foundation, 154
Coss, James, 118
Country Life Commission, 222, 247-8
Countryman Press, 148
Courser, Thomas, 225
Cox, Archibald, 126
Crafts, Ebenezer, 241
Crafts, Samuel, 241
Craftsbury, 241
Crane, Charles Edward, 27
de Crevecoeur, Hector St. John, 234
Crocker, Henry F. and Lawton V., 117
Crockett, Walter Hill, 51, 79, 172
Crystal Lake, 242
Cumberland County, 95
Cummings, Charles R., 247

Dake, Thomas Royal, 192
Dana House Museum, 173
Dana, John Cotton, 173
Danby, 33-4
Daniels, L.C.J., 215
Daniels, Reuben, 166
Danville, 240
Darling, Elmer, 243
Dartmouth College, 140
Davenport, Thomas, 42-3
Davis, Deane, 219-21
Davis, Jacob, 209
Davis, Thomas, 209
Dean, Cyrus, 78
Dean, Reuben, 124
Derby Line, 233
Deere, John, 2, 38
Deming, Martin, 26
DeVoto, Bernard, 7
Dewey, Albert G., 166
Dewey, Elijah, 18
Dewey, Admiral George, 2, 168, 183-5,
  211
Dewey, John, 2, 67-8
Dickens, Charles, 97

Dillingham, Paul, 205
Doe, Charles, 113
Dole, Minot, 160
Dorrilites, 104
Dorset, 32-3
Dorset Inn, 33
Douglas, Stephen A., 43-5
Dover, 145
Doyle, William, 106, 198
Drake, Edwin L., 192
Dresden Party, 138
Dresden School District, 130
Duane, James, 11,
Dummer, William, 95
Dummerston, 95
Dwight, Timothy, 45
Dwinell, Dwight, 210

Eagle Tavern, 195
East Burke, 243
East Fairfield, 83
Eden, 161
Eden Mills, 161
Edmunds, George F., 52, 84, 205-7
Ellis, A.H., 120
Ely, 133
Ely Copper Mines, 133-5
Ely, Smith, 134
Emerson, Lee, 7, 218
Emerson, Ralph Waldo, 159
Emery, Noah, 116
Equal Rights Amendment, 222
Equinox House, 27-8,
Essex Junction, 75
Estey, J. & Co., 102
Evarts, William Maxwell and Helen
  Wardner, 125-6
Everett, Edward H., 21-2

Fairbanks, Erastus, 128, 201, 234-5
Fairbanks, Franklin, 235, 237-8
Fairbanks, Horace, 235, 237
Fairbanks Museum of Natural
  Science, 237
Fairbanks, Joseph, 234
Fairbanks, Thaddeus, 234-6
Fairfield Pond ("Dream Lake"), 85
Fair Haven, 196
Farrar-Mansur House, 147
Fay, Jonas, 33, 121
Fay, Joseph, 121

259

Painter, Gamaliel, 45-7, 246
Park, Trenor, 19,
Parker, Robert, 225
Parmalee, Annette, 215
Peach, Arthur Wallace, 250
Peacham, 239
Peacham Academy, 240
Perkins, Maxwell Evarts, 126
Perkins, Rev. Nathan, 10, 11, 36, 63-4
Perkins, William A., 151
Peters, Rev. Samuel, 38, 177
Pettingill, Helen M., 116
Pettingill, Samuel B., 115
Phelps, Charles, 96,
Phelps, Edward J., 17, 49-52, 75
Phelps, Marlan, 114
Phelps, Timothy, 96
Philadelphia, 77
Piccini, Aristede, 211
Pico Peak, 178
Pinchot, Gifford, 57
Pittsford, 42
Porter, J.J., 165
Poultney, 195
Powers, Hiram, 173
Pownal, 10
Pratt, John Lowell, 148
"Precision Valley," 118
Prescott, Gen. Richard, 191
Proctor, 181
Proctor, Fletcher, 178, 186
Proctor, Mortimer, 101, 178, 186, 218
Proctor, Redfield, 17, 75, 154, 182-7
Proctor, Redfield,Jr., 186
Prohibition, 232
Prouty, George, 243
Prouty, Winston L., 243
Putney, 103 ff.
Putney School, 5

Quechee, 165
Quechee Gorge, 165-6

Raymond, Henry Jarvis, 195
Rich, Charles, 86
Richardson, H.H., 71, 170
Richmond, 205
Riehle, Ted, 7
Rinn, J. Philip, 16
Robertson, Robert H., 58
Robbins & Lawrence, 125

Robin Hood Powder Co., 86
Robinson, Moses, 121
Robinson, Rowland E., 56
Rochester, 154
Rock of Ages quarry, 226
Rockefeller, Laurance S., 172
Rockefeller, Mary French, 172
Rockingham, 110
Rockwell, Norman, 24, 26,
Rogers, L.C., 203
Rokeby Museum, 56
Roosevelt, Franklin D., 66, 204
Roosevelt, James, 66
Roosevelt, Theodore, 9, 60, 183, 207
Rothman, Annie, 34
Round Barn Farm, 156
Round, George, 181
Ruggles, Carl, 26
Rupert, 33
Ruschp, Sepp, 160
Russell, George A., 26
Russell, William A., 110
Rutland, 35 ff., 179
Rutland and Canada Railroad, 39, 128
Rutland Herald, 35 ff., 249
Rutland Marble Company, 182

Sadawga Pond, 144
Saint-Gaudens National Historic Site,
    127
St. Albans, 77
St. Albans Raid, 78-9
Ste. Anne's Shrine, 76
St. Francis, Homer, 86
St. Johnsbury, 233 ff.
St. Johnsbury Academy, 236
St. Johnsbury Athenaeum, 236
St. Johnsbury & Lake Champlain
    Railroad, 233
St. Michael's College, 72
Salmon, Thomas, 5, 114, 221
Saltash, 149
Sample, Paul, 225
Sanders, Bernard, 71-2
Saratoga, 55
Sargent, John G., 148
Savitt, 5
Saxe, John, 88
Saxe, John Godfrey, 44, 88-9
Saxton's River, 110
Schumann, Peter, 241-2